D0208103

WHATEVER YOU RESOLVE TO BE

To Bruce "Stonewall" Baker —
a fellow admirer of the
General and a great student
of the Civil War —
with best regards,
Will Greene
Fredericksburg, Va
11/28/92

WHATEVER YOU RESOLVE TO BE:
ESSAYS ON STONEWALL JACKSON

by
A. WILSON GREENE

Baltimore
BUTTERNUT AND BLUE
1992

©1992 by A. Wilson Greene

All rights reserved by the publisher. No part of this book may be reproduced in any form or by any method without permission in writing from the publisher.

ISBN   0-935523-27-8   hardcover
ISBN   0-935523-28-6   softcover

Dust jacket painting by Don Troiani.
Photograph courtesy Historical Art Prints, Ltd.,
Southbury, CT, Telephone 203-262-6680

Maps by Blake Magner

Butternut and Blue
3411 Northwind Road
Baltimore, Maryland 21234

Dedicated to the memory of Janet F. Greene, 1926–1979

Whose Presbyterian faith and courage in the face of adversity
Thomas J. Jackson would have admired

CONTENTS

MAPS AND ILLUSTRATIONS

INTRODUCTION

When he died, newspapers eulogized Thomas J. Jackson "for his untarnished personal character, for his devout piety, and for his military genius." "Nowhere else will the name of Jackson be more honored," the same panegyric insisted—in a New York city newspaper! The Southern rebel who fascinated Northerners at the same time that he bedeviled their armies has remained at the front and center of America's military pantheon ever since. The incomparable essayist Robert Penn Warren has suggested that the Civil War continues to attract our attention because of the "gallery of great human images" it offers for our contemplation. No figure in Warren's "dazzling array...noble in proportion yet human, caught out of Time as in a frieze..." is more fascinating than that of "Stonewall" Jackson.

The Jackson Legend is compounded of varying parts of military success, humble origins, and human-interest elements, with more than a tincture of eccentricity thrown in for flavoring. The boy orphaned in his nonage sojourned with a succession of relatives through his youth and reached West Point unprepared for its challenges. North Carolinian John Gibbon, destined to become a Federal general officer, called Jackson "by far the most remarkable member" of the class of 1846. Gibbon marveled at the way the relatively untutored cadet grappled with difficult lessons "like a bull-dog," and then sweated so profusely during recitations "that it soon became a proverb with us that...he was certain to flood the section room."

Thomas's fellow Virginian William E. Jones observed that "Jackson's mind seemed to do its work rather by perseverance than quick penetration." Jones also witnessed an instance of fanatical inflexibility at West Point that foreshadowed more famous episodes of later years: a fellow cadet involved in an infraction "prompted only by laziness" seemed to Jackson "to show a moral depravity disgracing to humanity." Nonetheless Jones—whose well-earned nickname "Grumble" denoted a generally surly worldview—thought Jackson to be "the most perfect example of a Christian hero, either living or recorded in history or fiction." That glowing tribute may be the only one that Jones ever directed toward anyone in authority.

Jackson graduated from the Military Academy just in time to go off to the Mexican War with the rank of lieutenant. Service as distinguished as that of any junior officer in the American army won him brevets to captain and then to major. The post-Mexico army might have offered an ideal milieu, with its regimen and routine, had not Major Jackson inevitably run across more moral depravity, real or imagined. In the aftermath of a struggle over the perceived turpitude of a superior officer, Jackson resigned and went to Virginia Military Institute, where he spent the happiest years of his life. Modern Jackson enthusiasts may be surprised to learn that in that pastoral setting Mighty Stonewall learned to play the violin, and "achieved some proficiency" in that apparently incongruous undertaking.

In beautiful Lexington the major-turned-professor afflicted hundreds of young cadets with his stern style, but achieved the respect of most. A literate youngster who fell under the professor's rigid aegis in 1860, and later served on the staff of Stonewall's protege General E.F. Paxton, left a thoughtful cadet's-eye view of the Lexington years. Randolph Barton concluded that Jackson "*possibly*...had the respect of the little community in which he lived. He certainly did not have their admiration. His personal qualities furnished nothing specially attractive or particularly unattractive. He was a neutral. He gave no offence, and except to his immediate and very small family...he gave no pleasure." The same cadet declared that a favorite trick while drilling with the light guns, hauled by cadet-power, "was to whirl the gun on Major Jackson in order to force him undignifiedly to skip about for a safe place." The victim of this youthful torment solved his problem eventually when, "bracing himself, he held his sword pointed towards the rapidly advancing team and forced a deflection without moving from his tracks." Despite their devilment at Jackson's expense, the cadets had enough admiration for the major's Mexican War reputation to hold him "in high estimation"; and yet there was "no enthusiasm felt for him." Barton wrote in summary, probably aptly: "He was not praised; he was not abused."

The vast Civil War that erupted in 1861 supplied the only tapestry upon which Thomas Jackson could have left a discernible design. Had he not entered that arena, it is hard to imagine Jackson earning even a footnote in the thick histories of Lexington and Rockbridge County. We might suppose that the four-volume history of V.M.I. surely would have mentioned Professor Jackson in any event, perhaps in the same paragraph as his colleagues Robert Gatewood, Hamilton L. Shields, and John H. Pitts. Instead the war catapulted Jackson within a few months to international renown. An element of his fame, then and now, unquestionably was the fortuitous *nom de guerre* "Stonewall." Had Thomas Jackson accomplished precisely what he did but earned a less euphonious nickname, his fame hardly could have spread with such random universal force. Confederate generals Adam R. "Stovepipe" Johnson, William W. "Old Blizzards" Loring, and H.H. "Mud" Walker would not be casually familiar today, and grist for mention in country music, had they conquered the entire known universe. Stonewall Jackson deserves to be greater than the sum of the parts of Thomas J. Jackson, the pedagogue and infantryman, but we also ought to recognize that quixotic fortune bestowed on him the perfect label.

Confederate General Jackson had a strong positive impact on his troops early in the war, and of course once he had crafted notable successes his fame grew exponentially. Sooner or later the wowsers will undertake to revise Stonewall Jackson, as they have done with Lee. In the process they will launch the breath-taking lie, as they have tried with Lee, that the general only became a hero after his death as part of a myth-making process necessary to sanitize the hideous Lost Cause. An enormous volume of contemporary writing makes it abundantly clear that the men in the ranks loved Jackson early and well, not that that sort of evidence will daunt the earnest nay-sayers. When a Shenandoah Valley boy who had heard of Jackson's mistreatment by the maladroit tandem of

Judah Benjamin and Jefferson Davis learned that the general would not resign after all, he wrote in early February 1862: "everyone is rejoicing over it[,] he is beloved by all." James Cooper Nisbet, whose familiar postwar book is adulatory, felt the same way in the spring of 1862 when he wrote home to Macon, Georgia, that Jackson was a reincarnation of Federick the Great: "We cheerfully move wherever our glorious leader orders....His soldiers all love the old fighting cock....We are panting to redeem Maryland and to make Olde Abe and his minions fly...."

On the other hand, Stonewall's much-mooted difficulties with his high-ranking subordinates pose a serious question about his capabilities to manage men. A.P. Hill's letter denominating Jackson a "crazy old Presbyterian fool," and suggesting that Jackson will "get the d—ndest thrashing" once "the Almighty" tired of bailing him out, has been printed. A great deal of manuscript material bearing on the subject awaits the work of a scholar bent on reviewing the matter in detail. The Romney mutiny of early 1862, for instance, is illuminated by the original letter of complaint signed first by William B. Taliaferro (whom Jackson loathed, with apparent cause; Taliaferro's postwar leap aboard the Stonewall Bandwagon is either amusing or disgusting) and second by Colonel S.V. Fulkerson (who is elsewhere identified as Jackson's favorite colonel). General Charles S. Winder, who replaced Jackson's unfortunate victim Dick Garnett, committed his disgust with his superior to paper in an unpublished diary. On the morning of June 8, 1862, moments before one of Jackson's most exciting episodes of the war, Winder "wrote note to Genl Jackson requesting to leave his command." Winder of course did not succeed; he died still in the same role two months and one day later.

Turner Ashby's bitter contest with his chief over control of the ill-organized Valley cavalry is widely recorded, but a great deal more material survives. For instance Ashby wrote to his congressman on April 25, 1862, seeking to resign and declaring that Jackson had regularly humiliated him—despite the fact that "for the last two months I have saved the army of the Valley from being utterly destroyed....This I have done without the aid of Gen. Jackson's command." An interesting uncited letter to Ashby from the Secretary of War vindicates Jackson's position on cavalry organization, something that Ashby never acknowledged and that historians have overlooked. Jackson's position on appointing subordinates, which was not as unreasonable as his treatment of them once in place, is nicely outlined in a May 6, 1862 letter expressing disgust over the promotions and assignments of Taliaferro, Ashby, Garnett, and John Echols, and of artillery Major William McLaughlin.

The North Carolinian volley that struck Jackson down in the smoke-streaked moonlight on May 2, 1863, changed the course of American history and at the same time probably launched the Jackson Legend more thoroughly than a more pedestrian demise could have done. The Tarheels quit firing when they saw A.P. Hill outlined in their muzzle flashes, much closer to them than was the stricken corps commander. Why had they hit Jackson and missed Hill? Some eventually concluded that it was God's will, in a bit of cosmic historiography. (Thomas Jackson would have liked that, a lot). In the short term, his men were prostrated. A member of the 32nd North Carolina heard uncertain word of Jackson's death and wrote: "I hope it ant so for hee is one of our smartes men." A lad in the 21st Georgia declared: "A greater hero never lived....If we could only see Jackson, we was all right, we would take off our hats and hollow....He was thought more of than are nother general that we have got."

The general's apotheosis had strongly religious overtones. A Georgian major (a few weeks from a battlefield death himself at the time) heard a sermon the next spring based on Jackson's life delivered for nearly three hours by the dead general's favorite preacher. The crowd that jammed a rude camp chapel overflowed onto its roof, which collapsed onto the worshippers, leaving two in extremis. Despite that inauspicious beginning, the major reported that he had "never heard anything more sublime, nor had anything to make so great an impression in my life. Every man who heard him, I know, is a better man, and a better soldier."

Jackson's best political friend, A.R. Boteler, quickly began waving the dead general as a political totem. Before May 1863 ended Boteler had published a broadside assailing the opposing candidate—who had been a colonel in the Stonewall Brigade!—as not the sort of fellow for whom Jackson would have voted. In military affairs, of course, Jackson was irreplaceable. Lee sadly commented soon after the war in talking of Gettysburg that he "often thinks that if Jackson had been there he would have succeeded."

The Jackson Legend includes a substantial component of eccentricity in its formula. How much of the attention focused on such things is warranted remains open to question. At this writing the redoubtable Jackson student Lowell Reidenbaugh is preparing a paper on the subject for a seminar to be presented at the Jackson Home in Lexington. The effect of personality quirks on the Legend is understandable. Humans expect most of their geniuses to be somewhere between quaint and certifiable, and appreciate signs confirming their expectations.

A story comes to mind that is particularly apposite because it involves A. Wilson Greene, the author of this book. Years ago I enjoyed a collegial fraternity with a brilliant Fredericksburg genealogist and local historian of richly deserved national reputation for his accomplishments. The man also combined a fabulous mixture of old Virginian form and style with eccentricities as egregious as I ever have seen. Will Greene, then a young historian working in town, would go with me from time to time to meet my colleague in the midst of his cluttered files, primarily for the ambience. The subject of his scrutiny discerned this, and would say—loudly and colorfully—"That Mr. Greene, he thinks I'm a *curiosity* or somethin'." He did, and he was. The Fredericksburger's very substantial historical achievements could readily stand alone, but his picturesque style gave them a patina unmistakable to Will and to everyone else who met him. On a much larger scale the same was true of Stonewall Jackson.

The consuming hunger for details about the great man that developed after his early success found adequate raw material to work with. Stories of Jackson's unusual religious ardor found support when an Ohio soldier met the general's sister in western Virginia and she allowed that Thomas "was very religious[,] fanatically so." Some men in the army knew that Colonel (later General) James A. Walker had tried to kill Jackson at V.M.I. after suffering substantive mistreatment. Everyone heard about the general's difficulties with virtually every near subordinate. Men who saw the living Legend invariably noticed the absence of visible distinction. A disappointed Louisianian wrote that the "ordinary looking" Jackson "looked to me like a Jew pedlar." The resultant elaborations and exaggerations eventually yielded a counter reaction when men saw the rather plain reality. A Columbus, Georgia correspondent was almost disappointed when "surprised at Stonewall Jackson's appearance. He has been described as a sort of a clown. I never yet saw him riding with his knees drawn up like a monkey....But the imagination is piqued, you know, by the absence of pretension....The boys keep him bareheaded [by cheering him] all the time." That absence of pretension was central to the man, and to the Legend—in the latter case often gilded a good deal, as befits legendary things.

The wartime growth of the Legend in the North obviously moved on a different axis, but it was by no means sluggish. In August 1862 a captive Yankee sergeant was found yanking tufts of hair from the tail of Jackson's famous war horse, "Little Sorrel." His explanation, that "each one of these hairs is worth a dollar in New York," prompted a Southern onlooker to ask: "Was there ever a more delicate compliment to a man's reputation?" In the fall of 1862 a New York paper launched a very clever satire on the subject. So much was being made of the notorious rebel that the paper professed to be confused. Jackson had been described physically as resembling everything from a "Hindo idol" to a winged statuette of Apollo. His descent was whimsically traced from such origins as "Jackaloe the Chinese Pirate" and "Jack surnamed the Giant Killer." The satirist ascribed the general's nickname to a beating young Tom took from a washboard-wielding mother, which she concluded by wailing in frustration, "You might as well larrup a stonewall." The Southern hero's success seemed the more remarkable, the New York article concluded, because of his physical handicaps: the Northern press had reported in detail the loss of each of his limbs at least once.

In a similarly fantastic (although entirely serious) vein the Federal matron of a military hospital near Frederick, Maryland reported a visit there by a civilian whose "keen eye seeming to take in everything" provoked curiosity. A check by the vigilant woman yielded the report that he was one "Dr. George," a veteran of the Crimean War, "very rich; a good Union man." The alert matron, however, was able to ascertain that the fellow really was Stonewall Jackson "in disguise," who often went into the Federal camps "and so acquaints himself with what is going on...." Any lieutenant general that sneaky deserves to be a legend; or, more accurately, anyone about whom such piffle accumulates has already *become* a legend.

The Northern fascination with Jackson cited at the beginning of this introduction is almost startling to one first exposed to it. Another New York paper compared the dead Virginian to Napoleon and reported him "popular even in our own" armies. A Washington journal admitted relief at removal of the skilled opponent, but added: "our sense of relief is not unmingled with emotions of sorrow and sympathy at the death of so brave a man." Vermonters recalled Jackson stopping in front of their downcast ranks after Harpers Ferry surrendered to provide encouragement dosed with religious fatalism: "Don't feel bad; you could not help it; it was just as God willed it." A brilliant Federal surgeon later wrote that Jackson's "death seemed to cause no elation in our army. All recognized how dangerous an enemy he was...how great a military genius. Yet with all this, the feeling...was one of pity, I might also say of regret, that so great a soldier was passing away."

Foreigners, especially those of the British sub-genus, were also much taken with Jackson. A leading journalist from London wrote from Guiney Station in May 1863, "It was impossible to look at the house where he lay...without a mist coming over the eyes and a choking sense of suffocation rising in the throat." In a stirring eulogy the Englishman compared the dead Confederate to Hannibal and Marlborough and said that "the sight of him, and of him alone, stirred the blood like a trumpet, and the words 'Stonewall is coming' carried confidence to his friends and terror to his foes." Comparing Jackson to Cromwell was popular, and remains so today (though I dislike the notion); but the London *Herald* used Havelock and the *Times* chose Nelson at Trafalgar. Those papers and the *Post* called Jackson a "Christian and patriot...doubly a martyr"; declared his "the foremost place" in the American war; and labelled him "a hero after our own heart."

Legends cannot survive unchanged from their infancy. They inevitably grow and thrive—and often transmogrify—for years until a vast body of material, but little of it precisely accurate, adheres to the corpus. Curios are part of the process. Memories burnished by time are another. Confederate memoirs, published or manuscript, always mention with understandable awe whatever brief contact the veterans enjoyed with Mighty Stonewall: how they saw him on the roadside; how he nodded from horseback; or at least how a distant cousin or a near neighbor once challenged the great man while on picket post. Few of these are unadulterated contemporary truth, and even fewer are arrant lies. Scraps of uniform, tiny locks of hair, his gloves, his raincoat—all of these have achieved status equal to (perhaps exceeding that of, in this secular age) a Vatican saint's wrist bone. In 1921, U.S.M.C. General Smedley Butler, himself eccentric without the overlay of genius, dug up Jackson's amputated arm in a frenzy of ghoulish admiration. Late in life dozens of Yankees claimed to have shot Jackson in the smoking Wilderness; none had. At the same time dozens of dying Confederate veterans admitted life-long convictions that their part in the volley had been the fatal one; three of them may have been right.

So early as the fall of 1863 General Jubal A. Early marveled at the fact that ladies were clamoring for a handkerchief of Jackson's in his possession. In 1891 a fellow drolly described as "the South's answer to the carpetbaggers" went to New York City and sold nine carefully autographed Stonewall Jackson Bibles to credulous antiquarian book dealers, each sale embellished with a lachrymose tale. This artisan, who was going by Thomas Chancellor of Chancellorsville, also peddled some autographed pictures. As the police closed in he successfully slipped away, "whistling, jes' a country boy from the South with his pockets full of Yankee dollars." One wonders who's buying those Bibles at auction today.

The modern manifestations of the indiscriminate Legend include a recent imbecilic novel about Jackson's wounding and death and a worse biography, laughably emblazoned with a photograph of someone resembling the general not at all. In the same vein, an amusingly earnest letter first circulated in the 1950's continues to crop up, reporting the deathbed admission of an old pioneer who knew Stonewall Jackson in the Wild West after the war. Stonewall had wearied of the war, by this account, skulked away through the Chancellorsville woods (Lee and his cohorts hiding this out of embarrassment), gone west, and fought at the Washita and with Crook. U. S. Grant learned of this skullduggery, however, and hired a team of Swiss assassins (big business and the CIA evidently being booked up) "to eliminate the traitor." They finally got poor Thomas in Nebraska in 1876. The corpse, as might be expected, was bedizened with a silver watch inscribed to Jackson from Lee. The watch has been misplaced somewhere, somehow.

An infinitely more seemly modern evidence of the survival of the Legend is the high level of serious study and scholarly interest in Stonewall Jackson. Will Greene's several essays in this book offer a fresh synopsis of the general in summary and in three of his most important campaigns. One of the five essays, that on the Seven Days, offers a markedly revisionist approach to Jackson's performance during that crucial week. Using nine manuscript letters written by members of the general's staff, together with the usual published sources, Greene defends Jackson from the animadversions that have become conventional wisdom about the campaign. He has undertaken to accomplish precisely what Jedediah Hotchkiss hoped the letters would do, see that Jackson's "military character will be fully vindicated and the miserable skeptics who say that he failed to do his duty...will be scouted from the field."

As an enthusiastic admirer of Jackson, I offer a sympathetic audience for such sorties, but I must admit to remaining unconvinced about the Seven Days. Greene establishes good reasons why a general performing as Jackson did does not deserve scathing criticism for struggling in vain with considerable difficulties—for being daunted, I think, by things that Jackson at his normal peak would have conquered. The exhaustion that eventually levels every organism, even one driving a Legend, apparently had floored Thomas Jackson. A staff officer serving under George T. Anderson who rode to army headquarters late in the campaign probably saw the Seven Days in microcosm when he noticed legs and feet, booted and spurred, protruding from beneath a group of tables. He asked an aide who it was. "That is Stonewall," came the reply, "he has had no sleep for forty-eight hours and fell down there exhausted."

Whether you buy or reject Greene's postulates on the Seven Days, and in his other essays, the transaction will be a profitable one. These gracefully written studies of slices of Jackson's history, before and during the war, will bring the reader into close contact with one of the most fascinating Americans of the Civil War era, and in fact of all of our national past.

Will Greene is particularly well suited to this undertaking. He studied at Louisiana State University under the famous Civil War scholar T. Harry Williams, then lived in Jackson's Shenandoah Valley before assuming historical duties at the scenes of crucial moments in Jackson's career. As historian at Fredericksburg and Spotsylvania County Battlefields Memorial National Military Park, Will was responsible for Fredericksburg Battlefield, where Jackson held one-half of the Confederate line; for Chancellorsville Battlefield, where Jackson won his last and greatest victory; and for the house at Guiney Station where the general died. Will's hometown of Fredericksburg is one of several claimants for the distinction of the place that originated Memorial Day, with Jackson in mind. A May 1865 women's meeting started the local movement. Then on May 10, 1866, "the stores and places of business were very generally closed...in commemoration of the death of that great and good man...and as a day to be remembered in respect for the Confederate dead." Will's association with these Jacksonian roots continues today. As the chief executive officer of the Association for the Preservation of Civil War Sites, based in Fredericksburg, he spends at least as much time and energy as anyone in the country on saving our vanishing Civil War heritage.

Robert K. Krick
Fredericksburg, Virginia
February 1992

PREFACE

INTEREST in the American Civil War has never been greater since the veterans themselves vanished from the scene. Commemorations of the war's 125th anniversary, the production of an immensely popular video documentary, and the realization that the great battlefields of the war are in danger of disappearing under a sea of asphalt and concrete have combined to resurrect the realization that the Civil War, more than any other chapter of our history, defines us as a people today.

The great leaders of the Civil War loom central not only to the events of the 1860s but to the rebirth of scholarship focusing on the period. New biographies of the leaders in blue and gray are appearing at an unprecedented pace, none more rapidly or provocatively than examinations of the commanders of the Army of Northern Virginia. Within the last few years, books on J.E.B. Stuart, James Longstreet, A.P. Hill, John B. Gordon, Richard H. Anderson, and a host of lesser lights have been written.[1] New treatments of Jubal A. Early (by Gary W. Gallagher), Richard S. Ewell (by Donald C. Pfanz), and James Longstreet (by Jeffry D. Wert) are forthcoming.

---

[1] Emory M. Thomas, *Bold Dragoon: The Life of J.E.B. Stuart* (New York: Harper and Row, 1986); William Garrett Piston, *Lee's Tarnished Lieutenant: James Longstreet and his Place in Southern History* (Athens: Univ. of Georgia Press, 1987); James I. Robertson, Jr., *General A.P. Hill: The Story of a Confederate Warrior* (New York: Random House, 1987); Ralph Lowell Eckert, *John Brown Gordon: Soldier, Southerner, American* (Baton Rouge: Louisiana State Univ. Press, 1989); Joseph Cantey Elliott, *Lieutenant General Richard Heron Anderson: Lee's Noble Soldier* (Dayton, Ohio: Morningside House, 1985). A good example of the third-level generals in the Army of Northern Virginia who are subjects of biographies is Gary W. Gallagher, *Stephen Dodson Ramseur: Lee's Gallant General* (Chapel Hill: Univ. of North Carolina Press, 1985).

No figure from that great army, however, has managed to capture and retain the imagination of new generations of students more than Thomas J. Jackson. Jackson's record on the battlefield, his seemingly inscrutable character and personality, and his larger-than-life image as symbolized by the equestrian statue at Manassas, continue to invite inquiry and interpretation. No Confederate personality, save the immortal Lee, has generated more books and articles during the last 125 years.[2]

In the composition of these essays, I have sampled most of the Jackson literature. It is virtually impossible to read anything on the Civil War in the Eastern Theater without encountering "Stonewall," so the outlines of his military career are not difficult to discover. Several writers, however, have tackled the more challenging task of surveying Jackson's entire life, the first appearing in 1863.

Southern novelist John Esten Cooke composed his *Life of Stonewall Jackson* that year and later expanded it into the more familiar *Stonewall Jackson, A Military Biography*.[3] Both of these books are as admiring as one would expect given their pedigree, and therefore are of interest as a contemporary gauge of Jackson's stature. Robert L. Dabney, Jackson's chief of staff during the Seven Days, wrote his laudatory tribute in 1866 at the invitation of Jackson's family.[4] This book retains surprising utility despite its age because of the primary material Dabney provides.

The late nineteenth century brought two notable additions to the Jackson lore. Mary Anna Jackson, the general's widow, first published her *Memoirs of Stonewall Jackson* in 1892.[5] This collection of reminiscences and letters is long on insights into Jack-

---

[2] Charles E. Dornbusch in his four-volume *Military Biography of the Civil War* (New York and Dayton: New York Public Library and Morningside House, 1961, 1967, 1972, 1987) lists 61 sources on Jackson and 77 on Lee. Stuart and Forrest have nine each and Longstreet six.

[3] John Esten Cooke, *The Life of Stonewall Jackson from Official Papers, Contemporary Narratives, and Personal Acquaintance, by a Virginian* (Richmond: Ayres & Wade Presses, 1863); *Stonewall Jackson, A Military Biography* (New York: D. Appleton and Co., 1866).

[4] Robert Lewis Dabney, *Life and Campaigns of Lieut.-Gen. Thomas J. Jackson (Stonewall Jackson)* (New York: Blalock & Co., 1866).

[5] Mary Anna (Morrison) Jackson, *Life and Letters of General Thomas J. Jackson (Stonewall Jackson) by his Wife Mary Anna Jackson* (New York: Harper & Brothers, 1892).

son's domestic life and predictably short on analysis of his military career. Its popularity and value may be judged by the many reprinted editions that have appeared.[6]

What Mrs. Jackson overlooked in her book, British military historian George Francis Robert Henderson treated in his 1898 *Stonewall Jackson and the American Civil War.*[7] This two-volume work for the first time systematically explored Jackson's performance in the field, using extensive correspondence with Stonewall's surviving comrades and opponents as the foundation for his conclusions. Henderson's tone is partial to Jackson, and modern evidence dates some of the Englishman's arguments. Nevertheless, Henderson's work still commands attention, and his book reappeared in a handsome set in 1987.[8]

As was true with most Civil War topics, the first half of the twentieth century yielded little useful Jackson biographical material. Allen Tate's *Stonewall Jackson, The Good Soldier* was a notable exception.[9] The approach of the Civil War Centennial created a renewed emphasis on Civil War research. Burke Davis wrote a readable biography in 1954[10] followed by arguably the best one-volume treatment of any Confederate officer, Frank E. Vandiver's *Mighty Stonewall.*[11] Vandiver unearthed primary sources that no one before him had used, and wove his information into a beautiful, balanced narrative. Lenoir Chambers, a journalist with a genius for history, produced a two-volume Jackson biography shortly after Vandiver's work appeared.[12] Chambers complemented Vandiver and, between the two of them, the definitive Jackson seemingly emerged.

---

[6] The subsequent volume was published as *Memoirs of Stonewall Jackson* by Prentice Press, Courier-Journal Job Printing Co. of Louisville, Ky. in 1895 and contained much new material. This volume was reprinted by the press of Morningside Bookshop of Dayton, Ohio in 1985.

[7] George Francis Robert Henderson, *Stonewall Jackson and the American Civil War* (London: Longmans, Green and Co., 1898).

[8] Published by the Blue and Grey Press, a division of Book Sales, Inc., Secaucus, N.J.

[9] Allen Tate, *Stonewall Jackson, The Good Soldier* (New York: Minton, Balch & Co., 1928).

[10] Burke Davis, *They Called Him Stonewall* (New York: Rinehart & Co., 1954).

[11] Frank E. Vandiver, *Mighty Stonewall* (New York: McGraw Hill, 1957).

[12] Lenoir Chambers, *Stonewall Jackson* (New York: William Morrow, 1959).

All of Stonewall's biographers relied upon contemporary accounts left by various articulate Confederates who either knew Jackson personally or fought under his command. Countless articles about the general appeared in the two most important Confederate serials, the *Southern Historical Society Papers* and *Confederate Veteran*.[13] Staff officers such as Dr. Hunter H. McGuire and James Power Smith wrote numerous pieces about Jackson's life on the battlefield and in bivouac. Several book-length memoirs contain generous glimpses of the general. Henry Kyd Douglas's *I Rode with Stonewall,* which some ungenerous critics believe should be entitled "Stonewall Rode with Me," is the source for many of the most familiar Jackson anecdotes.[14] William T. Poague, John O. Casler, Robert Stiles, Edward A. Moore, and many others produced enduring recollections that to various degrees focus on Jackson.[15]

The bibliography of Jackson's major battles and campaigns is voluminous but uneven. Some of his military exploits have been treated with microscopic attention while others are all but neglected. Robert K. Krick's *Stonewall Jackson at Cedar Mountain* is an example of the former.[16] It is hard to envision anyone ever finding anything else about that battle. On the other hand, the definitive treatment of the Seven Days, Second Manassas, or Fredericksburg has yet to appear.[17] Fortunately, talented historians

---

[13] The *Southern Historical Society Papers* were published between 1876 and 1959 in Richmond. *Confederate Veteran* appeared between 1893 and 1932 in 40 volumes published in Nashville. Both sets have been reprinted recently and are indexed.

[14] Henry Kyd Douglas, *I Rode with Stonewall* (Chapel Hill: Univ. of North Carolina Press, 1940).

[15] Monroe F. Cockrell, ed., *Gunner with Stonewall: Reminiscences of William Thomas Poague* (Jackson, Tenn.: McCowat-Mercer Press, 1957); John Overton Casler, *Four Years in the Stonewall Brigade* (Guthrie, Okla.: State Capital Printing Co., 1893); Robert Stiles, *Four Years under Marse Robert* (New York: Neale Publishing Co., 1903); Edward A. Moore, *The Story of a Cannoneer under Stonewall Jackson* (New York: Neale Publishing Co., 1907).

[16] Robert K. Krick, *Stonewall Jackson at Cedar Mountain* (Chapel Hill: Univ. of North Carolina Press, 1990).

[17] Clifford Dowdey, *The Seven Days: The Emergence of Lee* (Boston: Little, Brown, 1964) is the best source on the Seven Days, but slanted toward the Confederates and inadequate in its treatment of Jackson; Edward J. Stackpole, *Drama on the Rappahannock: the Fredericksburg Campaign* (Harrisburg, Pa: The Stackpole Co., 1957) is the only modern discussion of that battle, and it is largely unreliable. There is no good monograph on Second Manassas.

are at work on two of these historiographical gaps.[18] Naturally, anyone seeking to understand the context in which Jackson commanded needs first to turn to Douglas Southall Freeman's classic *Lee's Lieutenants*.[19]

I wrote the essays that appear in this book between 1986 and 1988. I dare say that few readers will find my interpretation of Thomas Jackson to be particularly revisionist, at least in the negative sense. However, I composed these thoughts during a time when Stonewall Jackson's performance on the battlefield received increasing critical evaluation. A growing number of speakers at historical forums found Jackson's military record seriously flawed and inflated. Invidious comparisons to James Longstreet, Dick Ewell, and Jubal Early still echo from podiums. We can look forward to a wider dissemination of these views, I predict, in new books and articles. The distinguished historian James I. Robertson, Jr., is at work on a full-length treatment of Jackson which, no doubt, will consider what the general's new critics have to say.

This volume, of course, does not attempt a comprehensive appraisal of Thomas Jackson. The five essays that follow instead examine three of his famous campaigns and attempt to address two questions: "What made the man tick?" and "How did he fare as a general?" I make no claim to original scholarship, but have relied on what I hope is a fresh look at published sources to achieve both reaffirmation and recasting of conventional views.

Nine years of walking in the shadows of Jackson at Fredericksburg, Chancellorsville, and Guinea Station during my work as a National Park Service historian have provided me an appreciation for the impact upon events that one man can create. My hope is that these words will contribute in some small way to the continuation of that impact on future generations.

---

[18] John Hennessy is at work on the definitive Second Manassas book and William Matter will do for Fredericksburg what he did for Spotsylvania in *If It Takes All Summer* (Chapel Hill: Univ. of North Carolina Press, 1988).

[19] Douglas Southall Freeman, *Lee's Lieutenants* (New York: Charles Scribner's Sons, 1942–1944.)

ACKNOWLEDGMENTS

I am greatly indebted to a number of colleagues and friends who deserve much of the credit for whatever value this volume possesses. It is virtually pro forma to thank Robert K. Krick in any book that addresses the Army of Northern Virginia or its commanders. Bob knows more about Lee's army than any historian working today and shares his knowledge with grace and enthusiasm. I owe part of my admiration of Thomas Jackson to years of working with Bob at Fredericksburg & Spotsylvania National Military Park. His guiding hand is also evident in these pages as a skilled editor.

Gary W. Gallagher of the Pennsylvania State University and president of the Association for the Preservation of Civil War Sites loaned me photocopies of the E. Porter Alexander papers before they found their way into print as his superb *Fighting for the Confederacy: The Personal Recollections of Edward Porter Alexander.* Gary and I toured various locales in 1988 lecturing about Jackson and Longstreet, and he unfailingly challenged me to rethink my views on Stonewall.

Kent Masterson Brown, formerly editor of *Civil War Magazine,* provided me an opportunity to speak about Jackson at the Seven Days and Second Manassas as a part of the Civil War Society's excellent seminar series. These talks eventually appeared in his magazine and reappear in these pages after several permutations. I am grateful to Tom Lewis, the current publisher of Civil War Magazine, for permitting the inclusion of these revised versions in this collection.

Likewise, John T. Hubbel, editor of *Civil War History,* allowed the Fredericksburg essay to appear after originally publishing it in 1987. Jeanne West of *Civil War History's* editorial staff substantially improved the prose in this article.

Many people aided me in my research but I wish to make special mention of Michael Anne Lynn of Lexington, Virginia and her staff at the Stonewall Jackson House. Thanks also to John Hennessy of the National Park Service in Harpers Ferry, West Virginia who shared his encyclopedic knowledge of the Second Manassas Campaign. Jim McLean of Butternut and Blue performed admirably as publisher and chief enforcer of deadlines, taking up where my friend John McGlone left off.

Finally I express gratitude to my wife, Margaret, who spent many hours alone upstairs while "Old Jack" and I cavorted in the library. It is her love and support that make my journeys to the 1860s possible.

A. Wilson Greene
Falmouth, Virginia
February 1992

ESSAY ONE

Stonewall Jackson:
The Man behind the Legend

ON MAY 10, 1863, Thomas Jonathan Jackson crossed over the river to rest under the shade of the trees. "Seldom in history has one been able, in so short a time, to write his name so deeply upon the hearts of his countrymen, and to raise the admiration of the world at large. Uniting the most beautiful simplicity with the most intense earnestness of character, with a religious consecration to duty as the regulative principle of his life, he was a true man in all the relations in which he moved."[1]

When the members of the Presbyterian Church of Columbia, South Carolina, penned this tribute to the departed general, voices throughout the South joined in honoring a man whose stature exceeded that of any other Confederate hero. An English observer pronounced Jackson "the greatest man America ever produced,"[2] and even people in the North sensed the passing of an extraordinary individual.

More than six-score years have not diluted our fascination with Stonewall Jackson. Most of us would still agree with Frank Vandiver's assessment that Jackson looms as "one of the most remarkable of all Civil War figures."[3] The general's fame, of course,

[1] *Southern Historical Society Papers (SHSP)*, v. 43, p. 103.

[2] *SHSP*, v. 13, p. 331.

[3] Vandiver, p. vii.

emanates from his exploits on the battlefield, but his legendary image is rooted in his singular nature and personality. We cannot hope to understand fully the twenty-two month career of Stonewall Jackson until we examine the thirty-seven years of Thomas Jackson that preceded it.

Americans prefer their idols to possess humble origins, and Jackson's boyhood seems, superficially at least, to satisfy that criterion. Born on January 21, 1824, in Clarksburg, Virginia, Thomas was the third child of Jonathan and Julia Beckwith Neale Jackson. Clarksburg, while not on the literal frontier, offered few amenities of high society. The Jacksons, though, moved in Clarksburg's best circles, Julia aided by a good education and an eastern Virginia upbringing, and Jonathan's successful law practice earning him a comfortable living and the community's esteem.

Thomas's father, however, indulged in the risky business of co-signing notes of credit for numerous acquaintances, liabilities that left Julia practically penniless following her husband's sudden demise from typhoid fever in 1826. The young widow supported her family by teaching school, but in 1830 married an attorney named Blake Woodson and moved to Fayette County. Soon, Julia's health also failed. Her death made orphans of Thomas, his brother Warren, and younger sister Laura. His older sister Elizabeth had perished earlier from the same illness that claimed his father.[4]

A few months before their mother's passing, Laura and Tom had gone to live with their grandmother and a collection of uncles and aunts at Jackson's Mill in Lewis County. This wholesome and hardy environment at last provided the future general with domestic stability, despite the early death of his grandmother and Laura's departure to make her home with other relatives.[5]

Thomas's bachelor uncle, Cummins Jackson, inherited primary responsibility for his older brother's son. Cummins operated a gristmill and sawmill and exposed his young charge to the benefits of hard work and a vigorous lifestyle. Thomas attended a num-

[4] *Ibid.*, pp. 2–5.

[5] Dabney, pp. 13–15.

ber of the primitive schools characteristic of western Virginia, evincing a thirst for education but an ordinary mind. One of his teachers remembered that "he was not what is now termed brilliant, but...was one of those untiring matter-of-fact persons who would never give up an undertaking until he accomplished his object.... What he got in his head he never forgot."[6]

The adolescent Thomas displayed many of the hallmarks for which Stonewall would be well-known. He enjoyed sports but appeared awkward. Honest to a fault, he was quick to defend a wronged schoolmate. His shyness reduced him to helplessness around girls and a nervous stomach compromised his otherwise robust constitution.[7]

Jackson dabbled in several occupations while in his teens. In 1836, Thomas and his brother set up shop as stokers on an island in the Mississippi River. This quixotic enterprise so weakened Warren that it eventually led him to the grave. Thomas subsequently helped build a turnpike to Parkersburg, taught at one of the area's country schools, and at age 17 served as a constable, or debt-collector, in Lewis County, discharging his duties with ingenuity and tenacity.[8]

Jackson's future, however, lay not as an officer of the court but as an officer in the army. Thanks to the influence of a prominent kinsman, the assistance of a sympathetic Congressman, and the cooperation of a disenchanted neighbor who resigned his cadetship, Thomas arrived at West Point in the summer of 1842. "Dressed in homespun, a hat of coarse felt on his head, and a pair of weather-stained saddlebags over his shoulder," cadet classmate Dabney Maury deemed this newcomer, "altogether an uncommonly awkward and green appearing specimen." Nevertheless, Maury admitted that his fellow Virginian had a sturdy air about him and looked as if he "had come to stay."[9]

---

[6] Roy Bird Cook, *The Family and Early Life of Stonewall Jackson* (Charleston, W.V.: Charleston Print. Co., 1948), pp. 56–57.

[7] *SHSP*, v. 22, pp. 157–159; Thomas Jackson Arnold, *Early Life and Letters of General Thomas J. Jackson* (New York: Fleming H. Revell Company, 1916), pp. 31–34.

[8] Vandiver, pp. 9–12.

[9] *SHSP*, v. 27, p. 337.

Jackson arrived at the Military Academy ill-prepared for the academic achievement required of new cadets. He struggled with the material, sweating profusely whenever an instructor required him to recite at the board.[10] He compensated for his weak background with unusual study habits that attracted the attention of his peers. "No one I have ever known," wrote a roommate, "could so perfectly withdraw his mind from surrounding objects or influences, and so thoroughly involve his whole being in his subject under consideration."[11]

Jackson's hard work and long hours earned him steadily improving marks. He eventually graduated 17th in a class that included George B. McClellan near the top, George E. Pickett at the bottom, and eighteen other future Union or Confederate generals somewhere in the middle.[12]

Viewed at first by his comrades as humorless and rigid (Maury once referred to him as a "jackass"),[13] Jackson's fidelity, honesty, and industry won him the respect and even the affection of his fellow cadets. They called him "the General" after Andrew Jackson, and admired the rough-hewn lad who seemed to demonstrate that he could indeed be what he resolved to be.[14]

Lt. Jackson celebrated his graduation in 1846 with a Bacchanalia at Brown's Hotel in Washington that featured raucous singing, barefoot dancing, and a spontaneous full-volume recitation of self-composed verse.[15] During calmer moments, Jackson talked of pursuing a legal career after completing a brief tour of active duty with the artillery, but the war with Mexico altered his plans.[16]

The army assigned Jackson to Company K of the 1st Artillery and dispatched him to Point Isabel, Texas. The anxious new officer spoiled for a fight, and before hostilities concluded he would realize his goal in spades.

[10] Henderson, p. 11.

[11] *Ibid.*, p. 15.

[12] Chambers, v. 1, p. 74.

[13] *SHSP*, v. 25, p. 310.

[14] Vandiver, pp. 9–12.

[15] *SHSP*, v. 25, pp. 311–12.

[16] Arnold, pp. 71–72.

Jackson first participated in the campaign to Saltillo and then joined Winfield Scott's expedition from Vera Cruz to Mexico City. In July 1847, Lt. Jackson obtained an appointment to a new field battery commanded by John Bankhead Magruder, and for the first time truly exhibited his abilities as a warrior.

Magruder cited his lieutenant's performance at the battles of Contreras and Churubusco, for which Jackson received promotion to Brevet Captain. The highlight of his Mexican War career, however, came on September 13, 1847, at the Battle of Chapultepec. Here, outside the City of Mexico, Jackson commanded two guns in the fore of the entire American army. Amidst staggering losses to his men and horses, Jackson persevered under heavy fire until infantry support arrived and carried Santa Anna's position. He then fearlessly followed the fleeing foe and repulsed repeated counterattacks.[17]

Magruder wrote of Jackson, "If devotion, industry, talent, and gallantry are the highest qualities of a soldier, then he is entitled to the distinction which the profession confers."[18] The army rewarded Jackson's bravery with a promotion to Brevet Major.

The Americans remained in Mexico City until June 1848, Major Jackson passing a pleasant and stimulating interlude in the capital of the Aztecs. The Virginian developed into a competent dancer and regular attendee at the city's many social events. Jackson acquired a taste for fresh citrus fruits in this southerly climate, and his correspondence with Laura intimates that he may have acquired a taste for something even sweeter.[19] "I think that probably I shall spend many years here," he wrote his sister, "and may possibly conclude to make my life more natural by sharing it with some amiable Senorita."[20]

Jackson's intellectual pursuits included a study of the Spanish language and serious inquiries into the Roman Catholic Church. He approached the reading of the Bible systematically, as he would any technical text, but for the first time gave vent to a

---

[17] See Chambers, v. 1, pp. 77–123 for a thorough review of Jackson's war record in Mexico.

[18] Quoted in Vandiver, p. 41.

[19] *Ibid.*, p. 42.

[20] Arnold, pp. 128–30.

religious affinity that would soon blossom into the central feature of his personality.[21]

In the meantime, the army withdrew from Mexico and Jackson repaired to Fort Columbus in New York Harbor. He served on a court-martial board at Carlisle Barracks, Pennsylvania, visited Laura during a much-deserved furlough to Virginia, then returned to New York for duty at Long Island's Fort Hamilton. Jackson could frequently be seen striding along the streets of Manhattan exploring book shops and adding to his expanding personal library.[22]

The peacetime army offered little opportunity for adventure, excitement, or promotion. Duty at Fort Hamilton may have been dull, but the proximity of New York at least promised outside stimulation. All the stimulation at Jackson's next post would be self-generated.

Fort Meade, Florida, located about thirty miles southeast of Tampa, epitomized the unattractive way of life in the United States Army in the 1850's. Its isolation and meager comforts helped set the stage for the first serious internal confrontation of Jackson's military career.

Stonewall's biographers have thoroughly documented Jackson's feud with William H. French, an episode that contributed significantly to Jackson's decision to leave the army. We need only observe that each officer contributed equal parts of obstinacy, pride, and pettiness to an affair that discredited both men. Jackson would evidence these same shortcomings during the Civil War, although untainted by the personal nature of his altercation with French.[23]

The unpleasantness at Fort Meade prompted Jackson to seek a transfer to a new regiment and an extended leave of absence. In the midst of the Florida imbroglio, the embattled major received an inquiry from Superintendent Francis H. Smith of the Virginia Military Institute in Lexington. Would the Major consider a nomination for the chair of Natural and Experimental Philosophy at the Institute for the new academic year? This unforeseen opportunity

[21] Chambers, v. 1, pp. 141–45.

[22] Vandiver, pp. 45–46, 53–55.

[23] Chambers, v. 1, pp. 167–199.

Thomas Jonathan Jackson wearing a "uniform" apparently painted on by the portrait photographer.
[*Leib Image Archive*]

appealed to Jackson and he responded in the affirmative, little expecting, however, to be selected.

Thanks to a series of fortuitous events and the advocacy of Daniel Harvey Hill, a Mexican War acquaintance and professor at Lexington's Washington College, Jackson received the offer. He eagerly accepted and as soon as French's superior released him from arrest, Jackson gladly left Florida. Following visits to Laura and Jackson's Mill, the new professor reported for duty at V.M.I. in August 1851.[24]

Thomas Jackson's experience at the Institute is most often perceived as a melange of incompetence and eccentricities. While such simplistic analysis does Jackson injustice, no one can argue that his classroom performance met reasonable standards.

In truth, the Major made a terrible teacher. He memorized each day's lesson and delivered it verbatim to an audience of glazed-eyed young scholars. If the subject matter's inherent interest overawed the professor's dreadful presentation, an inquisitive student enjoyed little hope for satisfactory elucidation from Jackson. The Major knew only one way to explain a concept: the way he himself had learned it. Questions thus met with merely a repetition of the original lesson, a technique that tended to suppress lively classroom discussion.[25]

Jackson's absolutely unbending demeanor saddled him with a reputation as a martinet and made him generally unpopular if grudgingly respected. Behind his back the cadets called him, among other nicknames, Hickory, Tom Fool, and Square Box, an illusion to the unusual size of his shoes.[26] "Old Jack...was so plain in manner and attire...his feet were so large and his arms and his hands fastened to his body in such an awkward shape, that the cadets didn't take much pride in him as a professor," confessed one Lexington student.[27]

Jackson certainly brooked no disobedience in his section-room. Once, he saw to the expulsion of cadet James A. Walker, a future commander of the Stonewall Brigade, for refusing his order

[24] Vandiver, pp. 70–73.

[25] *Ibid.*, pp. 76–77.

[26] *SHSP*, v. 38, pp. 270–72.

[27] *SHSP*, v. 9, pp. 41–42.

to stop talking in class. This extreme punishment so infuriated Walker that he challenged Jackson to a duel, a provocation the professor ignored.[28]

The cadets ridiculed their apparently humorless mentor in various ways. Jackson occasionally arrived in his classroom to discover the outline of a huge shoe drawn on the blackboard. Taking advantage of the professor's habit of stalking across campus with his eyes fixed rigidly ahead, audacious cadets would follow him in lockstep, imitating his ungainly gait unbeknown to the object of their derision. Cadet Randolph Barton testified, "No one recalls a smile, a humorous speech, anything from him while at the barracks," and concluded that Jackson was "an automaton."[29]

The Major's literal obedience of orders in contravention of common sense and self-preservation qualified him, in the eyes of the students, as eccentric at best. Who could forget Tom Fool Jackson pacing up and down in front of the Superintendent's office in a violent hailstorm refusing to seek admittance until precisely the time of his appointment? Jackson's insistence upon wearing a thick wool uniform one summer because he had somehow failed to receive the customary orders to change it struck witnesses as awfully irrational.[30] "If asked to name the professor at the Institute most likely to rise to the highest rank and win the greatest fame in the event of war," wrote cadet William A. Obenchain, "probably four cadets out of five would have thought of Jackson last."[31]

The professor initially enjoyed little more popularity in Lexington. An observer understated the case when she wrote, "In social life, Major Jackson was not what is called a 'society man.'"[32] He received but few invitations, being a dismal conversationalist, so unimaginative as to misunderstand the slightest witticism or exaggeration. Furthermore, Jackson adopted a most disconcerting posture when taking a chair. He sat perfectly erect, his back never

---

[28] Chambers, v. 1, p. 229.

[29] *SHSP*, v. 38, pp. 270–72.

[30] *SHSP*, v. 19, p. 145.

[31] *SHSP*, v. 16, pp. 45–46.

[32] Mrs. Jackson, p. 63.

Mary Anna Morrison Jackson
[from *Memoirs of Stonewall Jackson*]

touching the furniture, reminding one witness of Egyptian rendi-
tions of the Pharaohs.[33]

This is not to suggest that Jackson was friendless or an out-
cast. He struck up a relationship with Lexington book dealer and
Presbyterian elder John B. Lyle, who helped cultivate the Major's
religious interests. He also renewed his acquaintance with Harvey
Hill, the man most responsible for Jackson's presence at V.M.I.

Hill introduced his friend to other Lexingtonians, including Washington College president George Junkin. Reverend Mr.
Junkin had two unmarried daughters in his household, and Jackson fell in love with the less popular one. He and twenty-eight-
year-old Elinor conducted a quiet courtship that culminated in
their marriage on August 4, 1853.[34]

Following a honeymoon excursion to New York, West Point,
Niagara Falls, Montreal, and Quebec, Thomas and Ellie returned

---

[33] *SHSP*, v. 9, pp. 41–42.

[34] Vandiver, pp. 84–86; 90–96.

to Lexington and shared the Junkins' home at Washington College. The Major thrived on domestic life. Ellie playfully teased him, took him places, and dispelled his shyness. Jackson, in turn, loved his wife deeply, and her death in childbirth on October 22, 1854, left him desolate. He seemed obsessed with her passing and talked darkly about joining his wife and stillborn baby in the grave. Jackson's gradual drift toward religious devotion accelerated upon Ellie's demise, and his faith in God helped sustain him in his bereavement.[35]

The widower also coped with his loss by embarking upon actual as well as spiritual journeys. He spent the summer of 1855 visiting with his family in western Virginia and exploring his boyhood haunts at Clarksburg and Jackson's Mill. The next summer found Jackson on a junket to Britain, France, Germany, Switzerland, and Italy. Exposure to the wonder of the Old World's art and architecture at last lifted the mourner out of his malaise. It also seemed to kindle a smoldering spark that had ignited three years previously.[36]

Mary Anna Morrison, Harvey Hill's sister-in-law, had visited the Valley in 1853. Jackson remembered the vivacious North Carolina girl, like Ellie, the daughter of a Presbyterian minister, but had not seen her since his wedding day. Upon his return to Lexington, however, the Major launched a determined campaign. First he reconnoitered, using earnest correspondence. Then he assaulted the Morrisons' home with a personal visit in December.

By all accounts, Jackson's offensive met with complete success. He left Lincoln County engaged to be married and exchanged long, tender letters with his fiancée until Anna's formal surrender on July 16, 1857. The victorious suitor paraded his bride on a lengthy honeymoon that included some of the same destinations that he had toured with Ellie.[37]

The Jacksons returned to Lexington in time for the new school term, residing initially in a local hotel. Later, they moved to a private boarding house but ardently wished for a home of

---

[35] *Ibid.*, pp. 97–107.

[36] Chambers, v. 1, pp. 260–266.

[37] Jackson's courtship is covered in Vandiver, pp. 112–116.

their own. In November 1858 they realized their dream. Thomas and Anna selected a simple brick house on Washington Street, located only a moderate walk from the Major's classroom at the Institute.[38]

Although the building required a few repairs, the lack of a child was its greatest deficiency. In April, Anna had given birth to a daughter named Mary Graham, but within four weeks the infant had died of jaundice. His wife's reassuring presence, however, and his own implicit faith helped Jackson accept the tragedy.[39]

The two years in his Lexington home mark one of the happiest and most settled chapters of Jackson's life. Anna, described by a contemporary as a "lady of simplicity of character and cheerfulness of spirit, and most amiable and pleasing manner,"[40] captivated her husband's complete attention. The couple shared prayers each morning at 7:00, ate all their meals together, and indulged in afternoon strolls and evening conversation. The Jacksons often ended their day with Anna reading aloud to her adoring mate.[41]

Of course, the professor adhered to his regimen of study, lesson preparation, and teaching amidst his pleasant domestic routine. Added to family, professional, and church activities, the Major spent hours tilling his backyard garden or working on his little farm outside of town.[42]

During the winter of 1861–1862, Thomas Jackson's innate domesticity most belied his image as a grim-visaged warrior. Stonewall had playfully implored his wife to visit him during the campaign hiatus, and Anna joined her general at the home of Reverend and Mrs. James Graham in Winchester. There they passed, as Anna recalled, "as happy a winter as ever falls to the lot of mortals on this earth."[43] The Grahams' home echoed with the sounds of harmony and bliss, and, just as in Lexington, Jackson found no

---

[38] Chambers, v. 1, pp. 281; 287.

[39] Mrs. Jackson, p. 111.

[40] *SHSP*, v. 40, p. 323.

[41] Mrs. Jackson, pp. 109–111.

[42] *Ibid.*, pp. 110–111.

[43] *Ibid.*, p. 212.

contradiction in his duty-bound approach to business and his loving, gentle relationship with his "esposita."[44]

In Winchester, the Jacksons conceived another child—a daughter who would gladden Stonewall's heart more than all his victories combined. Anna delivered on November 23 at the Morrison home near Charlotte, and the happy parents named their infant Julia, after Thomas' mother.[45]

Jackson once mentioned a preference for a son, but withheld no affection from Julia. "Give the baby-daughter a shower of kisses from her father," Jackson wrote Anna upon learning of the newborn's arrival, "and tell her that he loves her better than all the baby-boys in the world." The new father could not resist admonishing Anna to avoid spoiling their daughter, and privately worried that if he loved Julia too much, God might summon her home just as he had taken Mary Graham.[46]

Throughout the winter, the General expressed a ceaseless desire to see his child but refused to take a furlough in order to do so. In March, Jackson moved his headquarters to Hamilton's Crossing, south of Fredericksburg, and the nearby Yerby House offered satisfactory accommodations for a new mother and infant. He soon called his little family to join him, and they united at Guinea Station, an ironic rendezvous, on April 20.

It would be difficult to imagine a more heartwarming vignette than Stonewall Jackson's first contact with his daughter. Afraid to handle the baby while wearing his sopping raincoat, the General waited until the party arrived safely in the warm, dry confines of the Yerby House. He picked up Julia in his arms and caressed the infant with unbounded affection.[47] Jackson spent every leisure minute of the next nine days with his baby, holding up a mirror and cooing, "Now, Miss Jackson, look at yourself." Anna claimed that Julia looked like her father, but Stonewall protested that she was too pretty for such a comparison.[48]

---

[44] *Ibid.*, pp. 211–215.

[45] *Ibid.*, pp. 360.

[46] *Ibid.*, p. 363.

[47] Vandiver, pp. 451–452.

[48] Mrs. Jackson, p. 409.

During this radiant interlude, Jackson found it necessary to divide his time between Anna and Julia, and his military obligations. The spring sun dried the roads, and on April 29 word at last arrived that Union commander Joseph Hooker had crossed the Rappahannock. The General rushed from the Yerby House instructing Anna to repair immediately to Guinea Station whence the next southbound train could whisk her from the combat zone. He would try to see her off, but could not promise to do so. Who could predict when they would be a family once again?[49]

The military exigency detained Jackson, so corps Chaplain Beverly Tucker Lacy escorted Anna and Julia to the depot. As their carriage rumbled south along the rough road to Guinea, Anna might well have reflected upon the husband and father whose every battle might be his last.

Jackson's aide-de-camp, James Power Smith, described his commander as "a man of good size, a little under six feet...with square shoulders, large bones, [and] large feet and hands." His brown hair and beard, grown reddish from the sun, contrasted with his dark blue, piercing eyes.[50] Other observers noticed a stern bearing that failed to conceal a "deep benevolence" in Jackson's face.[51] The General spoke in short, terse sentences, always preferring listening to speaking.[52]

Beyond physical appearance or superficial mannerisms dwelled a personality that has intrigued students of the Civil War for generations. While no great man can be reduced to a single quality, Reverend Moses Drury Hoge believed that "to attempt to portray the life of Jackson while leaving out the religious element would be like undertaking 'to describe Switzerland without making mention of the Alps'...."[53]

Jackson's youth included limited exposure to theological matters, but his serious study of Christianity commenced in Mexico City. His original battery commander, Captain Francis Taylor,

---

[49] *Ibid.*, pp. 415–416.

[50] *SHSP*, v. 43, p. 59.

[51] *SHSP*, v. 9, pp. 94–95.

[52] *SHSP*, v. 43, p. 59.

[53] *SHSP*, v. 13, p. 326.

discussed spiritual affairs with Jackson and encouraged him to read the Bible. Taylor's influence extended to Fort Hamilton, where in April 1849 the Captain sponsored Jackson's baptism at St. John's Episcopal Church.[54] The Major endorsed no specific denomination, but no one could doubt the sincerity of his commitment. "Rather than wilfully violate the known will of God, I would forfeit my life," he wrote his sister in 1850. "Such a resolution I have taken and I will by it abide."[55] Jackson's Lexington friendship with Lyle and Hill led him to Dr. William White, the local Presbyterian minister. In short order, the new professor formally joined White's church.[56]

Richmond reporter George W. Bagby described Jackson as "a Presbyterian who carries the doctrine of predestination to the borders of positive fatalism...."[57] James Power Smith, himself a Presbyterian divine, offered a different interpretation of his General's creed: "It was not only that he was a religious man, but he was that rare man...to whom religion was everything."[58]

Smith identified two primary components of Jackson's faith. First, the General subscribed to "the providence of a present God, ruling and directing in wisdom, power and goodness in all affairs of men."[59] Francis H. Smith of V.M.I. wrote that Jackson's views of divine truth "were as simple as a child's, and his life was that of an earnest Christian man, taking the word of God as his guide, and unhesitatingly accepting all therein revealed."[60] As Confederate memoirist Robert Stiles said, Jackson's life found consistency "by complete dependence upon Divine Providence and entire submission to divine decrees."[61]

---

[54] Dabney, p. 55; Mrs. Jackson, p. 50.

[55] *SHSP,* v. 43, p. 92.

[56] Vandiver, p. 87.

[57] J. Cutler Andrews, *The South Reports the Civil War* (Princeton, N.J.: Princeton Univ. Press, 1970), p. 181.

[58] *SHSP,* v. 43, p. 67.

[59] *SHSP,* v. 43, p. 68.

[60] *SHSP,* v. 6, p. 265.

[61] *SHSP,* v. 21, p. 26.

Secondly, Jackson implicitly relied upon the power of prayer.[62] Reverend D.B. Ewing of Gordonsville observed Jackson in July 1862 and described the General's supplications: "He did not pray to men, but to God. His tones were deep, solemn, tremulous. He seemed to realize that he was speaking to Heaven's King. I never heard anyone pray who seemed to be pervaded more fully by a spirit of self-abnegation."[63]

Jackson not only prayed frequently, his communication with God virtually never ceased. As he explained to the Junkins one evening:

> I have so fixed the habit in my own mind, that I never raise a glass of water to my lips without a moments asking of God's blessing. I never seal a letter without putting a word of prayer under the seal. I never take a letter from the post without a brief sending of my thoughts heavenward. I never change my classes in the section room without a minute's petition on the cadets who go out and those who come in. The habit has become as fixed almost as breathing.[64]

Those who knew him well recognized a pattern in his devotions. For example, the General's black body servant, Jim Lewis, testified that "Yes, the general is a great man for praying at all times, but when I see him get up a great many times in the night to pray, then I know there is going to be something to pay...."[65]

Jackson's faith made him happy. "I do rejoice to walk in the love of God," he once told Smith, and he sought to share the word of the Lord with others.[66] The blacks of Lexington comprised his most famous flock. He organized and taught a special Negro Sunday School at the Presbyterian Church despite the reservations or outright objections of the town's white community. Eventually more than 100 slaves or free blacks attended Deacon Jackson's services.[67]

---

[62] *SHSP*, v. 43, p. 69.

[63] Mrs. Jackson, p. 309.

[64] Cook, pp. 131–32.

[65] *SHSP*, v. 19, p. 161.

[66] *SHSP*, v. 43, p. 70.

[67] Chambers, v. 1, pp. 268–70.

He also advocated religious activity in the army, and "Old Jack's" personal example compelled many a sinner to patronize the regimental chaplain. This is not to suggest, however, that Jackson limited his religious veneration to Presbyterians alone. His corps medical director, Dr. Hunter Holmes McGuire, remembered an episode that transpired prior to the Battle of Chancellorsville that illustrates this point. Jackson had ordered the army to travel light and leave behind all surplus baggage and tents. This directive prompted the chaplain of a Louisiana regiment, a Roman Catholic, to tender his resignation on the grounds that he could not hear confession without the privacy of a tent. Jackson instantly suspended his order as it applied to the priest, and allowed the Louisianan to retain his shelter, the only man in the corps to enjoy that privilege.[68]

If Jackson's religiosity contained a downside, it lay in the way the General's devotion contributed to his unyielding personal conduct. He strove to live his life according to divine will and thus hesitated to stray from a very straight and narrow path. He gave up dancing, for example, although he could find no explicit proscription against it, because he knew that it was not wrong *not* to participate. He viewed life as the discharge of a sacred duty—man's half of a bargain with God. Therein lay the motivating spirit behind his remarkable self-discipline and his legendary inflexibility.[69]

We can easily understand how such rigidity might be viewed as fanatical, but Stonewall abetted his reputation as an eccentric by means of several other peculiarities. Jackson suffered real problems with his health, but sometimes dealt with them in manifestly irrational ways, even by the medical standards of his era. He also indulged in imagined ailments that lent him the aura of a hypochondriac, and before the war spent an inordinate amount of time trying to improve his physical condition.

Jackson's frailties included rheumatism, weak eyes, and poor digestion—or as the General called it "dyspepsia." He endured the rheumatism as best he could, rested his eyes, bathing

---

[68] *SHSP,* v. 25, p. 108.

[69] Mrs. Jackson, pp. 60–61.

them in cold water during especially bad bouts, and experimented with a variety of cures for his stomach distress.

Jackson's physicians, particularly at Fort Hamilton, recommended various dietary and exercise therapies to relieve their patient's digestive disorders. In 1849, for example, the Major consumed only water, unbuttered stale bread, and plainly dressed meat with apparently positive results. He followed a strict workout regimen of walking, leaping, and violently swinging his arms. At other times Jackson adopted a buttermilk diet or sought hydropathic relief at the mineral springs.[70]

Acquaintances raised their eyebrows, however, when in addition to these legitimate maladies and treatments Jackson would complain that the two halves of his body did not act in accord, or that the origin of his sore throat could be found in his liver. Dabney Maury reported that Jackson would occasionally thrust an arm in the air because he believed one of his limbs to be heavier than the other. By elevating the offending appendage, Stonewall thought, the blood would rush back into his body and thus temporarily rectify the imbalance. Dick Ewell remembered that his commander refused pepper to avoid weakening his left leg, and D.B. Conrad claimed that Jackson would sometimes pack himself in wet sheets before attending Sunday services.[71]

An odd correlation existed between Jackson's health and his physical environment. He suffered the most during periods of relative inactivity, such as at Fort Hamilton or in Lexington, but seemed to improve when stimulated by outside influences. With the exception of the "fever and debility" he endured during the Seven Days battles and an earache in December 1862, the General enjoyed robust health during the war until contracting pneumonia after his mortal wound.

Another of Jackson's physical traits enhanced his notoriety as an oddball. Stonewall required regular and significant sleep in order to function efficiently, and gratified this need at unusual times and in unusual places. Numerous witnesses remark upon the General's proclivity to snooze in church. Jackson felt ashamed of

---

[70] Vandiver, pp. 48–50.

[71] *Ibid.*, p. 123; *SHSP,* v. 25, p. 316; v. 19, p. 83; v. 20, p. 33.

this behavior, realized that people disapproved of it, and accepted their criticism as just punishment for his transgression, but could not overcome the habit.[72]

Old Jack would doze off in fence corners, on trains, or one time at Fredericksburg while sitting bolt upright on his camp stool posing for an artist.[73] Dr. McGuire wrote that Jackson was "the most difficult man to arouse I ever saw. I have seen his servant pull his boots off and remove his clothes without waking him up...."[74]

Random idiosyncrasies unrelated to religion, health, or sleep—such as his custom of holding his belted saber horizontally well up under his left arm—solidified Jackson's renown.[75] Many agreed with Jim Lewis' assessment that "General Jackson was mighty peculiar."[76]

During the war, Stonewall preferred plain, simple food, such as cornbread and milk, and evinced a considerable appetite. He never used tobacco and rarely consumed whiskey or wine.[77] Various accounts, however, document Jackson's self-professed attraction to liquor, typical of which is the episode in Winchester described by Confederate Congressman A.R. Boteler.

On the evening of May 30, 1862, Boteler arrived at Jackson's headquarters carrying two whiskey toddies. Old Jack declined his friend's hospitality, protesting that "I never drink intoxicating liquors."

"I know that, General," Boteler replied, "but though you habitually abstain, as I do myself, from everything of the sort, there are occasions, and this is one of them, when a stimulant will do us both good."

Jackson took a few tentative sips, then turned to his companion: "Colonel, do you know why I habitually abstain from intoxicating drinks? Why sir, because I like the taste of them, and when

[72] *Century Magazine*, v. 32, p. 936.

[73] Freeman, *Lee's Lieutenants*, v. 1, p. 415; *SHSP*, v. 43, p. 32.

[74] *SHSP*, v. 19, p. 311.

[75] *SHSP*, v. 16, pp. 44–45.

[76] Douglas, p. 155.

[77] *SHSP*, v. 19, p. 315.

I discovered that to be the case I made up my mind at once to do without them altogether."[78]

On at least one occasion during the war, although apparently by accident, Jackson did overindulge in spirits. The army had left Winchester on New Year's Day 1862 to embark on a new campaign, and the first night in camp the weather turned bitterly cold. Jackson remembered a bottle given him that morning by a gentleman from the city, and assumed that the gift contained wine. As Henry Kyd Douglas related the story:

> Asking for the bottle, he uncorked it, tilted it to his mouth and without stopping to taste, swallowed about as much of that old whiskey as if it had been light domestic wine. If he discovered his mistake he said nothing but handed the bottle to his staff, who, encouraged by the dimensions of the General's drink, soon disposed of all that he had left. In a short while the General complained of being very warm, although it was getting still colder, and unbuttoned his overcoat and some of the buttons on his uniform. The truth is, General Jackson was incipiently tight. He grew more than usually loquacious, discussed various interesting topics and among them the sudden changes of temperature to which the Valley is liable.[79]

Jackson held the line better with profanity. No one claims to have heard him take the Lord's name in vain. "Coarseness and vulgarity from anybody under any circumstances he would not brook," wrote Dr. McGuire. "Swearing jarred upon him terribly and he generally reproved the man."

The reverent warrior, while never blasphemous himself, occasionally forgave those who did stumble. When Isaac Trimble learned that the government had failed to promote him in 1862, he told Jackson, "By God, General…I will be a Major-General or a corpse before the war is over." Stonewall let it slide. Colonel Lindsay Walker at the Battle of Cedar Mountain turned the air blue as he attempted to rally the men at a point of crisis. "That's right, give it to them," advised the General. Jackson's acerbic quartermaster, Major John A. Harman, customarily employed in-

---

[78] *SHSP*, v. 40, p. 168.

[79] Douglas, p. 20.

THE JACKSON DWELLING, LEXINGTON.

The only home that Jackson ever owned, this brick house on Lexington's Washington Street is now (1992) a museum furnished to reflect the Jacksons' occupancy.
[from *Memoirs of Stonewall Jackson*]

delicate language when communicating with his mules at which Jackson only smiled.[80]

Thomas Jackson's precision, piety, and peculiarities only partially explain the character of this great and good man. He possessed numerous virtues beyond those practiced as an outgrowth of his faith.

Few men laid higher claims to honesty and integrity. An incident at V.M.I. illustrates the point. Tom Fool had upbraided a student in class for arguing some technicality of physics in contravention of the textbook and Jackson's own instruction. That night, the offending scholar received a summons to meet Major Jackson outside of the barracks. Fearing some unspeakable penalty for his impertinence, the lad descended with trepidation. To his utter surprise, the boy discovered that his professor had returned to the Institute in a blinding snowstorm to apologize. Jackson had determined, upon further study at home, that both he and the manual had been in error. He wished to acknowledge that fact at the earliest possible moment. Jackson then dismissed the stunned cadet and tramped back toward Lexington in the snowy gloom.[81]

Anna Jackson noted "a painstaking fidelity" in every one of her husband's undertakings. He never broke his word nor failed to meet a commitment. James Power Smith remembered his General's kindness and manners. "No one who ever entered his house or obtained access to his office...can forget the marked courtesy with which he was received. His attention was the same to his guest, whether he was the general commanding, or a private soldier."[82] Jackson abhorred anything that savored of display or pretension and he maintained a personal demeanor as humble and unassuming as the average man in the ranks.[83]

Those who knew him intimately—his wife, members of his army family, and close friends—frequently remarked upon Jackson's humanity and compassion. Admitting that the General's

---

[80] *SHSP*, v. 19, pp. 314–15.

[81] *SHSP*, v. 9, pp. 424–26.

[82] *SHSP*, v. 43, p. 74.

[83] *SHSP*, v. 43, p. 59; v. 38, pp. 282–83.

very soul burned in combat, Hunter McGuire remembered that off the field, Stonewall's milder nature held sway. "As I look back on the two years that I was daily, indeed hourly, with him," wrote the doctor, "his gentleness as a man, his great kindness, his tenderness to those in trouble and affliction…impress me more than his wonderful prowess as a great warrior."[84]

Jackson unfailingly provided for the welfare of his servants, even during the war. As a testimony to the esteem in which black Virginians held him, a Negro church in Roanoke installed a memorial window in the General's honor after his death.[85]

Numerous other events attest to Jackson's selflessness. Thanks to Stonewall's appeal, the Second Corps raised $30,000 for the women, children, and elderly of Fredericksburg who suffered so severely during the winter of 1862–1863. Many a private soldier drew a lifetime of pride from Jackson's habit of personally commending acts of bravery and consoling the wounded and sick.[86]

Stonewall's image as a dour and serious soul, although not entirely undeserved, fails to recognize the General's very real sense of humor. McGuire did confess that his commander's literal use of language and his absolute sincerity rendered him a difficult man with whom to jest. "I used to tell him some little jokes…but they had to be very plain ones for him to see them."[87] Still, many sources recount snippets of Jackson's wit.

Colonel J.T.L. Preston, Jackson's staff officer and brother-in-law, remembered that the General would sit at the dinner table as "grave as a signpost, till something chances to overcome him, then he breaks out into a laugh so awkward that it is manifest he had never laughed enough to learn how."[88] McGuire stated that "when he laughed (as I often saw him do) he did it with his whole heart. He would catch one knee with both hands, lift it up, throw his body back, open wide his mouth, and his whole face and form would be convulsed with mirth—but there was no sound."[89]

[84] *SHSP,* v. 25, p. 106.

[85] *SHSP,* v. 43, p. 60.

[86] *Ibid.,* p. 84.

[87] *SHSP,* v. 19, pp. 311–12.

[88] Quoted in Vandiver, p. 184.

[89] *SHSP,* v. 25, p. 106.

Anna Jackson's memoirs are replete with tales of her husband's playfulness. In Lexington, he was fond of hiding behind doors and leaping out suddenly to startle his wife, occasionally adding to the effect by wielding his saber above his head. Thomas's letters home during the war mix tender solicitations with affectionate teasing.[90]

Jackson often shared a smile with staff members and headquarters visitors. He particularly enjoyed the carefree jocularity of J.E.B. Stuart, whose yarns and antics around the campfire consistently entertained the General.

Kyd Douglas' memoir, *I Rode with Stonewall,* provides ample evidence of Jackson's good humor. One evening in March 1862, the General asked a staff officer, Sandie Pendleton, if the newspapers contained any important information. Pendleton discovered a story in the New York *Mercury* entitled, "The Life and Character of the Rebel General, Stonewall Jackson." Old Jack usually had little patience for such claptrap, but Pendleton, barely concealing his glee, recited the article nonetheless. The Yankee reporter waxed ridiculous about Stonewall's childhood and moral qualities, concluding with a tribute to Jackson's remarkable self-control that allowed the Confederate to "subsist for a fortnight on two crackers and a barrel of whiskey."

"The General listened attentively," remembered Douglas, "his expression relaxed. A smile appeared which grew broader as the 'Life' continued, kindled into audible delight, and at the end he broke into the loudest burst of laughter I ever heard him indulge in. This is the only time I ever heard him listen to what the press had to say about him."[91]

Jackson not only enjoyed a joke, but occasionally crafted one himself. One spring afternoon in 1863, he directed Jimmy Smith to fetch a bottle of wine from the headquarters wagon and asked his campmates to join him in some refreshment. Jackson knew the wine to be a homemade variety acquired from a vineyard in Front Royal, but ingenuously inquired of his well-travelled staff in what part of Europe they thought the intoxicant originated. McGuire,

[90] Mrs. Jackson, pp. 121–23.

[91] Douglas, pp. 35–36.

Colonel Charles J. Faulkner, and others earnestly debated the question, the partisans of France and Italy unreconciled to the end. The General quietly observed the dialogue and managed to smother his amusement in a pillow.[92]

We so often read of the simplistic Thomas Jackson, concerned solely with God and duty, that it is easy to overlook the man's many dimensions. He loved children, others' as well as his own, and delighted in play with the Grahams' offspring in Winchester.[93] Jackson read voraciously. His favorite subjects included military science, history, and background material for his classes in natural philosophy.[94]

Stonewall apparently possessed a poor ear for a tune. In July 1862, while breakfasting at a private home in Ashland, the General and his staff enjoyed songs and music provided at the piano by one of the owner's daughters. Jackson frolicked with the younger children of the house while listening to the impromptu concert. At one point, the General politely requested that the pianist play "Dixie." "I heard it a few days ago and it was, I thought, very beautiful."

The girl looked quizzically at Jackson and replied, "Why, general, I just sang it a few minutes ago—it is about our oldest war song."

"Ah, indeed," answered Old Jack "I didn't know it."

Kyd Douglas smirked that his commander had heard "Dixie" a thousand times. "Perhaps he thought he would startle the young lady with his knowledge of music: if so, he succeeded."[95]

Stonewall received mixed reviews in two fields of endeavor important to a general officer. Dabney Maury testified that Jackson "was singularly awkward and uncomfortable to look at upon a horse....He had a rough hand with the bridle, an ungainly seat, and he seemed in imminent danger of falling headlong from his [mount]...."[96]

[92] *SHSP*, v. 43, pp. 64–65.

[93] Mrs. Jackson, p. 358.

[94] *SHSP*, v. 43, pp. 2–3.

[95] Douglas, pp. 120–21.

[96] *SHSP*, v. 25, p. 315.

A postwar article in a riding periodical, however, declared the Virginian to be "a great horseman. He sat in the saddle easily, while there was a sort of abandon visible which showed his familiarity with horseflesh from boyhood. His seat was very erect, and though it had none of the stiffness of the cavalry style, it was very correct."[97] Despite this endorsement, we may safely conclude that the General was not a classic equestrian.

Jackson also enjoyed little reputation as a declaimer. The record reveals but few memorable Jacksonian addresses. He did, however, speak up at an 1860 political meeting in Lexington, making a favorable impression on the audience. Washington College student George H. Moffatt heard the talk and thought the Major "displayed one quality of an orator not always exhibited by political speakers; when he was done he quit."[98]

Jackson belonged firmly in the Democratic fold and voted for the Southern-Rights candidate, John C. Breckinridge, in the 1860 Presidential canvass. Like many Breckinridge stalwarts, the Major supported preservation of the Union consistent with the recognition of state sovereignty. He subscribed to the South's "peculiar institution," but viewed slaves as children of God with souls to save and deserving of humane treatment.[99]

Following the secession of seven Deep South states early in 1861, the V.M.I. professor recorded his opinion of the simmering sectional crisis in a letter to his nephew:

> I am in favor of making a thorough trial for peace, and if we fail in this, and the state is invaded, to defend it with a terrific resistance....People who are anxious to bring on War don't know what they are bargaining for; they don't see all the horrors that must accompany such an event.[100]

He once told Anna that "war was the sum of all evils," and from his headquarters frequently wrote her of his ardent hope for peace.[101] Yet the Confederacy claimed no more devoted a patriot.

[97] *SHSP*, v. 19, p. 173.

[98] *SHSP*, v. 9, p. 43.

[99] *SHSP*, v. 43, pp. 62–63; v. 19, pp. 158–59; *Century Magazine*, v. 32, p. 935.

[100] Arnold, pp. 293–94.

[101] Mrs. Jackson, pp. 101, 284.

Jackson informed Robert L. Dabney, his chief of staff, that "I don't profess any romantic indifference to life, and certainly in my own private relations, I have as much that is dear...to live for as any man. But I do not desire to survive the independence of my country."[102]

Hunter McGuire reported that Jackson, unlike Lee, thoroughly disdained his enemies:

> He believed that when the people of the North came down and stole our property, ran off the slaves...burned down the houses and barns of his people, insulted our defenseless women, hung and imprisoned our helpless old men, [and] behaved like an organized band of cut-throats and robbers...that they should be treated like highwaymen and assassins. He hated no individual Northerner... but he hated the whole Northern race.[103]

Jackson's contemporaries and biographers usually identify one additional characteristic of the General's personality, a trait that created a good deal of internal turmoil. Dr. McGuire illustrated what he termed Jackson's "intense earthly ambition" with a quote from an early battlefield. The physician met his commander after the contest and confessed that he had derived no enjoyment from the combat until the fighting concluded. He asked Jackson how *he* had felt the first time in battle. Stonewall promptly replied, "Afraid the fire would not be hot enough for me to distinguish myself."[104]

General Richard Taylor, who served under Jackson in the Valley, suggested one motivation for his commander's religious zeal: "His ambition was vast, all-absorbing. Like the unhappy wretch from whose shoulders sprang the foul serpent, he loathed it, perhaps feared it; but he could not escape it....He fought it with prayer, constant and earnest."[105]

In October 1862, Anna requested Thomas' permission to prepare a biographical article about her husband to satisfy the

[102] *SHSP*, v. 11, p. 255.

[103] *SHSP*, v. 19, pp. 309–10.

[104] *SHSP*, v. 25, p. 104.

[105] Richard Taylor, *Destruction and Reconstruction* (New York: D. Appleton and Company, 1879), p. 91.

public's insatiable demand for information about its national hero. Jackson reacted with humility, only hinting at the satisfaction he derived from his justly-deserved fame: "It is gratifying to be beloved and to have our conduct approved by our fellow men, but this is not worthy to be compared with the glory that is in reservation for us in the presence of our glorified Redeemer....I would not relinquish the slightest diminution of that glory for all this world can give."[106]

The events of early May 1863 rendered moot the General's dilemma. The last week of Jackson's life ensured that the Southern people would enshrine his memory with enduring and unprecedented reverence, as much as for who he was as for what he accomplished.

Nowhere did Stonewall Jackson display his strength of character more dramatically than during the eight-day ordeal following his wounding at Chancellorsville.[107] His self-control allowed him to suppress all expressions of suffering during his removal from the field, save a single groan emitted as his stretcher-bearers stumbled and dropped him painfully to the ground. His concern for others appeared when he advised his aides not to worry about him, but to look after their own safety. His devotion to duty clearly showed as Jackson summoned his waning strength to order a brigadier to hold his ground at a moment of crisis.

The wounded General calmly faced the prospect of death. He told Smith that he preferred to avoid the use of painkillers when preparing to meet his maker. The will of the Lord remained uppermost in Stonewall's mind following the amputation of his left arm on May 3 at a field hospital near Wilderness Tavern. When a visitor expressed regret at the loss of his limb, Jackson replied that the wisdom of his Heavenly Father should never be questioned. R.E. Lee's message crediting Jackson with the victory at Chancellors-

---

[106] Mrs. Jackson, p. 349.

[107] The literature on Jackson's wounding and subsequent events leading to his death on May 10 is voluminous. Among the better accounts are Cooke, *A Military Biography*, pp. 438–85; Dabney, pp. 685–725; Mrs. Jackson, pp. 427–57. Chambers, v. 2, pp. 410–47 is the best synthesis of the numerous conflicting details.

A postwar view of the Fairfield Plantation office building near Guinea Station belonging to Thomas Coleman Chandler. Jackson died in the room on the right of the first floor. [*Special Collections Department, Duke University Library*]

ville elicited a predictable response. "General Lee is very kind, but he should give the praise to God."[108]

The army commander insisted that Jackson be moved somewhere to safety behind Confederate lines, preferably to a place convenient to the Richmond railroad. Stonewall's physicians anticipated the General's recovery but advised that their patient be transferred to formal medical facilities as soon as his condition would permit.

Jackson wanted to remain at the field hospital. "If the enemy does come I am not afraid of them; I have always been kind to their wounded, and I am sure they would be kind to me."[109]

Furthermore, Jackson had always objected in principle to the practice of detailing surgeons to attend to individual officers. A doctor's duty lay with the soldiers at the front. But when Lee ordered McGuire to accompany the wounded General to Guinea Station, Jackson seemed relieved. "General Lee has always been very kind to me and I thank him."[110]

During the long ambulance ride from the Wilderness to Thomas Coleman Chandler's "Fairfield" plantation, Jackson conversed on a variety of topics. He explained that his famous *nom de guerre* belonged wholly to the men of his brigade, "for it was their steadfast heroism which...earned it at First Manassas."[111]

Once ensconced in Chandler's small frame office, the General frequently found pleasure in intellectual and theological discourse with Smith. He told the future minister that "Many would regard [my wounds] as a great misfortune, [but] I regard them as one of the blessings of my life." Smith observed that "All things work together for good to those that love God." "Yes, that's it," Jackson replied.

On the morning of May 7, the telltale symptoms of Jackson's fatal disease unmistakably appeared. Medical science had little

---

[108] Robert U. Johnson and Clarence C. Buel, eds., *Battles and Leaders of the Civil War (B&L)* (New York: Century Co., 1888), v. 3, p. 214.

[109] Hunter McGuire, *The Confederate Cause and Conduct in the War between the States* (Richmond: L.H. Jenkins, 1907), p. 224.

[110] *Ibid.*

[111] Dabney, p. 713.

capacity to treat pneumonia and the doctors resigned themselves to the inevitable prognosis. When Anna and Julia arrived that day, the General welcomed them with a full heart but requested that his wife not look so forlorn: "My darling you must cheer up and not wear such a long face. I love cheerfulness and brightness in a sick room. My darling, you are very much loved. You are one of the most precious little wives in the world."[112]

As the hours passed, Jackson's condition continued to deteriorate. On May 10, McGuire whispered that the end was near. Not surprisingly, Stonewall accepted the news without a blink: "It is the Lord's day; my wish is fulfilled. I have always desired to die on Sunday."[113] Twelve-year-old Lucy Chandler vocalized the sentiments of many people at Fairfield that day when she prayed that "God would let [me] die...for then only [my] mother [will] cry; but if [General] Jackson dies, all the people of the country [will] cry."[114]

The little girl's poignant emotions proved prophetic. Jackson's death shook the Confederacy more than any single event of the war: more than Gettysburg, more than Vicksburg, more than Appomattox. "News of the death of General Jackson, the true hero of the war, fills the whole army with grief," read a typical diary entry.[115]

Raleigh Colston, the commander of Jackson's old division at Chancellorsville, remembered what happened when word of Stonewall's passing reached the field:

> Ah! my countrymen, could you have seen and felt as I did, the sudden change in those camps of the Wilderness, when the dread announcement came..."Jackson is dead!" it would be a memory never to be effaced from your hearts. The sounds of merriment died away as if the Angel of Death himself had flapped his muffled wings over the troops. A silence profound, mournful, stifling and oppressive as a funeral pall succeeded to the voices of cheerfulness, and many were the veterans...whose bronzed cheeks

[112] Mrs. Jackson, p. 451.

[113] *SHSP*, v. 14, pp. 162–63.

[114] *SHSP*, v. 7, pp. 583–84.

[115] *SHSP*, v. 26, p. 9.

were now wet with burning tears, and whose dauntless breasts
were heaving with uncontrollable sobs.[116]

Lee wrote his son, Custis, that the death of General Jackson
was "a terrible loss. I do not know how to replace him. Any victory would be dear at such a cost."[117]

Mrs. Thomas J. Semmes, the wife of a Confederate congressman, believed that:

> The death of General Jackson cast a shadow on the fortunes
> of the Confederacy that reached to the catastrophe of the war. His
> death was not only a loss to his country; it was a calamity to the
> world. As someone has nobly said: "It was a subtraction from the
> living generation of genius; the extraction of a great light in the
> temple of Christianity!" Thousands followed him to the grave and
> consecrated it with their tears.[118]

The authorities removed Jackson's body to Richmond where
it lay in state at the capitol, draped with the new national flag. The
Richmond *Dispatch* reported that it had "never before seen such
an exhibition of heartfelt and general sorrow in reference to any
event as has been evinced...since the announcement of the death
of Stonewall Jackson."[119]

On May 13, Jackson's remains began a journey that concluded the following day in Lexington. The Presbyterian Church
conducted the funeral service and eight companies of V.M.I.
cadets, joined by veterans of the Stonewall Brigade, escorted
Jackson's coffin a few blocks to the town cemetery. There, beside
his first wife and daughter, while grievers heaped flowers over the
grave, the cadets laid Stonewall to rest.[120]

Succeeding generations have never abandoned the memory
of this extraordinary man. Jackson, of course, sealed his fame in
the crucible of combat, and had there been no Civil War there

---

[116] *SHSP,* v. 35, pp. 96–97.

[117] *SHSP,* v. 21, pp. 45–46.

[118] *SHSP,* v. 25, p. 328.

[119] Quoted in Chambers, pp. 451–52.

[120] Chambers, v. 2, p. 455–58.

would have been no Stonewall. But the legendary dimensions of T.J. Jackson exceed the sum of his brilliant victories. Our enduring fascination derives its inspiration as much from attempts to decipher his personality as it does from our admiration of his success on the crimson field.

ESSAY TWO

Failure or Scapegoat?
Jackson at the Seven Days

"**H**E NOWHERE, even distantly, approached his record as a soldier won in every other battle, either before or afterward."[1] So wrote one Confederate officer referring to Thomas J. Stonewall Jackson and his performance during the Seven Days Battles of June and July 1862. Other Southerners, like Robert Toombs of Georgia, shared this opinion: "Stonewall Jackson and his troops did little or nothing in these battles of the Chickahominy."[2]

Did Jackson's alleged poor showing affect the outcome of the campaign? Brig. Gen. Edward Porter Alexander was emphatic on the question:

> Gen. Lee's best hopes & plans were upset & miscarried & … he was prevented from completely destroying & capturing Mc-Clellan's whole army & all its stores & artillery by the incredible slackness & delay & hanging back which characterized Gen. Jackson's performance of his part of the work.[3]

---

[1] Edward Porter Alexander, *Military Memoirs of a Confederate* (New York: Charles Scribner's Sons, 1907), p. 116.

[2] Quoted in Freeman, *Lee's Lieutenants,* v. 1, p. 628.

[3] Gary W. Gallagher, ed., *Fighting for the Confederacy: The Personal Recollections of General Edward Porter Alexander* (Chapel Hill: Univ. of North Carolina Press, 1989), p. 96.

Explanations abound for Stonewall's presumed failures during Gen. Robert E. Lee's first campaign at the head of the Army of Northern Virginia. Lt. Gen. James Longstreet found Jackson "a very skillful man against such men as Shields, Banks and Frémont, but when pitted against the best of the Federal commanders, he did not appear so well."[4] More kindly, if less tangibly, Alexander concluded that at the Seven Days, Jackson was "under a spell."[5]

The campaign that generated such serious indictments against the Confederacy's most brilliant corps commander began in an atmosphere of crisis and hope. Maj. Gen. George B. McClellan and his Army of the Potomac presented the crisis. Their march up the Peninsula between the York and James rivers had carried them within easy hearing of Richmond's church bells.

The hope lay in the Shenandoah Valley, some one hundred miles northwest of the embattled Southern capital. There, a small Confederate army under an obscure professor from the Virginia Military Institute had electrified the South with a series of improbable victories over three Union commands. Stonewall Jackson and his army were on their way to glory.

Maj. Gen. Thomas J. Jackson wished to follow up his victories in the Valley with an offensive thrust into Maryland and Pennsylvania.[6] Reinforcements rushed to him by rail from Richmond on June 11 in the form of Brig. Gen. W.H.C. Whiting's small division and an oversized brigade of Georgians under Brig. Gen. Alexander R. Lawton, but these troops were not destined to march beside the Blue Ridge or splash across the Potomac.[7] Although Lee admired Jackson's aggressive instincts, he viewed McClellan's presence as his primary concern.[8] The addition of Whiting and Lawton would allow Jackson to crush the enemy in his immediate front, and then, after leaving a scratch force in the Valley and guarding the mountain gaps with cavalry, Old Jack's army was to

[4] *B&L*, v. 2, p. 405.

[5] Alexander, pp. 116–17.

[6] Chambers, v. 2, p. 10.

[7] Alexander, p. 111; Dowdey, p. 137.

[8] Chambers, v. 2, p. 11.

"move rapidly to Ashland...and sweep down the Chickahominy...cutting up the enemy's communications...while this army attacks General McClellan in front."[9] This message, dispatched on June 11, marked the genesis of Jackson's participation in the plan that would result two weeks later in the commencement of the Seven Days Battles. Thanks to a spectacular reconnaissance by Lee's cavalry chieftain, Brig. Gen. J.E.B. Stuart, Lee learned enough about the Federal dispositions astride the Chickahominy River and their supply base at White House on the Pamunkey River to devise a scheme for delivering the capital from the blue host on its eastern doorstep.

Reinforced by Maj. Gen. Theophilus H. Holmes' division from North Carolina and Jackson from the Valley, Lee would muster 86,000 men to face McClellan's 100,000. He would hold the Richmond entrenchments with the combined commands of Maj. Gens. John B. Magruder, Benjamin Huger, and Holmes, while those of Maj. Gens. Longstreet, Ambrose Powell Hill, Daniel Harvey Hill, and Jackson struck Brig. Gen. Fitz John Porter's isolated corps on the north bank of the Chickahominy. In this way, one wing of the Union army would be smashed and its supply line severed. Several opportunities might accrue from this, all of them preferable to submitting to a formal siege of the capital.[10]

On June 16, Lee sent specific orders to the Valley for Jackson to join him in Richmond. Somewhat in the manner of carrying coals to Newcastle, Lee warned Stonewall to guard his intentions from friend and foe alike in order to ensure the movement's secrecy. Discretion and deception, of course, were Jackson's strong suits.[11]

Col. Thomas T. Munford, his former student at V.M.I. and present cavalry commander, threw out a screen that effectively blocked all outside awareness of Jackson's preparations. The information that did reach the Yankees came from intentionally

---

[9] *Official Records of the War of the Rebellion (OR)* (Washington: Government Printing Office, 1884), Series I, v. 11, part 3, p. 589. All subsequent references are to Series I.

[10] Shelby Foote, *The Civil War: A Narrative, Fort Sumter to Perryville* (New York: Random House, 1958), pp. 470–71.

[11] *OR*, v. 12, part 3, p. 913.

released Federal prisoners who overheard dramatically staged conversations designed to persuade them that an offensive down the Valley was imminent.[12]

To his own officers, Old Jack said nothing, causing some of them, like Chase Whiting, to question the Virginian's sanity. Whiting's brigades had just joined Jackson via Gordonsville when Stonewall ordered them, without explanation, to countermarch back to that town. Whiting poured out his frustration in an outburst to a comrade: "Didn't I tell you he was a fool, and doesn't this prove it? I believe he hasn't any more sense than my horse!"[13]

The Valley army began to move on June 18 and crossed the Blue Ridge at Rockfish Gap the next day. The army consisted of 18,500 troops, including Whiting, Lawton, Maj. Gen. Richard S. Ewell's division, and Jackson's old division, now under Brig. Gen. Charles S. Winder.[14]

While the infantry filed through the mountain pass, Jackson called his chief of staff, Maj. Robert L. Dabney, into his hotel room at Mechum River Station. Carefully locking the door behind them, Jackson confided in the Reverend Dr. Dabney about the army's plans to join Lee at Richmond. Pledging the cleric to secrecy, Jackson indicated his intention to travel ahead of the men to meet with Lee. Dabney would assume control of the march in Jackson's absence.[15]

The two officers then repaired to the station, where Old Jack had his trunk put on a train, shook hands all around without telling anyone anything, "saying good bye as earnestly," remembered Henry Kyd Douglas, "as if he was off for Europe."[16]

One inquisitive old fellow, inexperienced about asking questions of the former professor, blurted out, "General, where are you going?"

"Can you keep a secret? Yes? Ah, so can I," came Stonewall's reply.[17]

[12] Dowdey, p. 138; Dabney, pp. 433–34.

[13] B&L, v. 2, p. 297.

[14] Vandiver, p. 290; Foote, p. 470; Freeman, Lee's Lieutenants, v. 1, p. 506.

[15] B&L, v. 2, p. 348. Dabney, p. 434, mistakenly places the conference in Charlottesville.

[16] Douglas, p. 97.

[17] Ibid., p. 98.

Many members of Jackson's military family became famous in their own right thanks to their wartime association with Stonewall and as a result of their popular postwar publications.
[*Leib Image Archive*]

As Jackson's train disappeared to the east, the army followed in its wake. There was not enough rolling stock to transport all the troops simultaneously, so arms, stores, some artillery, and baggage were loaded on freight cars. The rear brigades jammed the passenger cars and rode for awhile. Then they would disembark and the locomotives would return for the troops now in the rear. The army thus advanced by alternately riding and marching.[18]

Most of the army reached Gordonsville on June 21. There, Dabney met Jackson, who had waited to investigate a rumored enemy advance from the north. That night, Stonewall asked his aide, "Will you take a railroad ride with me?" The men boarded a special train composed of an engine and mail car, and Jackson promptly fell asleep in the mail clerk's bunk. On Sunday morning the 22nd, the train arrived in Fredericks Hall. There Jackson spent the Sabbath in worship and called the whole march to a halt, providing the troops a welcome and much-needed day of rest.[19]

But the General did not retire that evening. At 1:00 a.m. June 23, accompanied by two aides and a guide whom he instructed to call him "Colonel," Jackson embarked on a fifty-two-mile ride via a relay of commandeered horses and arrived fourteen hours later at Lee's headquarters at the Dabbs House, one and one-half miles northeast of Richmond. Joined by the two Hills and Longstreet, Jackson heard Lee's specific plan for the first time.[20]

The key to the Confederate scheme was maneuver. Jackson's approach eastward, well to the north of the Chickahominy, would allow the other three divisions to cross to the north side of the river. While Stuart's troopers protected his left, Jackson would clear the head of Beaver Dam Creek, outflanking Porter's Federal troops, who had assumed a strong position along the east bank of that stream. In this way, there would be no fighting until the enemy had been flushed from his entrenchments and, by then, Longstreet and the Hills would be on hand. With all four commands in line, the grayclad juggernaut would sweep down the left bank of the Chickahominy, reestablish contact with their outnumbered

---

[18] Dabney, p. 435.

[19] Dabney, p. 435; Vandiver, p. 293; Hunter H. McGuire to Jedediah Hotchkiss, March 30, 1896, in the Jedediah Hotchkiss Collection, Manuscript Division, Library of Congress.

[20] Henderson, v. 1, pp. 395–97; *B&L*, v. 2, p. 350.

forces south of the river, and press forward to interpose between "Little Mac" and his base of supplies at White House.[21]

After articulating this complex concept, involving the independent concentration of four separate divisions, Lee unwisely left the room to allow his lieutenants to discuss the plan among themselves. Longstreet asked Jackson to set the date for the attack because his column had the farthest to travel. When Jackson unrealistically named the 25th, Longstreet objected, advising the Virginian to take an extra day to allow for poor roads and possible Federal interference. Stonewall agreed. The offensive would begin on the 26th.[22] Lee then returned and promised to send written orders the next day.[23] The conference disbanded about nightfall, and Jackson remounted to begin another sleepless night with a marathon ride on rain-soaked roads. He reached Beaver Dam Station, east of Fredericks Hall, on the morning of the 24th.[24]

While Jackson conferred with Lee, Dabney directed the march. The delicate preacher had been miscast in his martial role. A domesticated professor from the theological seminary at Hampden-Sydney College, he initially appeared in camp wearing a Prince Albert coat, and on a ride with the staff raised an umbrella over his beaver hat, creating a ridiculous image for the soldiers.[25]

Dabney proved wholly unsuited for the responsibility Jackson assigned him on the movement to Richmond. The overmatched minister collapsed under the strain and took to his bed with a bad case of what he called "camp diarrhea."[26] The leaderless troops straggled badly on June 23 and spent the 24th merely closing the column on its advance at Beaver Dam Station. On this essentially wasted day, the physically exhausted Jackson sought unprecedented relaxation from a novel and then went to sleep.[27]

---

[21] Douglas Southall Freeman, *R.E. Lee: A Biography* (New York: Charles Scribner's Sons, 1934–1935), v. 2, pp. 111–12. Chambers, v. 2, p. 20; Foote, pp. 474–75.

[22] James Longstreet, *From Manassas to Appomattox* (Philadelphia: Lippincott, 1896), pp. 121–22.

[23] Dowdey, p. 157.

[24] *B&L*, v. 2, p. 348; Chambers, v. 2, pp. 23–24.

[25] Dowdey, p. 199.

[26] Dabney to Hotchkiss, March 31, 1896, Hotchkiss Collection.

[27] Freeman, *Lee's Lieutenants*, v. 1, p. 498; Dabney to Hotchkiss; Vandiver, p. 299.

Lee's written orders for the attack arrived about midnight June 24–25.[28] The passages relevant to Jackson instructed the Virginian to camp on the night of the 25th at "some convenient point west of the Central Railroad," move at 3:00 a.m. on the 26th from that point down the road leading to Pole Green Church and communicate his presence to the troops poised to cross the Chickahominy. Once joined by these other divisions, Jackson, with D.H. Hill in direct support on his right, would "sweep down the Chickahominy and endeavor to drive the enemy from his position above New Bridge, General Jackson bearing well to his left, turning Beaver Dam Creek and taking the direction toward Cold Harbor." Lee's orders said nothing about Jackson's responsibility for combat, and in fact implied that the main point of contact with the enemy would come at New Bridge on the opposite end of the four-division front.[29]

Jackson knew that the 25th would be a long day of marching.[30] He needed to cover some twenty-five miles to reach his jump-off point and do so in time to rest his troops before their scheduled 3:00 a.m. departure on the 26th.[31] He did not know that a Confederate deserter had entered Federal lines and warned McClellan of the Valley army's approach.[32]

Although Union intelligence placed Jackson's command at various locations from Luray to Richmond, McClellan characteristically believed the worst and made preparations to meet an attack against his right. Federal cavalry obstructed roads and destroyed bridges on Jackson's anticipated routes. Little Mac also alerted his guards at White House, cancelled plans for his own attack south of the Chickahominy, and contemplated falling back to the James in the face of what he estimated to be vastly superior numbers. In this way, Jackson's impending presence seized the

---

[28] Freeman, *Lee's Lieutenants*, v. 1, pp. 500–501.

[29] *OR*, v. 11, part 2, pp. 498–99. Chambers, v. 2, pp. 26–28, provides insightful analysis of Jackson's responsibilities as outlined in General Orders No. 75.

[30] Freeman, *Lee's Lieutenants*, v. 1, pp. 500–501.

[31] Chambers, v. 2, p. 25.

[32] Alexander, p. 114.

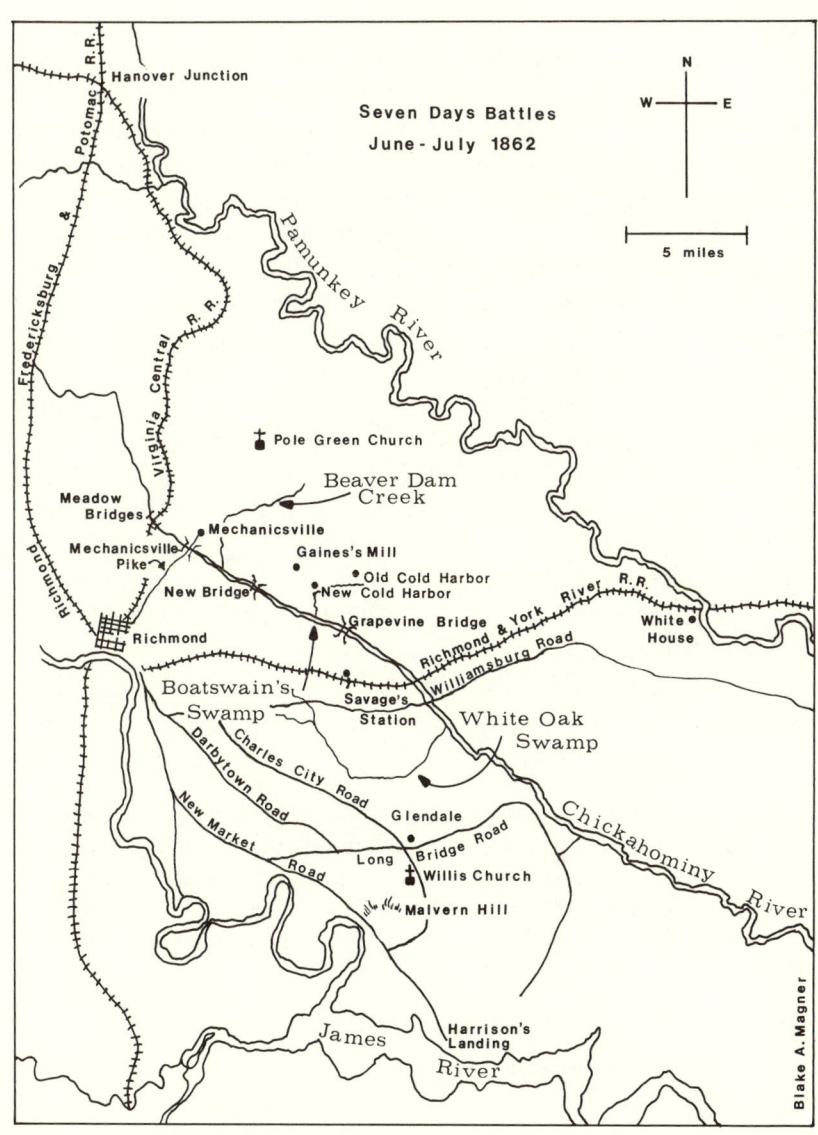

Seven Days Battles
June - July 1862

5 miles

Hanover Junction

Potomac R.R.

Fredericksburg & Potomac R.R.

Virginia Central R.R.

Pamunkey River

Pole Green Church

Beaver Dam Creek

Meadow Bridges

Mechanicsville Pike

Mechanicsville

Gaines's Mill

Old Cold Harbor

New Bridge

New Cold Harbor

Richmond

Grapevine Bridge

Richmond & York River R.R.

White House

Boatswain's Swamp

Savage's Station

Williamsburg Road

White Oak Swamp

Charles City Road

Darbytown Road

New Market Road

Glendale

Long Bridge Road

Willis Church

Malvern Hill

Chickahominy River

James River

Harrison's Landing

Blake A. Magner

initiative from McClellan and accomplished the primary mission of the campaign without pulling a trigger.[33]

The march on the 25th did not begin until an hour after sunrise, "by reason of the indolence and carelessness of julep-drinking officers," thought Rev. Dabney.[34] The troops encountered boggy roads, high, bridgeless streams, and reports of Union cavalry. Under the circumstances, Dabney judged the celerity of the march to be remarkable, but by day's end the soldiers had covered only about twenty miles when they flopped down west of Ashland, which was west of the designated jump-off point.[35] Jackson issued revised orders to resume the march at 2:30 a.m., sent a courier to Lee with news of his delay, and spent the moonlight hours "devoted...to the review of his preparations and to prayer," thus missing another night's rest.[36]

Ewell and Whiting visited Jackson after midnight with questions concerning roads. Jackson put them off with a promise to think matters over and they left. Ewell understood his chief's reticence. "Do you know why General Jackson would not decide at once?" he asked Whiting. "It was because he has to pray over it first." "Old Baldhead" was not surprised, therefore, upon returning to Jackson's quarters for his forgotten saber, to find his superior kneeling in search of divine guidance.[37]

The country into which Jackson's men now entered differed substantially from the ground where they had won their laurels west of the mountains:

> The roads were mere tracks, channels which served as drains for the interminable forest. The deep meadows, fresh and green to the eye, were damp and unwholesome camping-grounds. Turgid streams, like the Chickahominy and its affluents, winding sluggishly through rank jungles, spread in swamp and morass across

---

[33] Foote, pp. 476–77; Dowdey, p. 162.

[34] Dabney to Hotchkiss.

[35] *Ibid.;* Chambers, v. 2, pp. 28–29; Freeman, *Lee's Lieutenants,* v. 1, pp. 503–504.

[36] Freeman, *Lee's Lieutenants,* v. 1, p. 504; Dabney, p. 439. Lee reported the contents of Jackson's dispatch in correspondence with President Davis. Clifford Dowdey, ed., *The Wartime Papers of R.E. Lee* (Boston: Little, Brown, 1961), p. 201.

[37] Dabney, p. 440.

the valleys, and the languid atmosphere, surcharged with vapor, was redolent of decay.[38]

Whiting's troops led Jackson's nine brigades of infantry and nine batteries of artillery on the 26th, another day marred by a slow start. Despite Old Jack's instructions to leave at 2:30 a.m., his men paused to fill their canteens and prepare rations, failing to step out until after sunrise. They reached the Virginia Central Railroad east of Ashland at 9:00 a.m., six hours behind schedule. There Jackson sent word to A.P. Hill of his presence.[39]

As Lee's orders read, Jackson's successive tasks from this position were to: (1) advance toward Pole Green Church; (2) communicate with A.P. Hill, which he had done; (3) make contact with D.H. Hill on his right; (4) lead a combined movement in echelon down the Chickahominy; (5) bear well to his left (northeast); (6) turn Beaver Dam Creek; and (7) take the direction toward Cold Harbor. The orders said nothing about Jackson passing over the creek, and the turning movement was dependent upon the arrival of D.H. Hill and the other divisions in support.[40]

Jackson marched cautiously on the 26th, as indeed circumstances required deep in enemy-held territory.[41] He did appear to be in good humor and pointed out Henry Clay's birthplace as the head of his column moved east.[42] Dr. Hunter H. McGuire, de facto medical chief of Jackson's command, testified after the war that his General "pushed along his army as rapidly as it was possible."[43] Porter's cavalry had obstructed the road to Pole Green Church and destroyed the bridge over Totopotomoy Creek, and now harried the lead units of the Confederate column.[44]

Thanks, according to McGuire, to "almost superhuman exertion," Jackson's men reached Hundley's Corner, a little beyond

---

[38] Henderson, v. 2, p. 2.

[39] Freeman, *Lee*, v. 2, pp. 116–17; Dabney, p. 140; Dabney to Hotchkiss; Freeman, *Lee's Lieutenants*, v. 1, pp. 506–508.

[40] Freeman, *Lee*, v. 2, p. 568. Freeman provides a careful analysis of Jackson's march in an appendix, v. 2, pp. 566–72.

[41] Chambers, v. 2, p. 33.

[42] Douglas, p. 100.

[43] McGuire to Hotchkiss.

[44] *B&L*, v. 2, p. 327; Dabney to Hotchkiss.

Pole Green Church, at 4:30 p.m.[45] Jedediah Hotchkiss, Jackson's topographical engineer, noticed his commander's "anxious and perplexed countenance" at the crossroads.[46] Jackson had heard nothing from Lee all day, had received no response from signals he had fired from a battery announcing his presence, and saw no signs of D.H. Hill, who was supposed to support him on the downriver sweep. Although six hours late, Jackson had otherwise conformed precisely to his orders.[47]

The sounds of battle now reached Stonewall and his officers. This "furious cannonade," as Whiting called it, came from the south and west.[48] Unbeknown to Jackson and contrary to orders, A.P. Hill had independently decided to tackle Porter's defenses along Beaver Dam Creek in the uninformed hope that Jackson would appear on his left to aid him. Hill's attacks proved as costly as they were impetuous and the Battle of Mechanicsville turned into a Confederate slaughter pen.[49] While Powell Hill hurled his brigades into the deadly bottomlands of Beaver Dam Creek, Jackson, five miles away, closed up his columns and went into bivouac.

After the war, various writers noted Jackson's proximity to Hill's struggle and blamed the Valley commander for not rushing to the sounds of battle.[50] Jackson's march on the 26th covered sixteen difficult miles. McGuire called it "a constant fight" and the men were exhausted.[51] Nevertheless, was Stonewall Jackson culpable for the Confederate disaster at Mechanicsville? The answer lies primarily in the difference between Lee's intentions and Lee's actual orders.

The gray chieftain expected Jackson's advance to Pole Green Church to be such a threat to Porter as to compel that officer to retire without offering battle. After the war, Lee called the engagement at Mechanicsville "unexpected." "Marse Robert" based his

---

[45] McGuire to Hotchkiss; Freeman, *Lee*, v. 2, p. 140.

[46] Hotchkiss to Henderson, April 6, 1896, Hotchkiss Collection.

[47] McGuire to Hotchkiss; Dabney to Hotchkiss.

[48] *OR*, v. 11, part 2, p. 562.

[49] See Chambers, v. 2, p. 38, for an analysis of Hill's responsibility for launching the attack.

[50] For example, see Alexander, p. 119; *B&L*, v. 2, p. 403.

[51] Chambers, v. 2, p. 35; McGuire to Hotchkiss.

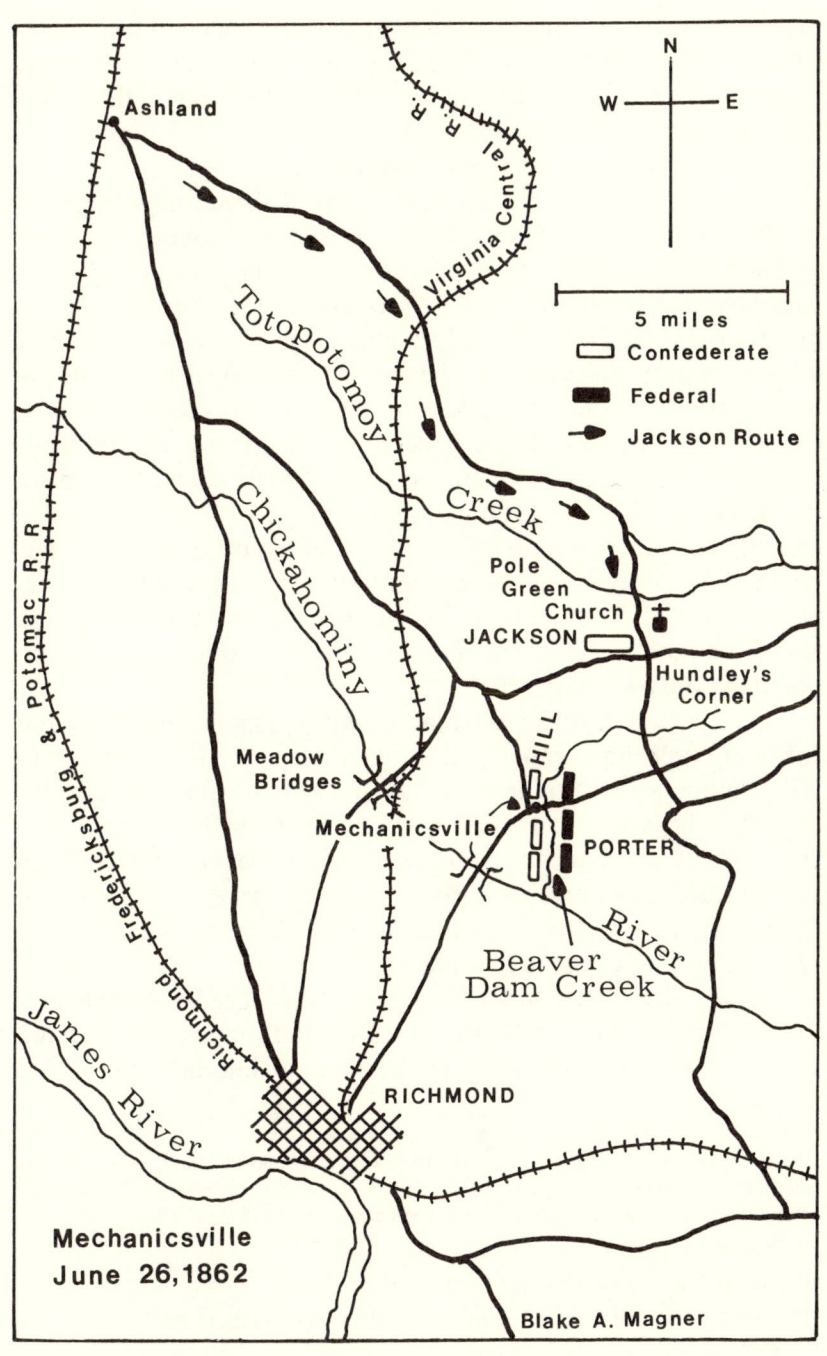

Mechanicsville
June 26, 1862

Blake A. Magner

expectations on a faulty map that incorrectly placed Pole Green Church close to but beyond the headwaters of Beaver Dam Creek. In other words, Lee predicated his orders to Jackson on the belief that Jackson's presence at the church would turn the creek and leave Porter no rational choice but to retreat.

In fact, Pole Green Church lay almost three miles from the headwaters of Beaver Dam Creek, and even at Hundley's Corner Jackson was nowhere near a position to turn Porter out of his entrenchments. Furthermore, Jackson understandably interpreted his orders for the 26th as merely a preparatory movement toward a decisive action the next day. His goal, then, consistent with his written orders, would be Cold Harbor. The only way Jackson at Hundley's Corner could have accomplished Lee's objective of flushing Porter away from Beaver Dam Creek would have been by attacking. This Lee did not order.[52]

Jackson received no communication from Lee or any other commander all day. He stood singularly alone at Hundley's Corner on the afternoon of June 26, on the edge of an unanticipated and ill-defined battle. In the absence of new instructions, Jackson opted to hold his ground.[53]

Furthermore, with hindsight, we know that it is doubtful that Jackson could have moved his road-weary troops five miles to Hill's aid via unfamiliar roads obstructed by blueclad cavalry even had he attempted to do so.[54] While Jackson's critics may speculate as to events had Stonewall's troops moved into position sooner, direct responsibility for the Confederate debacle on the 26th rests with A.P. Hill for disobeying orders and with Lee for drafting poor ones in the first place.[55]

Ironically, Lee's strategy ultimately succeeded in the pre-dawn hours of June 27. Porter's scouts and outposts discovered Jackson's relative proximity to the Federal line and due to the

---

[52] Freeman, *Lee*, v. 2, pp. 570–72, includes copies of both the incorrect map upon which Lee relied and an accurate map depicting the relevant features. See also Chambers, v. 2, p. 40, for a concise analysis of Jackson's interpretation of Lee's orders.

[53] Chambers, v. 2, p. 35.

[54] Dabney to Hotchkiss; Dowdey, pp. 193–95.

[55] Hotchkiss wrote, "Hill disobeyed orders and had no business making an attack." Hotchkiss to Henderson.

presence of the Valley army, not Hill's fruitless assaults, McClellan ordered Porter to withdraw east from Beaver Dam Creek.[56]

The Federals executed their retreat with stealth and skill, leaving behind one brigade of infantry and two batteries of artillery as a rear guard. Even these troops had fled by 8:00 a.m. when Jackson appeared after a slow southward march of three miles across the Old Church Road toward Walnut Grove Church.[57]

Sometime after 9:30 a.m., Lee rode into the yard of that country sanctuary and met Jackson for the first time since the Dabbs House conference of the 23rd. As the curious staffs peered at one another and the generals from a respectful distance, Lee sat on a cedar stump and Jackson, removing his battered old cadet cap, stood before him. The two talked earnestly but quietly and no one recorded the conversation. We may safely assume, however, that Lee outlined his plan for the day.[58]

It resembled, in many ways, the concept that misfired on the 26th. Lee expected to find McClellan drawn up behind Powhite Creek, a mile east of Walnut Grove Church and the only nearby stream on which Lee believed the Federals could make a stand while maintaining direct contact with their forces south of the Chickahominy. Jackson's role would be to march to Old Cold Harbor, in command of D.H. Hill's division as well as his own troops, where he would be well beyond and behind the Union right flank.

Just as the day before, Lee anticipated that Jackson's very presence at a designated spot would force the Federals to retire. If, however, they failed to fall back, A.P. Hill and Longstreet would press them irresistibly from the west, and as they recoiled from this pressure, Jackson, astride McClellan's logical line of retreat toward the Union supply base, would assail their flank. Stonewall nodded his agreement, mounted, and rode away.[59]

Unfortunately for the Army of Northern Virginia, General Lee predicated his strategy on erroneous assumptions for the sec-

[56] Foote, p. 484; Chambers, v. 2, p. 42; *B&L,* v. 2, p. 331; Alexander, p. 121.

[57] Dowdey, p. 204; Alexander, p. 122; Chambers, v. 2, p. 43.

[58] *B&L,* v. 2, p. 353; Dowdey, p. 205; Vandiver, p. 304.

[59] Freeman, *Lee,* v. 2, pp. 140–41; Dowdey, p. 206; Foote, p. 485.

ond consecutive day. The Yankees were not where he thought they would be. Moreover, they had no intention of defending their supply line to the Pamunkey. McClellan had already determined to establish a new base on the James and abandon the one at White House. Porter's job on June 27 would be to defend the north side of the Chickahominy long enough to allow McClellan to evacuate White House and move south with his ponderous wagon train in Porter's rear.[60]

Porter chose to accomplish this mission not from behind Powhite Creek as Lee expected, but east of that water course in rear of a sluggish stream called Boatswain's Swamp. There, behind a semicircle that curved from the northeast to the southwest and then straightened to flow southward to reach the Chickahominy, Porter placed some 35,000 troops well supported by artillery. The banks of both sides of the stream, covered by tangled underbrush, rose steeply, and Porter's men stood six ranks deep on some portions of the line.[61]

Just as on the 26th, A.P. Hill began the action at the Battle of Gaines' Mill. Scattering the thin Union skirmish line at Powhite Creek about noon, Hill plunged blindly ahead into the main Federal position at Boatswain's Swamp. And for the second day in a row, "Little Powell" found himself fighting in a lethal trap at a watery obstacle in the bottom of a ravine.[62]

When Lee discovered the Federals behind this drainage, which did not even appear on his map, he reasoned that his original strategy still applied. Jackson's presence on the Union right would still threaten McClellan's supply line to the Pamunkey. "The arrival of Jackson on our left was momentarily expected," Lee wrote in his report, "and it was supposed that his approach would cause the extension of the enemy's line in that direction."[63] Therefore, a frontal attack by A.P. Hill would catch Porter shift-

---

[60] Dowdey, p. 207.

[61] *B&L*, v. 2, p. 337; Henderson, v. 2, p. 27; Alexander, pp. 122–23. Estimates of Federal troop strength vary from 27,000 to 36,000. Chambers, v. 2, p. 44 provides the best modern description of the Federal position.

[62] Dowdey, p. 216.

[63] *B&L*, v. 2, p. 353; *OR*, v. 11, part 2, p. 492.

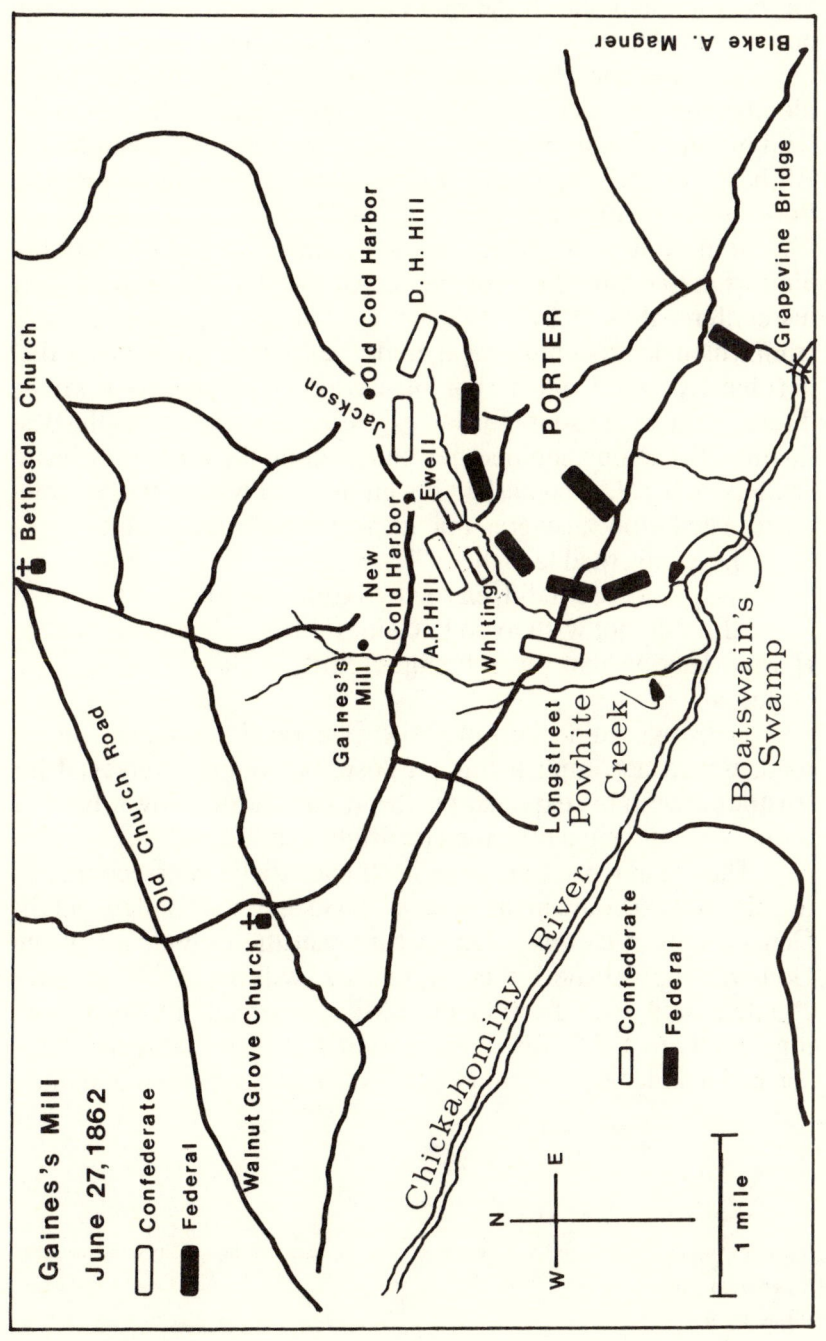

Gaines's Mill
June 27, 1862

Confederate
Federal

ing his men and smash the moving Federal front while Jackson pounded the enemy right and blocked his escape route.

Hill, accordingly, moved forward at 2:30 p.m. but met a bloody repulse.[64] Evidently Porter had not weakened his left to defend his supply line from Jackson's threat. Lee's plan had failed. All bets were off. Now, only a general assault would accomplish Porter's destruction, but where was Jackson?

Stonewall, as we know, was to move to Old Cold Harbor behind what Lee thought would be the Union rear. On the road after his conference with Lee, Jackson spotted a company of cavalry from which he procured a local guide. Telling the trooper only that his objective was Cold Harbor, the cavalcade proceeded down the direct road that led south to Gaines' Mill, then bent east to the destination. Some one and one-half miles along the route they heard artillery firing. Jackson asked his guide from where the fire emanated. The fellow answered that it came from Gaines' Mill.

"Does this road lead there?"

The guide said it did, en route to Cold Harbor.

"But I do not wish to go to Gaines' Mill. I wish to go to Cold Harbor, leaving that place [Gaines' Mill] to the right," Jackson protested.

Jackson's guide informed the General that another, longer road, would accomplish this purpose, but boldly conveyed his frustration with his explanation. "Had you let me know what you desired, I could have directed you aright at first."[65]

The column had to reverse itself back to the intersection, losing almost two hours in the process. Jackson's staff boiled, but the General took it calmly: "Let us trust that the providence of our God will so overrule it that no mischief will result."[66] Jackson's countermarch away from Gaines' Mill prevented him from moving directly to A.P. Hill's support, for it was Hill's battle that Jackson had heard.[67] But, of course, Jackson had been ordered to move

[64] Freeman, *Lee*, v. 2, pp. 146–49.

[65] Dabney, p. 443; Vandiver, p. 305; Dowdey, pp. 212–13, questions the veracity of this anecdote.

[66] Dabney, p. 444.

[67] Dowdey, p. 215.

to Cold Harbor, north of Gaines' Mill, and received no modification of his original instructions.

Meanwhile, Harvey Hill had not fallen victim to the tangled road net and successfully moved by a separate route via Bethesda Church to Cold Harbor. He made contact with the Federals who faced him across the east-west extension of Boatswain's Swamp. When Jackson arrived at Cold Harbor around 3:00 p.m., he withdrew Hill from the Union front. Jackson was, to quote his report, "hoping that Gens. A.P. Hill and Longstreet would soon drive the Federals toward me." He also harbored fears that "our troops would be mistaken for the enemy and be fired into."[68]

To mitigate those contingencies, Jackson shifted Hill to a position from which he might slash the Yankees if they retired toward their supply line and where his men would not be in Longstreet's and Powell Hill's lines of fire as those divisions pressed forward. This decision remained consistent with Lee's original plan, though by now the army commander had determined upon a general assault.[69]

Soon, Jackson independently came to the same conclusion. He could hear that Little Powell's attacks were making scant progress, so he ordered D.H. Hill to drive ahead against Porter's right. He called on Ewell's division to support Harvey Hill's right and sent word back to Lawton, Whiting, and Winder to move up from reserve and support Ewell's right. Once in position, all of Jackson's 27,000 men would surge forward.[70]

Normally, Dabney would have carried his chief's orders back to the waiting reserves. But out of concern for the minister's health, Jackson sent instead his rough-tongued quartermaster, Maj. John A. Harman.[71] Hotchkiss called Harman "a most efficient quartermaster who was always bungling when he had anything to do with matters strictly military."[72] Harman dashed back to Whiting and attempted to repeat Stonewall's orders. Whiting

---

[68] *OR*, v. 11, part 2, p. 553; William Allan, *The Army of Northern Virginia in 1862* (Boston: Houghton, Mifflin, 1892), p. 90.

[69] Chambers, v. 2, pp. 45–46; Dowdey, p. 217.

[70] Chambers, v. 2, p. 46.

[71] Dabney to Hotchkiss.

[72] Hotchkiss to Dabney, March 24, 1896, Hotchkiss Collection.

called Harman's instructions "a farrago of which I could understand nothing." He opted to stay put, as did Winder and Lawton.[73]

After a delay of more than an hour, the ailing Dabney, who had noticed Harman's confusion upon receiving Jackson's orders, rode to Whiting's headquarters. "Whiting was in liquor and received my explanations and new instructions very captiously," remembered Dabney primly, but the cleric managed at last to put the reinforcements in motion.[74]

Jackson's command filed into position for the attack haphazardly, due to the confusing terrain and the botched orders. Lee personally deployed Ewell between the two Hills, where Old Baldhead encountered vicious opposition. Lawton stumbled into place behind Ewell, and Whiting and Winder drifted even farther to the right in support of Little Powell.[75]

Although Jackson thus lost personal control of much of his command, his spirits remained high, cheek and brow blazed red, and his eyes, under the old drab cap, glowed with the fire of battle.[76] He instructed one regimental commander to "make your men shoot like they are shooting at a mark, slow and low, hit them here and here," illustrating his point by thrusting a finger at the Colonel's waist.[77] Impatient of the delays, he turned to waiting couriers with messages for all commanders: "Tell them," he shouted, "this affair must hang in suspense no longer; sweep the field with the bayonet!"[78]

This directed, Jackson trotted along the road to New Cold Harbor. Lee saw him approaching, a dust-covered figure, the dingy cap pulled over his eyes, and chewing enthusiastically on a lemon.[79]

---

[73] Dowdey, p. 218; Dabney to Hotchkiss, March 3, 1896, Hotchkiss Collection.

[74] Dabney to Hotchkiss, March 3, 1896; Dabney to Hotchkiss, December 28, 1896, Hotchkiss Collection.

[75] Dowdey, pp. 218–19, 232; Freeman, *Lee*, v. 2, pp. 149–52; Chambers, v. 2, pp. 48–50.

[76] Dabney, p. 455.

[77] *SHSP*, v. 10, p. 150.

[78] Dabney, p. 455.

[79] Freeman, *Lee*, v. 2, p. 153.

"Ah, general, I am very glad to see you. I hoped to have been with you before."[80]

Jackson's bow contained a flinch, a reaction to the implied rebuke, and he mumbled something indistinguishable in the din. Lee continued the exchange. "That fire is heavy. Do you think your men can stand it?"

Jackson pondered for a moment, listening to the cannon. Then he raised his voice to be heard above the tumult: "They can stand almost anything! They can stand that!"[81]

The presence of the Valley troops heartened the battered brigades of Powell Hill and Longstreet. At last, the Confederate army presented an unbroken front from D.H. Hill on the left to "Old Pete" on the right. While Jackson sat on his horse and sucked a lemon, a sunset charge succeeded in breaking Porter's line and winning the day for Lee's weary soldiers.

But nightfall soon followed the Confederate triumph and brought confusion to all attempts to move troops save for Porter's skillful withdrawal across the Chickahominy. At one point, Jackson rode out in front of his men with a few staff officers and blundered into fifteen or twenty Federals. He recovered before they did and demanded their surrender. Later, as these captives marched to the rear, they boasted, "Gentlemen, we had the honor of being captured by Stonewall Jackson himself."[82]

The Battle of Gaines' Mill marked Lee's first triumph as army commander, but it came at a tremendous price. Some 8,000 Confederates fell on June 27, and writers frequently blame Jackson for the terrible toll. Critics point to the relatively vulnerable Federal right, a position Jackson did not press until the final assault. Moreover, instead of supporting A.P. Hill's frontal attacks, Stonewall actually disengaged D.H. Hill and then tardily marshalled the rest of his troops. Traditional interpretations grant that Jackson regained his energy late in the day, but because most of his brigades fought outside his immediate control, Jackson exer-

---

[80] Cooke, *A Military Biography*, p. 220.

[81] *Ibid.*; Chambers, v. 2, p. 50.

[82] *B&L*, v. 2, p. 359. Hill cites Maj. T.O. Chestney, then assistant adjutant-general of Arnold Elzey's brigade, as his source.

cised little direct impact on the happy conclusion to the day's fighting.[83]

This line of reasoning ignores Jackson's authorized role in the June 27 offensive. Lee misread the Federals' intentions and erroneously assumed that Porter would place himself in a position to be annihilated by Jackson.

Jackson arrived late in this position, but that proved irrelevant because Porter had no intention of protecting the now-abandoned supply line to White House. Jackson wisely seized the initiative when A.P. Hill's attacks failed to achieve their purpose of driving Porter across Jackson's front. The Harman failure conspired against the expedient and organized arrival of the rest of Jackson's brigades, but this had nothing to do with lethargy or lack of aggression on the part of their commander. The facts remain that Jackson did order a general advance and that his troops first pierced Porter's defenses behind Boatswain's Swamp.

Jackson rose early on the 28th looking "brisk enough, cheerful and pleasant."[84] He rode out to examine the ground where Whiting's brigades had executed their successful assaults the evening before and his admiration overcame his reserve. "The men who carried this position," Jackson marvelled, "were soldiers indeed."[85]

Old Jack could tour the battlefield at leisure because the Yankees had disappeared. Determining where they had gone occupied the Confederates all day.

Lee sent Stuart and Ewell down the Chickahominy, where they witnessed Union rearguards destroying the railroad bridge over the river, thus cutting any connection with the Pamunkey. Clearly, McClellan had abandoned his base, but Little Mac's uprooted columns still possessed two options. They could fall back down the Peninsula by the same route they had used to approach Richmond, or they could cut across country to the James River.

---

[83] Alexander, pp. 128–29, 132; Dowdey, p. 234; Gallagher, p. 103.

[84] G. Moxley Sorrel, *Recollections of a Confederate Staff Officer* (New York: Neale Publishing Co., 1917), p. 84.

[85] John Bell Hood, *Advance and Retreat* (New Orleans: Hood Orphan Memorial Fund, 1880), p. 28.

The ruins of Gaines' Mill circa 1887. Maj. Gen. Philip Sheridan probably destroyed the mill in May 1864 during the cavalry operations that also resulted in J.E.B. Stuart's mortal wounding. [*Leib Image Archive*]

Lee ordered Ewell and Stuart to remain on the lower Chicka-hominy to watch for a Federal passage to the north bank, which would signal a retreat toward Williamsburg. But, thought the gray commander, McClellan would more likely move south toward the James. He formulated his plans for the 29th accordingly.[86]

Jackson's troops rested opposite Grapevine Bridge over the Chickahominy. Lee directed them to repair that structure, which Porter had destroyed in his wake, and be ready to cross to the south side in order to harass the tail end of a Federal column mov-ing south. On the other hand, if Stuart turned up evidence of a Union retreat down the Peninsula, Jackson could slide along the north bank of the river and assist Ewell in contesting the Blue-coats' passage.[87]

By dawn of the 29th, all Lee's reports indicated that McClel-lan was hastening toward the James and a new supply line pro-tected by Union gunboats. This change of base, as Little Mac would style it, offered Lee another opportunity to destroy the Army of the Potomac—a much better opportunity, in reality, than had been available at Mechanicsville or Gaines' Mill. By neces-sity, the Federal soldiers, guns, and wagons would be moving on narrow roads across the morass of White Oak Swamp, which me-andered astride their path to safety on the James. Lee, however, had spotted them a one-day head start. Now speed, as well as au-dacity, counted more than ever.

Longstreet and A.P. Hill would negotiate the Chickahominy upstream and race south to the Darbytown Road to gain position near the head of McClellan's column. It would require all day to effect such a march, so Huger on the Charles City Road and Magruder on the Williamsburg Road would pin down the Federal flank and rear respectively to buy time for Little Powell and Old Pete to get into place. Jackson's job would be to repair and cross Grapevine Bridge, march east along the south bank, protecting the army from any threats to the north, and pass behind the extreme

[86] Freeman, *Lee*, v. 2, pp. 162–64; Allan, p. 97.

[87] Freeman, *Lee*, v. 2, pp. 167–68.

northern flank of McClellan's army. From there, Jackson could cooperate with Magruder's assault.[88]

Magruder did attack on June 29 in a battle known as Savage Station. Jackson did not help him. In fact, Jackson's men never crossed Grapevine Bridge and Magruder suffered on a smaller scale what Powell Hill had experienced at Mechanicsville and Gaines' Mill—a sound thrashing. Jackson, we frequently read, was to blame.

The Grapevine Bridge, a "rolling structure of loose logs, half-buried in the slushy soil," presented a difficult engineering challenge.[89] Heavy poles had to be fashioned from the forest and lugged into place manually, both for the long corduroy approach and the passage over the stream.[90] The loose-boweled Dabney superintended the project ineffectually until Capt. Claiborne R. Mason and his corps of black pioneers took over late in the morning. The bridge began to take shape and Jackson informed Magruder that he would be ready to cross in two hours.[91]

Mason's work would consume more time than this, but it had progressed sufficiently for Jackson to pick his way across the half-finished span and reconnoiter the right bank. In the distance, he heard the sounds of battle to the south, just as he had heard them three days earlier. But Lee's orders clearly called for him to move east, not south, toward the Union rear downstream.[92]

At that moment a courier appeared and handed Stonewall a dispatch from Lee via Stuart that resolved any question about Jackson's proper course of action. Lee's cavalry chief had remained downstream as instructed to watch the lower fords and bridges across the Chickahominy. Somehow, Lee now had the notion that McClellan might indeed fall back down the Peninsula rather than make for the James. Accordingly, Jackson should re-

[88] Dabney to Hotchkiss, March 31, 1896; Freeman, *Lee's Lieutenants,* v. 1, pp. 541–42; 560–61; Foote, pp. 495–96.

[89] Cooke, *A Military Biography,* p. 231.

[90] Casler, p. 92.

[91] Dabney to Hotchkiss, April 22, 1896, Hotchkiss Collection; Freeman, *Lee's Lieutenants,* v. 1, pp. 561–62.

[92] Freeman, *Lee's Lieutenants,* v. 1, p. 562; Chambers, v. 2, p. 61; Vandiver, pp. 311–12.

sist the passage of any Federal troops attempting to cross the Chickahominy.

Old Jack acknowledged receipt of this message at 3:05 p.m., informing Stuart that he would leave Ewell downriver and would himself remain on the north bank in a position to rush rapidly to Ewell's aid if necessary.[93] To a messenger from Magruder requesting help with his attack at Savage Station, Jackson responded only that he had "other important duty to perform."[94] Jackson personally recrossed the river, the fire of battle kindled in his heart, and issued orders to his troops to be ready to pursue the Federals.[95]

This communication from Stuart, unknown to Jackson's contemporary critics and overlooked by Douglas Southall Freeman in his account of the Seven Days, is the key to explaining Jackson's behavior on the 29th.[96] Jackson's failure to aid the distraught Magruder, who committed less than half his available troops at Savage Station and in general performed miserably, is far from "unextenuated," as is claimed in the most respected history of the campaign.[97] Ascribing Jackson's lack of action to his refusal to fight on the Sabbath (the 29th being a Sunday), as does E.P. Alexander, illustrates the unsupportable extremes to which Jackson's critics have stretched to make Stonewall the scapegoat.[98]

About midnight of the 29th–30th, a heavy downpour drenched Jackson, and after seeking shelter in an ambulance with Dr. McGuire, the General abandoned all idea of sleep at 1:00 a.m. Leaving word to have his men on the move by 2:30 a.m., he mounted and sloshed through the mud to Magruder's headquarters.[99] The two officers discussed their assignments for the day. Lee now understood that Little Mac was moving south and deter-

---

[93] Vandiver, p. 312. Vandiver cites a dispatch from R.H. Chilton to Stuart dated "Hd. Qrs., Charles City Road, June 29, 1862," in the Stuart Collection, Huntington Library.

[94] *OR*, v. 11, part 2, p. 675.

[95] Dabney, p. 461.

[96] See Freeman, *Lee*, v. 2, p. 174, for one explanation of Jackson's "strange" behavior. Foote, p. 498, is less charitable in his ignorance of the critical dispatch. William B. Franklin, "Rear-Guard Fighting during the Change of Base," in *B&L*, v. 2, p. 376, provides a contemporary Federal interpretation.

[97] Allan, p. 103; Dowdey, pp. 275–79.

[98] Alexander, pp. 136, 145; Gallagher, p. 105.

[99] Dabney, p. 461; Freeman, *Lee's Lieutenants*, v. 1, p. 568.; Chambers, v. 2, p. 61.

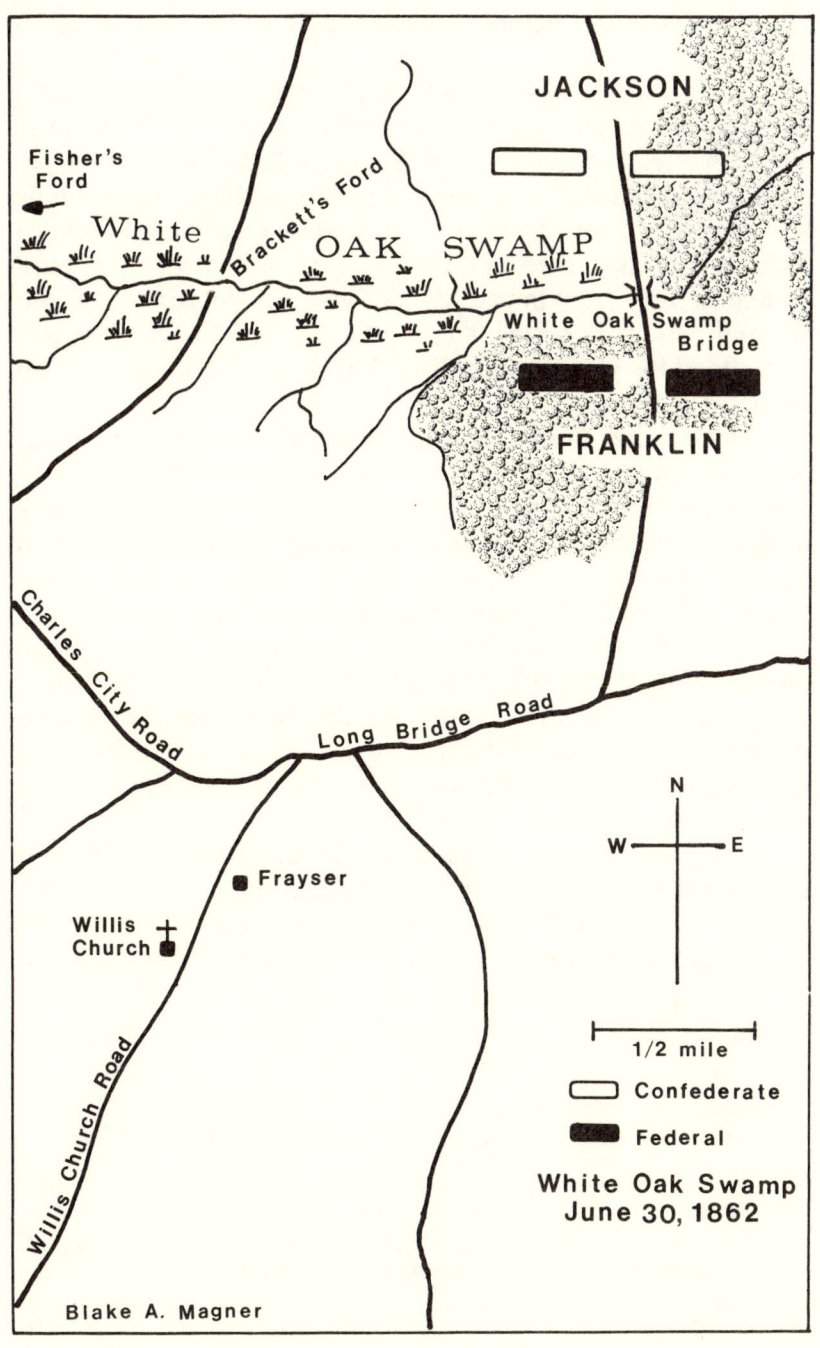

Fisher's Ford

White OAK SWAMP

Brackett's Ford

JACKSON

White Oak Swamp Bridge

FRANKLIN

Charles City Road

Long Bridge Road

Frayser

Willis Church

Willis Church Road

N
W E

1/2 mile

Confederate

Federal

White Oak Swamp
June 30, 1862

Blake A. Magner

mined to renew his attempt to cut off the Bluecoats and catch them in a vise.[100]

After sunrise, Jackson met Lee at Savage Station. The Valley General, "appeared worn down to the lowest point of flesh consistent with effective service...[and] began talking in a jerky, impetuous way, meanwhile drawing a diagram on the ground with the toe of his right boot." Describing two sides of a triangle in the dirt, Jackson carefully traced a third line. Suddenly as that line intersected the first, he stamped his foot and said decisively, "We've got him!"[101] There seems, then, little question that Jackson both understood the plan on June 30 and displayed the energy and enthusiasm to carry it out.[102]

His advance from Grapevine Bridge to White Oak Swamp, a march of seven miles, encountered abandoned Federal property, 1,000 prisoners, and 2,500 wounded Yankees left behind in a field hospital.[103] When someone protested that the captives would be of considerable expense to the government, Jackson shook his head. "It is cheaper to feed them than to fight them," he replied.[104]

While these housekeeping chores progressed, Jackson stole a moment to write the usual Monday morning letter to his wife.[105] The head of his column did not reach the swamp until about noon. By then, all the Federals had crossed and Jackson found the bridge broken and burned and the timbers tossed into the miry ford, rendering it impassable.[106]

The stream itself normally flowed ten to twenty feet wide, narrower in dry weather. After the previous night's rain, however, it resembled a broad bog. The banks and adjoining areas turned to muck and the underbrush was thick.[107] A pine forest on Jackson's

---

[100] Alexander, p. 138; Freeman, *Lee*, v. 2, pp. 176–78.

[101] Stiles, pp. 98–99.

[102] Freeman, *Lee*, v. 2, pp. 179–80.

[103] Alexander, p. 146; Dabney, pp. 460–61; *OR*, v. 11, part 2, pp. 556, 627.

[104] Mrs. Jackson, p. 298.

[105] *Ibid.*, p. 297.

[106] Wade Hampton as quoted in Alexander, p. 150; H.B. McClellan, *The Life and Campaigns of Major-General J.E.B. Stuart* (Richmond: J.W. Randolph and English, 1885), p. 80.

[107] Alexander, p. 146; Chambers, v. 2, p. 53.

left offered concealment, and on his right a considerable clearing atop a wide ridge provided an excellent position for artillery. Looking across the stream to his left, Jackson could see at least three Federal batteries with infantry supports and wagons retreating in the far distance. Opposite the Confederate right, a heavy fringe of tall timber limited his view to the thick foliage of early summer. Some 20,000 Federals under Brig. Gen. William B. Franklin defended the crossing, and Union Brig. Gen. George A. McCall thought the Northerners' position impregnable.[108]

At 1:45 p.m. Jackson opened with twenty-eight pieces of artillery from the ridge on the Confederate right. This barrage overwhelmed Franklin's guns, which fired only four shots before limbering up, and also stampeded a cluster of mules watering at the swamp. The startled Federal infantry took a cue from their long-eared companions and also fled.[109]

Jackson now ordered Col. Munford to lead the 2nd Virginia Cavalry across the swamp, secure a gun abandoned by the Federals, and hold the opposite shore. He sent a battery down to the north bank to disperse Union sharpshooters and directed a crew to repair the bridge. Stonewall joined his troopers across the creek to reconnoiter. Before long, however, the Confederates pounded back down the south slope and through the water to the north side to escape infantry and artillery fire emanating from the woods on the Union left.[110]

Jackson quickly withdrew the vulnerable battery from the road opposite the damaged bridge, concealed his infantry in the forest on his left, but renewed the orders for mending the bridge. He also focused his own artillery upon the hidden Union batteries and maintained an ineffectual long-range contest with the Federal gunners that Alexander termed an "absurd farce of war." Northern sharpshooters and stray artillery shells kept D.H. Hill's men from

---

[108] Gallagher, p. 108; Alexander, p. 150; *OR*, v. 11, part 2, pp. 389, 465; Dabney, p. 464; Chambers, v. 2, p. 64; Allan, p. 109.

[109] *B&L*, v. 2, pp. 378–79; *OR*, v. 11, part 2, p. 561; Freeman, *Lee's Lieutenants*, v. 1, p. 574.

[110] *OR*, v. 11, part 2, pp. 561, 627, 566; Chambers, v. 2, pp. 54–65; Dowdey, pp. 310–11; Dabney, p. 465.

their work at the span, and it became clear that under the prevailing circumstances, Jackson was stymied.[111]

Munford's horsemen had recrossed the swamp in haste slightly downstream from the bridge, but he admitted that his cavalry encountered "great difficulty" in doing so, implying a less-than-ideal ford for infantry.[112] At 2:30 p.m., however, Brig. Gen. Ambrose R. Wright's brigade on a reconnaissance from Huger's division, arrived from upstream and reported to Jackson. Stonewall merely ordered these men to return to their command, which they did by crossing four miles upstream from the bridge at Fisher's Ford, having found a closer crossing point, Brackett's Ford, apparently well guarded.[113]

Brig. Gen. Wade Hampton, in command of a brigade in Jackson's old division, presented yet a third alternative to the stalemate at the bridge. When Hampton reported that he had discovered a downstream crossing suitable for infantry and invisible to Yankee eyes, Jackson asked the brigadier if he could build a bridge there. Hampton thought he could, although it would only support soldiers, not wagons or guns. Jackson told him to do it.[114]

The impromptu span took little time, and soon the wealthy South Carolinian returned to his chief. He found Jackson seated on a fallen pine alongside the road, his head down and his cap over his eyes. Hampton spoke of the completion of his mission, to which his commander raised his head, peered out from beneath his cap brim and said, "H-M-M?" Hampton repeated his report. Jackson answered, "Um-H-m-m," and resumed his reclining posture. Hampton waited for further remarks until the situation became awkward and then returned to his brigade. Jackson rose, repaired to a nearby tree, and went to sleep.[115]

About an hour later he woke up, but sat placidly as though devoid of energy and incapable of action, with a seeming indif-

[111] Freeman, *Lee's Lieutenants*, v. 1, p. 576; Gallagher, p. 108; *OR*, v. 11, part 2, p. 566; Allan, p. 110; Dowdey, p. 312.

[112] Thomas T. Munford in Henderson, v. 2, p. 51.

[113] *OR*, v. 11, part 2, pp. 810–11; Alexander, pp. 142–43.

[114] Alexander, pp. 149–50; Chambers, v. 2, p. 69.

[115] Gallagher, pp. 108–109; Alexander, p. 151.

ference to his men behind him or his comrades ahead of him.[116] Those comrades, Longstreet's and Powell Hill's divisions, were fighting several miles south at Glendale, or Frayser's Farm. None of the other columns, including Jackson's, had participated in the engagement that might have removed McClellan's army from the map. As it happened, the Federals resisted numerous Confederate attacks and slipped beyond Lee's trap to a strong position near the James.

At supper that night, on the far side of White Oak Swamp, Stonewall dozed off with a piece of unchewed biscuit between his teeth. Startled to consciousness by his own nodding, he looked blankly about, then rose from the table. "Now, gentlemen," he addressed his staff, "let us at once to bed, and rise with the dawn, and see if tomorrow we cannot do something."[117]

Clifford Dowdey calls Jackson's performance on June 30 a "complete, disastrous and unredeemable" failure.[118] E.P. Alexander writes, "When one thinks of the great chances in General Lee's grasp that one summer afternoon, it is enough to make one cry...and to think too that our Stonewall Jackson lost them."[119] Even William Allan, an unabashed Jackson admirer, felt that White Oak Swamp "is best...set...down as one of the few great mistakes of his marvelous career."[120]

It is difficult to disagree with this assessment, although the case is not as one-sided as it may at first appear. Jackson himself reported that "the marshy character of the soil, the destruction of the bridge over the marsh and creek, and the strong position of the enemy for defending the passage prevented my advancing until the following morning."[121]

What then of the alternative crossings discovered by Munford, Wright, and Hampton? Lee's orders did specify that Jackson should cross White Oak Bridge, and despite being within forty

[116] Chambers, v. 2, p. 70.

[117] Dabney, p. 467.

[118] Dowdey, p. 308.

[119] Gallagher, p. 109.

[120] Allan, p. 121.

[121] *OR*, v. 11, part 2, p. 557.

minutes of Stonewall's position, Lee failed to communicate with his lieutenant all day.[122] As Jackson phrased it a few weeks later, "If General Lee had wanted me, he could have sent for me."[123] Furthermore, an upstream crossing would have removed Jackson from a position to turn east and pursue the Federals had Lee forced them to flee down the Peninsula, and would have put Jackson's troops in rear of Huger's jammed columns on the Charles City Road.[124]

D.H. Hill's suggestion that Jackson intentionally spared his troops under the belief that the Valley army had done more than its share of fighting is as full of nonsense as the camp rumor that Stonewall was unwilling to cooperate as a subordinate.[125] Finally, holding Jackson solely responsible for the futility on June 30 ignores the shortcomings of Holmes, Magruder, and especially Huger, who contributed their full measure to the failure.

Early on the morning of July 1, Jackson sent Whiting's men to test the crossing at White Oak Swamp. Discovering that the enemy had withdrawn, Jackson's troops swiftly repaired the bridge and pushed south, Stonewall in the lead of the unopposed column. Near the Willis Church, he spotted a knot of officers and rode toward them. They turned out to be Lee and his various commanders, and Old Jack joined them to discuss the day's strategy.[126]

Lee said nothing about the frustration of the 30th. Instead, he directed that the Confederates pursue south in a last attempt to bring McClellan to bay.[127] The Federals might be found several miles ahead on a plateau called Malvern Hill. Rev. L.W. Allen of Magruder's staff knew that terrain and had told D.H. Hill of its natural strength. Hill advised Lee at the conference: "If General McClellan is there in force, we had better let him alone." Long-

---

[122] Dowdey, p. 295; Henderson, v. 2, p. 57.

[123] Henderson, v. 2, p. 57. He cites Dr. McGuire as his authority.

[124] *Ibid.,* p. 58.

[125] Freeman, *Lee,* v. 2, pp. 572–82, provides an exhaustive review of these and other theories advanced to explain Jackson's torpor at White Oak Swamp.

[126] Vandiver, p. 317.

[127] Dowdey, p. 319.

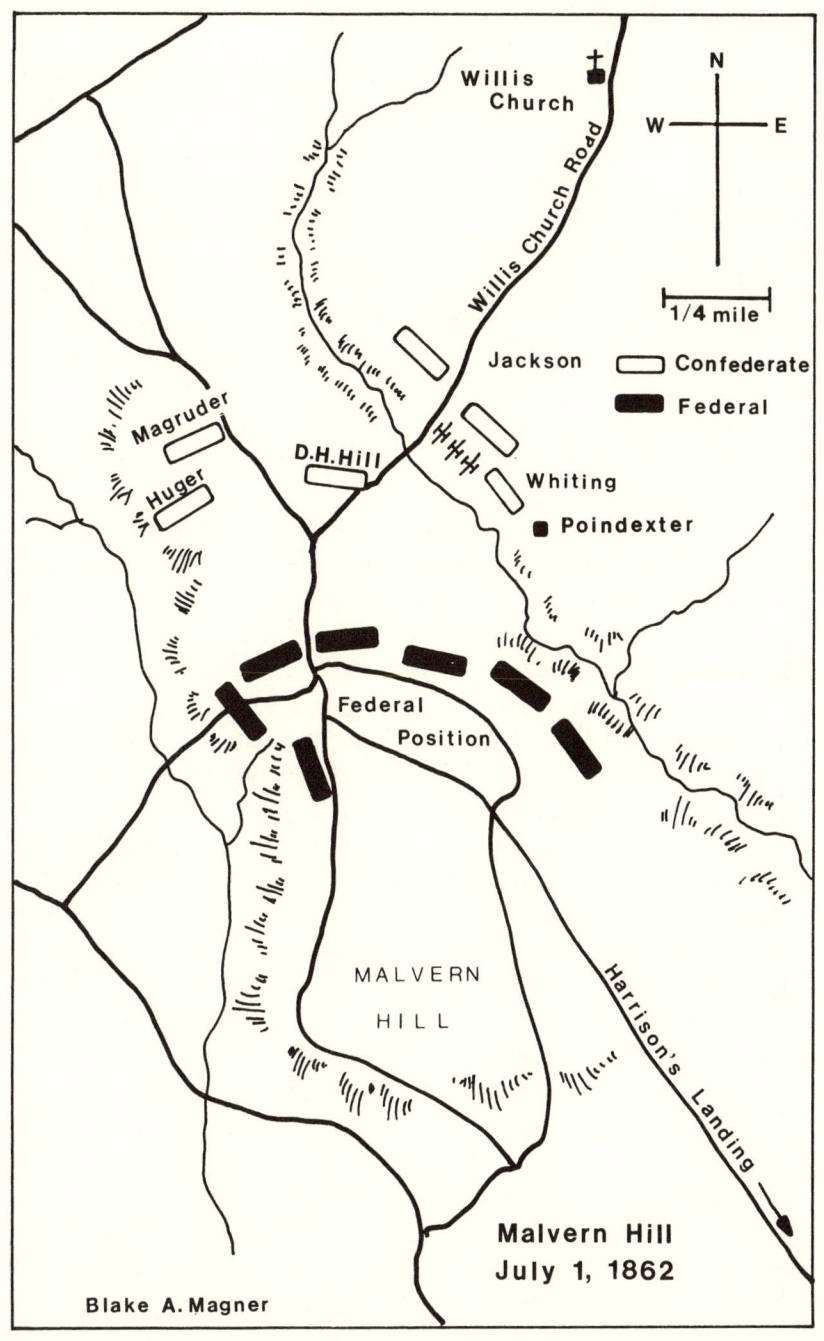

**Malvern Hill
July 1, 1862**

Blake A. Magner

street scoffed at Hill's trepidation. "Don't get scared, now that we have got him whipped!"[128]

Jackson's column led the pursuit. Halting at the base of Malvern Hill, Jackson sent Whiting to the left of the road into the fields of the Poindexter Farm where he found protection in a shallow woods. D.H. Hill took position to the right of Whiting across the Willis Church Road, the gap between them plugged later by Brig. Gen. Isaac R. Trimble's brigade of Ewell's division. Whiting held the extreme Confederate left and deployed by 11:00 a.m. The rest of Jackson's command filed into reserve behind Whiting and Hill, while Magruder and Huger eventually formed the Confederate right.[129]

McClellan had indeed occupied Malvern Hill in front of Lee's army. "Had the Union engineers searched the whole countryside below Richmond," wrote D.S. Freeman, "they could not have found ground more ideally set for the slaughter of an attacking army."[130] Fitz John Porter, who defended the eminence, called his position "better adapted for a defensive battle than any with which we had been favored"—high praise from the man who had already slaughtered Rebels from behind Beaver Dam Creek and Boatswain's Swamp.[131]

James Longstreet, however, thought he knew the solution to the Malvern Hill conundrum. He discovered two positions, one on the Confederate right and one on the left, that provided excellent artillery locations. A massive concentration of iron crossfired against the Yankees on the hill would soften them up, thought Old Pete, for a devastating infantry assault that would carry the Confederate battle flags over the high ground and down to the James. Lee agreed to try.[132]

Unfortunately, the bombardment Longstreet anticipated never occurred. The batteries unlimbered piecemeal and Union

---

[128] *B&L*, v. 2, p. 391.

[129] Vandiver, p. 318; Allan, p. 126. Dowdey, p. 327, cites Jackson's report in *OR*, v. 11, part 2, p. 557, to support his view that Taylor's brigade filled the interval between Whiting and Hill.

[130] Freeman, *Lee*, v. 2, p. 204.

[131] *B&L*, v. 2, p. 409; Gallagher, pp. 111–12 provides Alexander's concurrence.

[132] Longstreet, p. 143.

guns blasted them before they could make any impact. Brig. Gen. William N. Pendleton, in charge of the army's reserve artillery, spent the day searching for Lee while Lee searched for him, and none of his needed guns reached the front.[133] Jackson, on the left, managed to bring eighteen cannon into play, at times personally rolling them into place and dangerously exposing himself to counterbattery fire.[134] But such a weak show from the long arm—Harvey Hill called it "farcical"—clearly could not pave the way for the foot soldiers.[135]

Lee's orders circulated early in the afternoon: "Batteries have been established to rake the enemy's lines. If it [sic] is broken, as is probable, [Brig. Gen. Lewis A.] Armistead, who can witness the effect of the fire, has been ordered to charge with a yell. Do the same."[136]

As a combat directive, Lee's orders at Malvern Hill are almost unbelievable. They assigned the responsibility of where and when to attack to a mere brigade commander, one of fourteen such men whose troops covered more than a mile of densely wooded country. To expect one brigade's "yell" to be a clear signal to everyone to move forward in concert stretched credulity.

In fact, it was incredible. Lee predicated his infantry attack on the success of his artillery bombardment, which manifestly failed. He probably felt, therefore, that his orders no longer applied and forgot them. But John Magruder had not forgotten them.

As the sun lowered on the western horizon behind him, Lewis Armistead noticed the advance of Col. Hiram Berdan's Union sharpshooters toward his portion of the line and directed his men to repulse them, which they did. "Prince John," feeling keenly his failures of the last three days and the commanding general's criticisms of them, misinterpreted this isolated action as the signal from Armistead for a general advance. He so reported to Lee, who, after accepting Whiting's mistaken impression that the Federals were retiring, authorized the attack.[137]

---

[133] *OR*, v. 11, part 2, pp. 533–37; Gallagher, p. 112.

[134] *B&L*, v. 2, p. 392; Freeman, *Lee's Lieutenants*, v. 1, p. 596.

[135] Freeman, *Lee's Lieutenants*, v. 1, p. 597.

[136] *OR*, v. 11 part 2, p. 677.

[137] Dowdey, pp. 336–38.

Sitting on his horse with a leg thrown over the pommel and smoking a cigar, Harvey Hill heard the shouts to his right. Although fully realizing that the artillery had not done its job, Hill ordered his troops forward into the maelstrom of Malvern Hill. It was, as through all the Seven Days, Confederate infantry versus Union artillery—valor versus iron.[138] "Never was the courage of troops more severely tried and heroically exhibited than in this charge," wrote one Confederate officer.[139] Hill put it differently: "It was not war—it was murder."[140]

Hill suggested that Jackson push up his reserves. Stonewall ordered Ewell and Winder to the front, "but from the darkness of the night, and the obstructions caused by the swamp and undergrowth, through which they had to march, [they did not reach the front] in time to afford the desired support."[141]

Shortly before dark, Jackson discovered Trimble forming his troops under cover of the gathering dusk.

"What are you going to do, General Trimble," asked Jackson.

"I am going to charge those batteries, sir," Trimble answered bravely.

"I guess you had better not try it. General D.H. Hill has just tried it with his whole division and been repulsed; I guess you had better not try it, sir."[142]

Jackson then rode off. The assaults on the Rebel right met the same fate as Hill's, and the fighting at Malvern Hill sputtered out at dark.

G.F.R. Henderson called Malvern Hill "one of the very worst fought battles I ever read of,"[143] and who can argue? E.P. Alexander manages again to blame Jackson for this most hideous Confederate tactical failure of the Seven Days,[144] but few other writers

---

[138] *Ibid.*, p. 340.

[139] John B. Gordon in Allan, p. 132.

[140] *B&L*, v. 2, p. 394.

[141] *OR*, v. 11, part 2, p. 558.

[142] Freeman, *Lee's Lieutenants*, v. 1, p. 603.

[143] Henderson to Hotchkiss, February 7, 1897, Hotchkiss Collection.

[144] Gallagher, pp. 113–14.

share his opinion. Stonewall displayed great personal energy on July 1 and promptly obeyed every order he received.[145]

Jackson's failure to include Whiting in the suicidal attacks late in the day can hardly be tallied on the debit side of his ledger. Hill's request for reinforcements arrived too late for Jackson to honor it.[146] With hindsight, it is apparent that by moving around the Federal right, that is by extending Jackson's left, Malvern Hill might have been turned. Lee issued no orders for such a maneuver and, in fact, asked nothing of Jackson that day that required initiative or judgment.[147] Longstreet, Pendleton, Magruder, Whiting, and most of all Lee himself bear responsibility for the tragedy at Malvern Hill; this was not Jackson's battle.

That night, Stonewall found his headquarters wagon, and after consuming his first good meal in many days, stretched out to rest. At 1:00 a.m., Ewell and D.H. Hill disturbed their General's slumber with concerns about meeting a possible dawn attack from McClellan. Jackson arose, and one sleepy observer, seeing the three men squatting in a circle, thought they resembled a triumvirate of frogs. "No," Jackson said quietly, "I think he will clear out in the morning."[148]

Stonewall was right. The blue rear guard on Malvern Hill faded into the morning mist and Jackson spent the forenoon furiously superintending the burying of the dead. He cleansed the grim field of all its gore, and when asked why, he replied, "I am going to attack here presently...and it won't do to march the troops over their own dead.[149]

Later that day, while Jackson visited Lee at army headquarters, President Jefferson Davis appeared. Stonewall arose and stood at rigid attention. Lee saw Davis looking at him. "Why President, don't you know General Jackson? This is our Stonewall Jackson."

---

[145] Chambers, v. 2, p. 83; Alexander, p. 167.

[146] Dowdey, p. 341.

[147] *Ibid.*, p. 328.

[148] Dabney to Hotchkiss, May 7, 1896, Hotchkiss Collection; Dabney, p. 473.

[149] W.W. Blackford, *War Years with Jeb Stuart* (New York: Charles Scribner's Sons, 1945), pp. 80–82.

They did know each other, of course, but their relationship had been strained by the Loring incident at Romney a few months earlier. Observing Jackson's bristling manner, Davis did not advance to shake hands. Instead, he bowed, and Jackson responded with a stiff salute.[150]

Davis and Lee launched into a discussion of the proper Confederate reaction to McClellan's retreat. Jackson clearly favored maintaining the offensive. "They have not all got away if we go immediately after them," he said, but the poor weather and battered condition of the Southern army overcame his advice.[151] Dabney reported that when Lee made the decision not to pursue, Jackson's face "expressed first surprise, then dissent, mortification, sorrow, anguish."[152] McGuire remembered, "I never saw... Jackson show such mental agony as he did that day."[153]

Stonewall Jackson included his assessment of the Seven Days Battles in the report he wrote after the fighting: "Undying gratitude is due to God for this great victory, by which despondency increased in the North, hope brightened in the South, and the capital of Virginia and the Confederacy was saved."[154] Lee's evaluation of the campaign cut closer to the heart of the matter: "Under ordinary circumstances the Federal army should have been destroyed.[155]

The extraordinary circumstances of the Seven Days to which Lee referred, but did not define, are most frequently identified as shortcomings in Thomas Jackson's performance. This narrative has examined the indictments on each day's battlefield and attempted to discredit some of the unsatisfactory theories used by previous writers to account for Jackson's behavior. It is impossible, however, to evaluate Jackson at the Seven Days without addressing his physical condition.

[150] McGuire to Hotchkiss, May 28, 1896, Hotchkiss Collection.

[151] Jefferson Davis, *The Rise and Fall of the Confederate Government* (New York: D. Appleton and Co., 1881), v. 2, p. 150.

[152] Dabney to Henderson, cited in Henderson, v. 2, p. 70.

[153] McGuire to Hotchkiss, March 30, 1896, Hotchkiss Collection.

[154] *OR*, v. 11, part 2, p. 559.

[155] *OR*, v. 11, part 2, pp. 196–98.

Dowdey explains the General's alleged lethargy as a classic example of clinical stress fatigue—a medical phenomenon not yet defined in the 19th century.[156] Beginning with his ride from Fredericks Hall on June 23 and his return the following day, Jackson lost sleep that he never regained. Each night through June 30, with the possible exception of the 28th, Jackson's nightly rest was either interrupted or destroyed entirely. Throughout these eight days, he arose each morning at or before dawn—roughly 4:30 a.m. His only known naps occurred after returning from Lee's headquarters on the 24th and at White Oak Swamp on the 30th.[157]

Moreover, Jackson admitted to his wife on July 8 that he had been sick: "During this past week," he said, "I have not been well, have suffered from fever and debility, but through the blessing of an ever-kind Providence I am much better today."[158]

To recognize that Jackson suffered exhaustion and impaired health, however, is not to subscribe to any universal condemnation of his generalship during the campaign. At White Oak Swamp, his depleted physical resources certainly affected his judgment. Hampton's crossing point conformed so closely to his original objective that any general officer should have exercised the discretion to use the unexploited alternative. On the other fields, Jackson's command decisions are defensible. The mistakes he did commit are most accurately understood in terms of poor communications and staff work by army headquarters, lack of adequate maps or knowledge of the country, and a determined and skilled enemy. Under these criteria, A.P. Hill, Magruder, Huger, Holmes, Longstreet, and Lee himself all share the blame.

Why then do Jackson's errors consistently receive so much emphasis in analyses of the Seven Days? The answer may be that although Jackson failed only relatively, not abjectly, during this campaign, writers tend to obscure the distinction.

Historians often articulate an invidious comparison between the Stonewall of the Valley and the Stonewall of the Chickahom-

---

[156] Dowdey, pp. 196–98.

[157] Chambers, v. 2, pp. 73–74.

[158] Mrs. Jackson, p. 302.

iny.[159] Of course, Jackson at the Seven Days did not operate as an independent commander, as he had earlier, but functioned under direct orders from a superior officer. Lee would never again limit Jackson's discretion on the field so tightly, and the results of this adjustment define the high water mark of Confederate military destiny.

Therefore, to admit that Jackson, the new subordinate, did not display the aggressive initiative east of Richmond that he had shown beside the Shenandoah River should be neither surprising nor tantamount to acknowledging failure. Instead, to judge any officer by the standards Stonewall Jackson established in the Valley, on the Plains of Manassas, or at Chancellorsville is to pronounce that officer a relative failure—even if the officer is Jackson himself.

---

[159] Alexander, p. 167, for example.

ESSAY THREE

Artistry in August: Jackson and the Second Manassas Campaign

> For these great and signal victories our sincere and humble thanks are due unto Almighty God....In view of the arduous labors and great privations the troops were called to endure and the isolated and perilous position which the command occupied while engaged with greatly superior numbers of the enemy we can but express the grateful conviction of our mind that God was with us and gave us the victory, and unto His holy name be the praise.[1]

MAJ. GEN. Thomas J. Jackson's pious self-effacement represents a rare miscalculation concerning the command clinic he conducted in August 1862 known as the Second Manassas Campaign. For there can be no doubt about the identity of the earthly architect who crafted the dramatic series of maneuvers and engagements that combined the risks of Chancellorsville, the deep and mobile defense of Fredericksburg, and the independence and celerity of the Valley Campaign to blunt a Union offensive and pave the way for the Confederacy's first "invasion" of the North.

The road toward this singular achievement began in July when Gen. Robert E. Lee detached Jackson's original Valley army from the Richmond defenses to counter a threat posed to the Vir-

---

[1] *OR*, v. 12, part 2, p. 648.

ginia Central Railroad by a new Federal force under Maj. Gen. John Pope. Joined by Maj. Gen. Ambrose Powell Hill's division, Jackson defeated a portion of Pope's command at Cedar Mountain near Culpeper on August 9, but withdrew across the Rapidan River forty-eight hours later in the face of increasing Federal strength.

Despite this retreat, Jackson still cherished the offensive. He instructed his topographical engineer to prepare maps covering the whole area from Gordonsville to Washington, thus revealing his preference for a theater of operations. This proved to be a wise expedient, because on August 15 Lee arrived at Gordonsville with the bulk of Maj. Gen. James Longstreet's wing of the army and endorsed his lieutenant's strategic conception. Overruling Longstreet's preference for a movement by the Confederate left, Lee agreed with Jackson that the Federal left should be their target, thus interposing between Pope and his expected reinforcements from Fredericksburg. By means of a quick infantry thrust across the Rapidan and a cavalry foray aimed at destroying the vital railroad bridge across the Rappahannock in Pope's rear, the Federals could be trapped between the rivers and "suppressed" as Lee so passionately desired.[2] "Probably at no time during the war," wrote a Southern officer, "was a more brilliant opportunity put so easily within [Lee's] grasp."[3]

Jackson recognized the rare chance to strike a decisive blow and urged a crossing on the 16th, even though the cavalry would not then be present. When Longstreet objected to an immediate advance on the basis of possessing inadequate supplies, the Valley General offered to furnish rations from his own wagons and pointed to the abundant Federal provisions at Brandy Station that would supplement the green apples and ripening corn of the Piedmont. Each passing hour, Jackson knew, brought the Army of the Potomac closer to a rendezvous with Pope, whose augmented numbers already approached 70,000.[4]

But General Lee insisted that his mounted arm be included in the operations. Wishing also to respond to the concerns of his "old

---

[2] Chambers, v. 2, p. 119. Freeman, *Lee*, v. 2, pp. 277–81.

[3] Alexander, p. 186.

[4] Tate, p. 197; Chambers, v. 2, p. 125; Freeman, *Lee*, v. 2, pp. 280, 282.

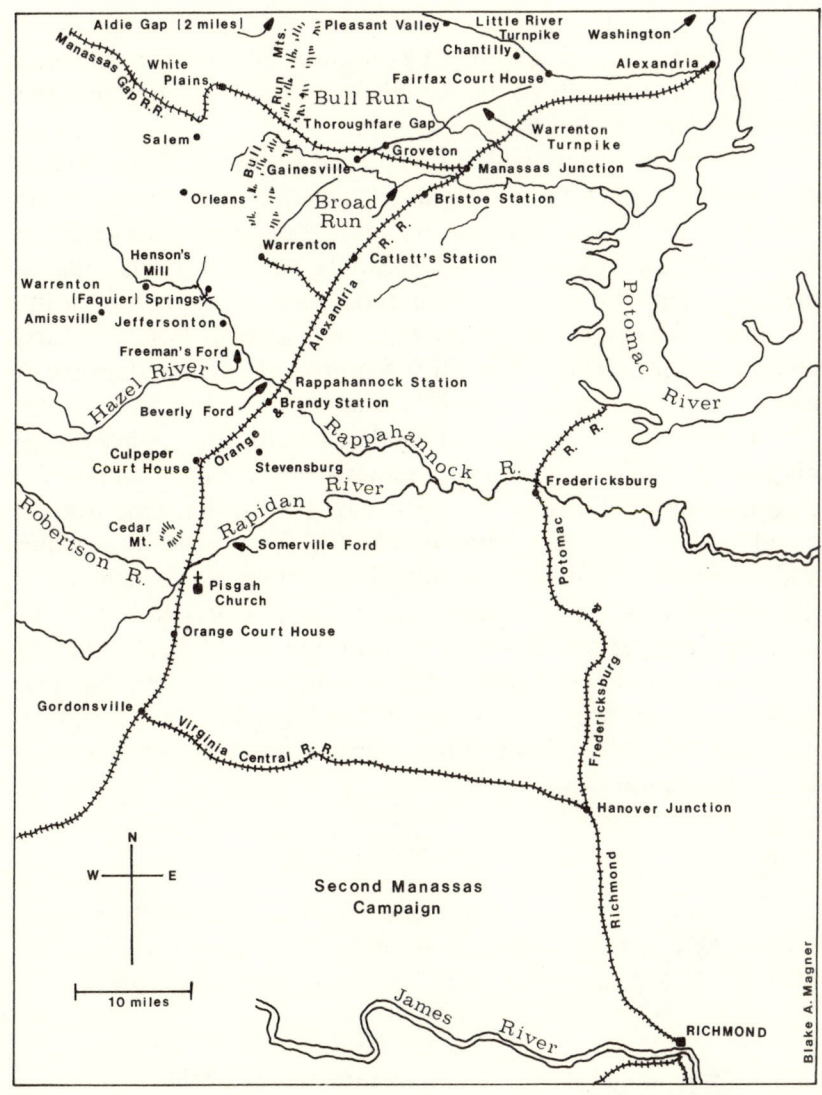

Second Manassas Campaign

10 miles

Blake A. Magner

war horse," he named instead the 18th as the day of battle.[5] At this, according to one eyewitness, Stonewall "laid down on the ground, under an adjoining tree, and groaned most audibly," prompting Longstreet to remark disapprovingly that such conduct was disrespectful of the council.[6]

The irony of being chastised by James Longstreet about civilities perhaps eluding him, Jackson joined his troops at Pisgah Church near the fords of the Rapidan and went into bivouac. He would remain here for five days.[7]

The cavalry upon which Lee placed so much reliance failed to arrive in time for the scheduled advance. Moreover, on the morning of the 18th, Pope barely missed capturing Confederate cavalry chieftain Maj. Gen. J.E.B. Stuart, but did liberate Stuart's precious plumed hat and cloak and a copy of Lee's orders for the offensive.[8] Thus apprised of his impending demise, Pope retreated "like a fleeting vision" toward the north side of the Rappahannock.[9]

Jackson chafed at the delay and vented his impatience on the night of the 19th by means of a moonlight reconnaissance in the company of a handful of staff officers and cavalry. One trooper concluded, "It was one of those freaks which sometimes seize him and which make many people think he is somewhat deranged."[10]

While Jackson galloped about in the darkness adding to his eccentric reputation, his soldiers stood poised to begin another campaign. "Great confidence in the abilities of our Generals pervades the whole army," wrote an officer. "It is the general impression…that the mass of the Yankee Army is much demoralized and will not fight too well."[11]

---

[5] Freeman, *Lee*, v. 2, p. 282.

[6] Dr. A.G. Grinnan, "General Lee's Movement against Pope, August 1862," Hotchkiss Collection.

[7] James I. Robertson, Jr., *The Stonewall Brigade* (Baton Rouge: Louisiana State Univ. Press, 1963), pp. 140–41.

[8] Chambers, v. 2, p. 125.

[9] Dabney, p. 512.

[10] Charles Minor Blackford III, ed., *Letters from Lee's Army* (New York: Charles Scribner's Sons, 1947), p. 113.

[11] James Power Smith to his sister, August 19, 1862. Typescript at Fredericksburg and Spotsylvania National Military Park.

Pope's escape may not have dampened the enthusiasm of the rank and file, but it did change the strategic imperatives for Lee. Union reinforcements from the east now precluded a movement against the Federal left where the Confederate right would lie dangerously exposed to Pope's accretions. Now, an advance up the Rappahannock aimed at turning Pope's right offered the only hope to thrash the Prairie State General before Maj. Gen. George B. McClellan's corps completed their long journey to northern Virginia from the Peninsula.[12]

With this in mind, Jackson pushed his columns across the Rapidan at Somerville Ford early on the morning of August 20. A.P. Hill, confused about his marching orders, failed to begin at the appointed hour, thus plunging himself deeper into Jackson's disfavor. Despite the tardy departure and the need to detour the march into a field to avoid a skunk—"one of Pope's scouts" according to the impertinent Confederates—Jackson's men covered nearly twenty miles and made camp near Stevensburg, not far from the Rappahannock.[13]

This creditable march and cavalry skirmishes during the day notwithstanding, the Federals successfully slipped the noose and scrambled through thigh-deep fords to the left bank of the Rappahannock.[14] That side of the river dominated the opposite shore and, in the words of an artilleryman, had Lee chosen to launch a frontal assault, it "would have been pie for Pope like Malvern Hill was for McClellan."[15]

Jackson reached the river on the 21st and exchanged cannon fire with the Bluecoats at Beverly Ford. Stuart probed across the stream with a single cavalry regiment, but the Confederates risked no further incursion into Pope's formidable lair. The Federals now had terrain as well as time on their side and offered Lee no alternative but to push farther upstream in search of an unguarded crossing.[16]

[12] Chambers, v. 2, p. 125.

[13] Freeman, *Lee's Lieutenants* v. 2, p. 66; Douglas, p. 130; Chambers, v. 2, p. 128.

[14] Cooke, *A Military Biography*, p. 269.

[15] Gallagher, p. 129; Vandiver, p. 349.

[16] Allan, pp. 185–86.

The following day, Jackson continued his leftward sidle past fortified Freeman's Ford and on toward the bridge at Fauquier Springs, leaving his wagons behind under the watchful eye of pugnacious Brig. Gen. Isaac R. Trimble. The span at the Springs lay in ruins, but the distant bank appeared unoccupied at the moment. Stonewall ordered a Georgia regiment to wade the current, supported on its right by Jubal Early's brigade, which tip-toed over a dilapidated dam a mile downriver.[17] But these Confederates were not the only troops to execute a crossing on the 22nd.

Back at Freeman's Ford, Brig. Gen. Henry Bohlen led three Union regiments through the swirling waters, intent on capturing Jackson's trains. Old Jack had anticipated such an attempt, however, and when informed of the Federal presence he laconically predicted, "General Trimble will attend to them."[18] The Marylander, who had confided to Jackson a few days previously that he intended to emerge from the war "a Major General or a corpse," made progress toward achieving the preferable status in his encounter with Bohlen.[19] Driving the Federals back to the Rappahannock in "great disorder," Trimble "pursued them closely and slaughtered great numbers as they waded the river or climbed up the opposite bank."[20] The stream filled with floating bodies and Bohlen himself lay among the slain.[21]

The threat to his rear thus dismissed, Jackson confronted a new enemy at the Springs—the rising Rappahannock. A light afternoon shower escalated into a deluge by dusk, stranding Early and the Georgians on Pope's side of the river. The Confederates passed a worrisome and uncomfortable night in their isolated position, but on the following day Stonewall unconsciously transformed this perilous predicament into a strategic advantage. Communicating via swimmers, Jackson deployed Early's contingent in the strongest available location, behind a swollen tributary, and personally superintended the construction of a new bridge on the

[17] Chambers, v. 2, pp. 128–29; Freeman, *Lee*, v. 2, pp. 288–99; *OR*, v. 12, part 2, pp. 705–706. The 13th Georgia made the crossing.

[18] *SHSP*, v. 35, p. 92.

[19] Douglas, p. 129.

[20] *OR*, v. 12, part 2, p. 719.

[21] Dabney, p. 514; Freeman, *Lee's Lieutenants*, v. 2, pp. 79–80.

23rd, "covered with mud from head to foot." Once the engineers completed their work, Jackson ordered the remainder of Brig. Gen. Alexander R. Lawton's troops across to support their comrades and Early. Stonewall then extricated all his men from the left bank before dawn on the 24th, "my command [being] thus rescued from almost certain capture," reported Early.[22]

Jackson's decision to reinforce his bridgehead before withdrawing it persuaded Pope, whose soldiers quiescently observed the drama at close range, that he had effectively thwarted the Confederate turning movement. Ironically, Jeb Stuart's daring and vengeful raid on Federal headquarters at Catlett's Station during the night of the 22nd seemed to the Northern commander further proof of Lee's failed offensive, for the gray cavalry also fell back across the river. Therefore, on the morning of August 24, John Pope once again reigned as undisputed master of the Rappahannock and basked in the illusion of accomplishment and security.[23]

Stuart's nighttime frolic at Catlett's not only produced the purest example of tables-turning in the annals of the war (Pope's uniform coat "going south" as hostage for the Virginia cavalier's headgear), but it provided Lee and Jackson vital information that dictated the direction of the campaign. Documents from a headquarters dispatch case revealed the approach of McClellan's vanguard merely a few days' march from Pope's position. Clearly, if the Army of Northern Virginia hoped to deal with Pope on anything like equal terms, the luxury of delay had expired.[24]

Lee summoned the Valley General to his headquarters at Jeffersonton on the 24th, where the two officers hatched a plan aimed at bringing the "blatherskite" Pope to grief. While Longstreet watched the river line, Jackson would sweep wide to the north well around the Federal right, pierce the Bull Run Mountains at Thoroughfare Gap, and pounce upon the Federal supply line leading to Washington. If successful, such a maneuver would force Pope to retreat from the Rappahannock, thereby lengthening the distance between him and McClellan's legions marching from

[22] Chambers, v. 2, p. 129; *OR*, v. 12, part 2, pp. 705-707; Douglas, p. 130.

[23] Henderson, v. 2, pp. 121–22.

[24] *OR*, v. 12, part 2, pp. 731–33; Chambers, v. 2, p. 131; Editors of Time-Life Books, *Lee Takes Command* (Alexandria, Va.: Time-Life Books, 1984), p. 125.

Fredericksburg. It would also exploit the established Federal sensitivity for the safety of their capital and relieve a portion of Virginia from the despot's heel.[25]

Lee recognized, of course, the perils of dividing his army and wished to avoid a general engagement until the wings reunited. The Southern commander designated no particular target on the Orange and Alexandria Railroad, leaving that decision and all other details of the operation to Jackson. In fact, some accounts credit the plan's conception to Stonewall himself, but the scheme more likely emerged as the joint product of two like-minded strategists.[26]

Jackson's ill humor experienced during the inconclusive probes along the Rappahannock dissipated at the prospect of offensive action. He instructed his chief engineer, James Keith Boswell, to select "the most direct and covered route to Manassas." Boswell suggested a course that led through Amissville, Henson's Mill, Orleans, Salem (present-day Marshall), Thoroughfare Gap and Gainesville. Jackson approved and told his engineer to guide the lead division the following morning.[27]

The column would march lightly with three days' cooked rations in haversacks, but no knapsacks or supply wagons.[28] A staff officer remembered that "there was so much disturbance, as marching orders had been issued, that we did not rest much" that night.[29] Jackson also slept but little, rose early on the 25th, and penned a note to his wife, saying, "I have only time to tell you how much I love my little pet dove."[30] The General then embarked upon what one of his biographers calls "the most adventurous and brilliant of his exploits."[31]

The force with which Jackson would attempt to discomfit John Pope numbered some 23,500 men, including fourteen brigades of infantry, two brigades of cavalry and eighteen light artil-

[25] Gallagher, p. 123; Foote, p. 611. Freeman, *Lee*, v. 2, pp. 298–99.

[26] Foote, p. 612; Chambers, v. 2, pp. 131–33.

[27] Chambers, v. 2, pp. 130, 134; *OR*, v. 12, part 2, p. 650; Freeman, *Lee's Lieutenants*, v. 2, p. 81.

[28] Chambers, v. 2, p. 134.

[29] *Ibid.*, quoting Jedediah Hotchkiss.

[30] Mrs. Jackson, p. 317.

[31] Dabney, p. 516.

lery batteries. Maj. Gen. Richard S. Ewell's division trailed closely behind Boswell and his cavalry escort, and Brig. Gen. William B. Taliaferro, in command of Jackson's old division, brought up the rear. Stonewall intentionally positioned Powell Hill's six brigades between Ewell and Taliaferro to prevent the red-bearded Virginian from committing another logistical faux pas.[32]

The day dawned cool but the late August sun soon sent temperatures soaring to steamy seasonal norms. Jackson demanded that the march be executed with "the utmost promptitude" and the commander worked tirelessly to keep his troops in motion. Boswell selected every available shortcut to lessen the distance, slicing through woods and across fields, leaving the soldiers baffled as to their destination.[33] No one in the corps, save Jackson and his young engineer, knew their objective, but as one member of the 2nd Virginia remembered, "Each felt that something extraordinary was contemplated."[34]

When the column passed the hamlet of Orleans at midday the relentless pace began to take its toll. Barefoot men left blood-stained impressions on the roads. Jackson's two-minute rest breaks did little to ease the fatigue, hunger, and thirst that plagued the weary marchers. Nevertheless, "Stonewall's foot cavalry" bore up remarkably well. Villagers and rural folk along the way distributed biscuits, cold chicken, ham, and dippers of water that met with instant acceptance by the troops.[35] One Palmetto State wag covered all his bases as he beseeched a Virginia matron: "Please ma'am give me a drink of water. I'm so hungry, I ain't got no place to sleep."[36]

Another soldier revealed what motivated the Confederates as they trudged along on their seemingly endless journey: "The fine weather, magnificent country, the mysterious march, through

---

[32] Gallagher, p. 130; Freeman, *Lee's Lieutenants,* v. 2, p. 84. Chambers, v. 2, p. 133, estimates Jackson's force to be 27,000 men; Vandiver, p. 353, says "more than 20,000."

[33] Vandiver, pp. 353–54; Freeman, *Lee's Lieutenants,* v. 2, p. 85; *OR,* v. 12, part 2, p. 678; Cooke, *A Military Biography,* pp. 274–75.

[34] *Confederate Veteran,* v. 17, p. 549.

[35] Tate, p. 201; *SHSP,* v. 13, p. 9; Dennis Kelly, "Second Manassas: The Battle and Campaign," *Civil War Times Illustrated* (Harrisburg, Pa.: Eastern Acorn Press, 1983), p. 22.

[36] Quoted in Kelly, p. 22.

fields and byways, the unknown destination, the possible collision at any moment with the enemy…all served to keep us intensely interested and all the time on the qui vive."[37]

Most of Jackson's men guessed that they were making for the Shenandoah Valley, and when Pope's elevated signal stations caught sight of the butternut parade as early as 8:00 a.m., the Federal commander similarly misjudged Jackson's intentions.[38] Edward A. Moore of the Rockbridge Artillery joked that Pope "possibly thought Jackson was on his way to Ohio or New York, and a week later no doubt regretted that one of those distant places had not been his destination."[39] The graybacks, however, disappeared from Pope's view at Orleans not to resurface for thirty hours, while the Unionists, content to let their opponents scurry over the mountains, squandered that precious time.[40]

Jackson hoped to reach Salem by day's end and mounted an outcropping of rocks just south of that settlement to observe the progress of his column. "His sun-burned cap was lifted from his brow, and he was gazing toward the west," wrote Maj. Robert L. Dabney, "where the splendid August sun was about to kiss the distant crest of the Blue Ridge, which stretched far away, bathed in azure and gold; and his blue eye, beaming with martial pride, returned the rays of the evening with almost equal brightness."[41]

As Dick Ewell's veterans swung into view, they spotted the peculiar figure whom they had learned literally to trust with their lives. They began to cheer their stoic leader framed above them in the setting sun when the word came down to maintain silence lest the enemy be alerted to their presence. The troops quickly obeyed but found an outlet for their admiration by filing beneath Jackson with raised hats in mute tribute. When the General's old Stonewall Brigade appeared, the Valley unit's enthusiasm overmatched its discipline and the Rebel Yell echoed off the surrounding granite. Jackson turned to his staff and said quietly, "It is of no use, you see I can't stop them." Then as an afterthought, as much to himself as

---

[37] Cockrell, ed., pp. 34–35.

[38] Alexander, p. 193; Time-Life, pp. 126–27.

[39] Moore, p. 101.

[40] Henderson, v. 2, p. 137.

[41] Dabney, p. 517.

to his listeners, he added, "Who could not conquer with such troops as these?"[42]

Lt. Col. E.P. Alexander characterized the march on the 25th as "very remarkable." The exhausted warriors flopped down after dark just short of Salem. They arose early the next morning, reached the nearby hamlet, then turned east toward White Plains and the Bull Run Mountains. The cavalry quickly discovered that the only substantial obstacle on Jackson's route, Thoroughfare Gap, lay undefended, and the procession passed through the narrow gorge and out onto the plains of Manassas.[43]

Locals still stared in amazement at so many Confederates shuffling through their neighborhood, but the men in the ranks responded less festively on the 26th. "The fine dust, which enveloped the column like a cloud," recalled a participant, "settled upon clothing and accoutrement, upon hair and beard, until there was no longer any distinction of color; only hands and faces showed a departure from the white-gray uniformity, as the mingled soil and perspiration streaked and crusted the skin."[44]

Stonewall himself cut a less than regal appearance during the second day of his flank march:

> It would have been easy to have mistaken him for the courier of one of his brigadiers…his single-breasted coat of rusty gray, sun-scorched about the shoulders until it was almost yellow, and his plain cadet-cap of the same hue, tilted forward until the visor rested almost upon his nose, were meaner in appearance than the make up of many a smart fellow in the ranks; and not a quartermaster in the corps but would have considered Jackson's gaunt old sorrel a bad swap for his own nag. But the eager look in his eyes …the firm set of his lips and the impatient jerking of his arm from time to time, were all signs by which we were to learn that something was up."[45]

The march itself proceeded less formally this day, "like each man was walking the distance alone, stopping to rest a moment or

[42] *Ibid.;* Henderson, v. 2, p. 127.

[43] Gallagher, p. 130.

[44] Cooke, *A Military Biography,* p. 276; Freeman, *Lee's Lieutenants,* v. 2, pp. 87–88; A.C. Redwood in the Maine *Bugle,* Hotchkiss Collection.

[45] Redwood.

drink." The men found their greatest motivation from the fear that their endurance would fail and they would miss the fun.[46] By now no question remained about the goal of the operation. These veterans realized that they were in Pope's rear and they thrilled at the prospects ahead. "Never in the history of warfare," thought a staff officer, "has an army shown more devotion to duty and the wishes of one man than the followers of Jackson exhibited during these days."[47]

The column encountered its first Union opposition at Hay Market and Gainesville in the form of a few pickets or stragglers, men "entirely ignorant of any movement of our army," according to cavalry colonel Tom Munford.[48] Stuart joined Jackson on the Warrenton Turnpike at Gainesville about 4:00 p.m. and Stonewall placed the welcome horsemen on his right flank. He then identified Bristoe Station, four miles below the Federal supply depot at Manassas Junction, as the army's immediate objective. The General reasoned that by destroying the bridge over Broad Run near Bristoe he would be able to seize Manassas without fear of early interference from Pope—the correct but by no means obvious strategic decision.[49]

As the troops forged ahead on the last leg of a march that had covered more than fifty miles in thirty-six hours, Jackson climbed onto the porch of a roadside cabin to await the concentration of his corps. He quickly dozed off, as was his custom, and slept peacefully until an aide shook him awake with distressing news. Apparently an officer had failed to place a picket at an intersection, causing subsequent regiments to take a wrong turn. "Put him under arrest and prefer charges" snapped the former professor, who then lowered his eyelids and resumed his nap.[50]

About sunset, the Confederates prepared to storm the unsuspecting garrison at Bristoe. Munford's cavalry, supported by Col. Henry Forno's Louisiana brigade of Ewell's division and one regiment from Trimble, stole to within one hundred yards of the sta-

[46] W.W. Blackford, p. 109.

[47] Douglas, p. 135.

[48] *OR*, v. 12, part 2, p. 747.

[49] *OR*, v. 12, part 2, pp. 733–34; Freeman, *Lee's Lieutenants*, v. 2, p. 89.

[50] W.W. Blackford, pp. 111–12.

tion before the Bluecoats detected them. In an instant, a startled company of Federal infantry and one of cavalry laid down their arms or fled precipitately, at a cost of only three wounded for Munford.[51] One of the incredulous Northern captives, stunned by the appearance of Rebel foot soldiers so far in Pope's rear, inquired, "What sort of man is your Stonewall Jackson anyway; are his soldiers made of gutta-percha, or do they run on wheels?"[52]

No sooner had the Confederates secured the depot than the shrill whistle of an approaching locomotive shattered the twilight stillness. The regular evening relay of empty trains returning to Alexandria from supplying Pope's voracious army along the Rappahannock promised the Confederates a rare opportunity. They scrambled eagerly to obstruct the tracks but the alert engineer, plowing through the hastily prepared ambuscade, chugged north with news of what he guessed to be another mounted raid, like the one four nights earlier at Catlett's.[53]

Undaunted, Jackson's raiders removed a stretch of rails and awaited the appearance of more cars. In a matter of minutes the steam locomotive "President," displaying a likeness of Abraham Lincoln on its dome and pulling twenty empty boxcars, entered Bristoe unaware of the trap. A hail of bullets perforated the engine, which quickly reached the iron gap and plunged off its course in a spectacular crash. A Confederate soldier named Foreman, familiar with operational procedures, boarded the derailed locomotive and sounded the "all clear" signal as another Federal train rumbled up from the south. It smashed into the smoking debris from the first wreck, much to the delight of the Rebel spectators.[54]

Jackson soon arrived on the scene and summoned one of the engineers for interrogation. An unidentified civilian passenger from one of the trains, learning of the great Stonewall's proximity,

---

[51] Freeman, *Lee's Lieutenants*, v. 2, p. 91; Allan, p. 214. The Union infantry regiment was the 4th New York.

[52] Douglas, p. 135.

[53] Foote, pp. 616–17; Freeman, *Lee's Lieutenants*, v. 2, p. 91.

[54] Glenn C. Oldaker, comp., *Centennial Tales: Memoirs of Colonel "Chester" S. Basset French* (New York: Carlton Press, 1962), p. 34; Cooke, *A Military Biography*, pp. 278–79; Chambers, v. 2, p. 143.

implored his captors to allow him to see the legendary figure so famous and feared in the North. Despite the injuries the man had sustained during the derailment, troops from the 15th Alabama agreed to honor his request. They carefully transported him to the fringes of the little campfire where a typically disheveled Jackson held court in his ragged, filthy uniform. In a voice filled with "disappointment and disgust," the disillusioned celebrity-seeker told the Alabamians, "O my God! Lay me down!" This story circulated throughout the army, and the soldiers from that time forward would exclaim "O my God! Lay me down!" when confronted with every situation from rancid rations to a charging Federal formation.[55]

Although Pvt. Foreman reprised his whistle ruse, the next northbound train became suspicious and halted before it reached the Bristoe barricade. The trainman backed down the tracks and into the night, spreading the alarm as he went.[56]

Jackson now faced another dilemma. His presence along the railroad would undoubtedly force Pope to abandon the line of the Rappahannock, thus achieving one objective of the campaign. However, Maj. Gen. Fitz John Porter's corps of McClellan's army rested southeast of Bristoe in a position to menace Jackson's flank. Moreover, Thoroughfare Gap now lay five miles closer to Pope than to Jackson, therefore threatening Longstreet's ability to use that mountain pass to reunite the Confederate army.[57]

Jackson could do little to aid Longstreet directly, but by drawing the Federals' attention upon himself he might provide Old Pete the time and means to allow Lee to concentrate his entire force. A victorious collision with Pope, the campaign's second objective, clearly depended upon a unified Army of Northern Virginia.

Stonewall learned from prisoners and local citizens that only a modest force guarded Manassas Junction, and he felt that the seizure of the Union supply base might create just the sort of dis-

---

[55] William C. Oates, *The War between the Union and the Confederacy* (New York: Neale Publishing Co., 1905), p. 134; Foote, p. 617.

[56] Cooke, *A Military Biography,* p. 279; Oldaker, p. 34.

[57] Vandiver, p. 357.

traction Longstreet required. Furthermore, his flank march had been so swift, secretive, and successful that he believed the Federals would need considerable time to react. The relief that the Federal provisions promised his famished men also figured significantly in the calculation.[58]

Trimble volunteered two of his regiments to undertake an agonizing extension of the day's march to Manassas. Joined by Stuart's cavalry, Trimble reached the Junction about midnight and snatched three hundred prisoners and two artillery batteries with a loss of only fifteen wounded. In the predawn darkness of August 27, the Maryland brigadier posted his exhausted troops around the huge supply depot to guard the newly acquired Confederate States property.[59]

Gray streaks of light appeared in the eastern sky a few hours later, revealing the enormity of Trimble's accomplishment. One square mile of sprawling warehouses, boxcars, and wagons bulging with every imaginable military necessity or luxury loomed before the hollow-cheeked and tattered Confederates.[60] An officer testified that "the supplies embraced everything eatable, drinkable, wearable, or usable, and in immense profusion."[61] A member of Jackson's staff added that "the valuable stores captured were far in excess of what any Confederate ever conceived to be in existence."[62]

Before dawn, Jackson directed the Stonewall Brigade, accompanied by the Rockbridge Artillery, to move from Bristoe to the Junction in support of Trimble. Hill's division marched next, followed by the remainder of Taliaferro's troops. Ewell remained at Bristoe with three brigades to resist any Federal threats from the south, but the wing commander ordered Old Baldhead to retire toward Manassas if he became hard-pressed. Jackson himself then

---

[58] *B&L*, v. 2, p. 503; VanLoan Naisawald, "The Little Known Battle of Manassas," p. 1, typescript at Fredericksburg and Spotsylvania National Military Park.

[59] Chambers, v. 2, pp. 143–44; Allan, p. 215; Foote, p. 617; Freeman, *Lee's Lieutenants*, v. 2, p. 93; Henderson, v. 2, p. 130; Dabney, p. 519.

[60] Foote, p. 618.

[61] Alexander, p. 194.

[62] Douglas, p. 136.

rapidly repaired to the supply depot.[63] When the General caught his first glimpse of the largesse he had inherited at Manassas, he acted immediately to eliminate the most potentially destructive commodity on the premises. He demanded that an ad hoc company, consisting of an officer and one hundred hand-picked men who never used alcohol, be charged with the prompt disposal of the whiskey in Pope's warehouses. "I fear that liquor more than General Pope's army," admitted Deacon Jackson.[64]

The requisite detail came forward and went about its business with a grim efficiency. "I shall never forget the scene," wrote a witness. "Streams of spirits ran like water through the sands of Manassas, and the soldiers on hands and knees drank it greedily from the ground as it ran."[65]

As more wide-eyed Confederates poured into Pope's cornucopia, Trimble's faithful sentries faced deteriorating odds. "It was with extreme mortification," protested the indignant Marylander, "that...I witnessed an indiscriminate plunder of the public stores, cars, and sutlers' houses by the army which had just arrived, in which General Hill's division was conspicuous, setting at defiance the guards I had placed over the stores."[66]

Members of the Stonewall Brigade joined their comrades of the Light Division in a frantic brand of pillaging characterized primarily by indecisiveness as to what loot to expropriate and maintain. The spectacle assumed ludicrous proportions as starving, unshod men in mendicants' rags consumed lobster salad washed down with Rhine wine, their haversacks and pockets overflowing with cigars, jars of mustard, and sundry other superfluous articles.[67]

The revelry ended, however, when word arrived that Union troops north of the Junction threatened to crash the party. These Federals consisted of two separate commands.

---

[63] Foote, p. 618; Freeman, *Lee's Lieutenants,* v. 2, p. 96.

[64] Time-Life, pp. 129, 131–32; *SHSP,* v. 23, pp. 333–34.

[65] *B&L,* v. 2, p. 529.

[66] *OR,* v. 12, part 2, p. 721.

[67] Casler, pp. 107–109; Cooke, *A Military Biography,* pp. 280–81; John H. Worsham, *One of Jackson's Foot Cavalry* (Jackson, Tenn.: McCowat-Mercer Press, 1964), pp. 70–71.

Richard Stoddert Ewell performed very capably while serving under Jackson, but never lived up to his promise when placed in corps command following the Battle of Chancellorsville.
[*Valentine Museum, Richmond, Virginia*]

The 2nd New York Heavy Artillery, serving as infantry, had been en route to reinforce the Manassas garrison when they became aware of its capture by unknown Confederate forces. Cautiously approaching the Junction from the northwest, the Heavies first encountered Brig. Gen. Fitzhugh Lee's troopers and later the Stonewall Brigade and Brig. Gen. Lawrence O'B. Branch's North Carolinians. The New Yorkers recognized a losing proposition when they saw one and fled back across Bull Run, chased by Lee's cavalry almost to Fairfax.[68]

Brig. Gen. George W. Taylor's four New Jersey regiments promised to create another problem. These Garden Staters had been dispatched from Alexandria to guard the railroad bridge over Bull Run in the face of the presumed cavalry raid against Manassas. Taylor, however, chose to exceed his instructions and oust the insolent Southern horsemen from the depot. Fortunately for Jackson, the New Jerseyans moved cautiously, affording Stonewall an opportunity to deploy most of Hill's division in strong positions well supported by artillery.[69]

The Confederate guns boomed out a metallic greeting before Taylor reached Hill's line, thus prematurely revealing Jackson's presence. Nevertheless, the Federals launched an intrepid attack, "made with great spirit and determination...under a leader worthy of a better cause," according to Jackson.[70] Taylor stood no chance of succeeding, despite his bravery. The Valley General drew a white handkerchief from his pocket, rode out in front of Hill's battle line, and called on the outnumbered Northerners to surrender. By way of reply, one of the Jerseymen fired a bullet that whistled past Jackson's ear. "Seeing his passion thus requited with treachery," as Reverend Dabney phrased it, "he hastened back to his troops and commanded them to let loose their full fury against their foes."[71] Upon the execution of Stonewall's orders, Taylor's men, boasted a Rebel cannoneer, ran like "a flock of sheep."[72] The Federal brigade suffered more than 335 casualties, including Gen-

[68] Naisawald, pp. 3–5.

[69] Foote, p. 619; Freeman, *Lee's Lieutenants*, v. 2, p. 98; Naisawald, pp. 4–6.

[70] Freeman, *Lee's Lieutenants*, v. 2, p. 98; *OR*, v. 12, part 2, p. 644.

[71] Chambers, v. 2, p. 147; Cockrell, ed., p. 35; Moore, p. 104; Dabney, p. 520.

[72] Moore, p. 105.

eral Taylor, who died while entreating his men to rally "and for God's sake…prevent another Bull Run."[73]

The danger over, Hill's troops returned to Manassas by noon. Here they discovered Taliaferro managing a more orderly distribution of the provisions. All the rolling stock, wagons, and ambulances soon filled with medicines and other scarce and valuable merchandise. When Taliaferro completed his mission, Jackson authorized the men free access to all that remained. "Fine whiskey and segars circulated freely, elegant…linen handkerchiefs were applied to noses hitherto blown with the thumb and forefinger, and sumptuous underclothing was fitted over limbs sunburnt, sore and vermin-splotched." Concluded a South Carolinian, "at the Junction there was a general jubilee."[74] Another Confederate estimated that "We destroyed millions of property at Manassas…. Alas! Poor Pope. Lee, Jackson & Co. have plucked the wings of this vain butterfly."[75]

While most of Jackson's corps partook of their grandest orgy of the War, Dick Ewell and his 5,500 men maintained their lonely vigil at Bristoe. About 3:00 p.m., Maj. Gen. Joseph Hooker's division from the Army of the Potomac made contact with Ewell south of Broad Run. The Confederates fought a flawless rear guard action, broke off contact after an hour, and crossed the stream destroying the bridge in their wake. Ewell then proceeded to Manassas and foraged through what remained of the spoils. The Federals, bloodied and nearly out of ammunition, did not pursue.[76]

Hooker's advance comprised only a fraction of Pope's response to Jackson's envelopment. Obsessed with the notion of bagging Jackson, the Union commander ordered his expanding army to concentrate at Manassas, revising his earlier instructions that had recognized the importance of holding Gainesville and

[73] Quoted in Foote, p. 620; *OR*, v. 12, part 2, pp. 260, 408; Naisawald, pp. 6–8.

[74] Freeman, *Lee's Lieutenants*, v. 2. pp. 99–100; J.F.J. Caldwell, *The History of a Brigade of South Carolinians, Known First as "Gregg's" and Subsequently as "McGowan's" Brigade* (Philadelphia: King and Baird, Printers, 1866), p. 31.

[75] Lexington (Va.) *Gazette*, September 11, 1862. The writer was a member of the Rockbridge Artillery.

[76] Chambers, v. 2, p. 148; Henderson, p. 136; Edward J. Stackpole, *From Cedar Mountain to Antietam* (Harrisburg, Pa.: Stackpole Co., 1959), p. 120.

keeping Longstreet at bay. By focusing exclusively upon the anni-
hilation of Jackson, General Pope ignored the critical necessity of
preventing the two wings of Lee's army from reuniting. This over-
sight cost Pope the campaign.[77]

Jackson, of course, could not divine his opponent's intentions with certainty, but he did know that several considerations
dictated the Confederates' next move. They needed a place on the
enemy's flank from which they could evade a full blow yet strike
effectively themselves in order to keep Pope from withdrawing
unscathed to Washington. This location had to permit them both
to connect with Longstreet upon that officer's arrival from Thoroughfare Gap or, should Old Pete find his path barred, allow Jackson to retire safely behind the Bull Run Mountains via an alternate
route. Stonewall glanced at his map and identified the low ridge
north of the Warrenton Turnpike behind the village of Groveton
as ideal for all these purposes. This deduction, claimed E.P.
Alexander, "was a masterful piece of strategy, unexcelled during the war."[78]

Jackson ordered the supplies that could not be carried or consumed to be put to the torch, then began his trek toward Stony
Ridge. "The appearance of the marching columns was novel and
amusing," remembered Henry Kyd Douglas. "Here one fellow
was bending beneath the weight of a score of boxes of cigars,
smoking and joking as he went, another with as many boxes of
canned fruits, another with coffee enough for a winter's encamp-
ment, or perhaps with a long string of shoes hung around his neck,
like beads. It was a martial masquerade by night."[79]

Taliaferro led the nocturnal operation, marched directly
north to Sudley Springs Ford on Bull Run as ordered, and went
into camp. Jackson accompanied his old division. Soon, he became so exhausted that he dismounted near the Stone House at the
intersection of the Turnpike and Sudley Road, curled up in a fence
corner and went to sleep, leaving instructions for a staff officer to

---

[77] Chambers, v. 2, p. 152; Douglas, p. 136.

[78] Chambers, v. 2, p. 150; Freeman, *Lee's Lieutenants*, v. 2, p. 103; Bruce Catton, *Terrible Swift
Sword* (Garden City, N.Y.: Doubleday, 1963), p. 424; Alexander, p. 197.

[79] Chambers, v. 2, p. 150; Douglas, p. 136.

awaken him in thirty minutes. His nap completed, the commander joined Talilaferro at the ford.[80]

A night march is always a hazardous undertaking. Jackson's other two divisions fell victim to a combination of the darkness, unqualified guides, and a reticent superior officer. Hill lost track of Taliaferro and blindly followed some local geographer who misled him across Bull Run and eventually to Centreville, miles from Sudley Springs. Ewell, possessing little knowledge of the movement's objective, shadowed Hill for awhile, crossed the Run at Blackburn's Ford, turned upstream, and used the Stone Bridge on the Turnpike to return to the rendezvous point. Hill did not rejoin the corps until noon on the 28th, converting a simple eight-mile march into a hike of twice that distance.[81]

The march from Manassas to Stony Ridge north of the Turnpike clearly represents the nadir of Jackson's generalship during the Second Manassas Campaign. Yet, the inefficiency and confusion ultimately redounded to the Virginian's favor. While the Confederate commander concealed his corps behind the low ridge in the woods, "packed like herring in a barrel," Pope learned of Hill's presence at Centreville. This information further befuddled the overmatched Illinoisan, who flailed about northern Virginia searching for his elusive quarry.[82]

Except for Hill's voyagers, Jackson's men spent a restful morning on August 28, snacking, snoozing and speculating about their immediate future. Officers prohibited the bands from playing and the men from shouting, but, remembered a soldier, there were "no restrictions as to laughing and talking...and the woods sounded like the hum of a beehive in the warm sunshine." Jackson hastened couriers back to Lee reporting his position, then indulged in another fence-corner nap.[83]

Mounted officers bearing a captured Federal dispatch discovered Jackson and his lieutenants about noon in this peaceful repose, but the contents of their appropriated correspondence

---

[80] William Allan to Jedediah Hotchkiss, October 22, 1886, Hotchkiss Collection.

[81] Chambers, v. 2, p. 151; Freeman, *Lee's Lieutenants*, v. 2, pp. 104–105; Stackpole, *Cedar Mountain to Antietam*, p. 143.

[82] W.W. Blackford, p. 116; Chambers, v. 2, p. 152.

[83] Freeman, *Lee*, v. 2, p. 312; *B&L*, v. 2, pp. 507–508; *SHSP*, v. 25, p. 100.

"aroused Jackson like an electric shock."[84] The message revealed that Union troops would be moving east on the Turnpike, possibly, feared Stonewall, toward an assemblage with McClellan on the far side of Bull Run. Jackson sprang to his feet and stalked toward his horse, buckling his saber as he went. He ordered Taliaferro to "Move your division and attack the enemy" and directed Ewell to "support the attack." He instructed Hill to remain on the left to protect the Confederate escape route via Aldie Gap.[85]

Taliaferro and Ewell moved southwest about two and one-half miles and searched in vain for a blue target. Jackson himself scanned the Turnpike in both directions and watched one Federal column turn south before it could blunder into his snare. The Confederate commander longed to strike a blow, particularly when he learned at 3:00 p.m. of Longstreet's arrival at Thoroughfare Gap. His mood turned sour, reminding one observer of "an explosive missile, an unlucky spark applied to which would blow you sky high."[86]

Late in the day, Jackson at last spotted a Union force marching east on the Turnpike that promised the opportunity he sought to pin Pope down by means of the sword. The Valley General cantered boldly along the high ground north of the roadway, his figure silhouetted against the evening sky in plain view of thousands of passing Northern marksmen. "We could almost tell his thoughts by his movements," recalled a staff officer. "Sometimes he would halt, then trot on rapidly, halt again, wheel his horse and pass again along the [flank] of the marching column." Satisfied that the time had arrived to commence the ball, Jackson pivoted his mount, dashed back to his concealed division, touched his cap, and calmly declared, "Bring out your men, gentlemen!"[87]

Lenoir Chambers calls Groveton "the strangest battle of Jackson's career."[88] Some 3,000 Federals of Brig. Gen. John Gibbon's renowned Iron Brigade, assisted by three additional regi-

[84] *B&L,* v. 2, p. 508.

[85] *Ibid; SHSP,* v. 25, p. 100.

[86] W.W. Blackford, p. 118; Chambers, v. 2, p. 153; Foote, p. 625.

[87] W.W. Blackford, pp. 120–21; Stackpole, *Cedar Mountain to Antietam,* p. 158; Catton, pp. 426–27; Foote, p. 625.

[88] Chambers, v. 2, p. 157.

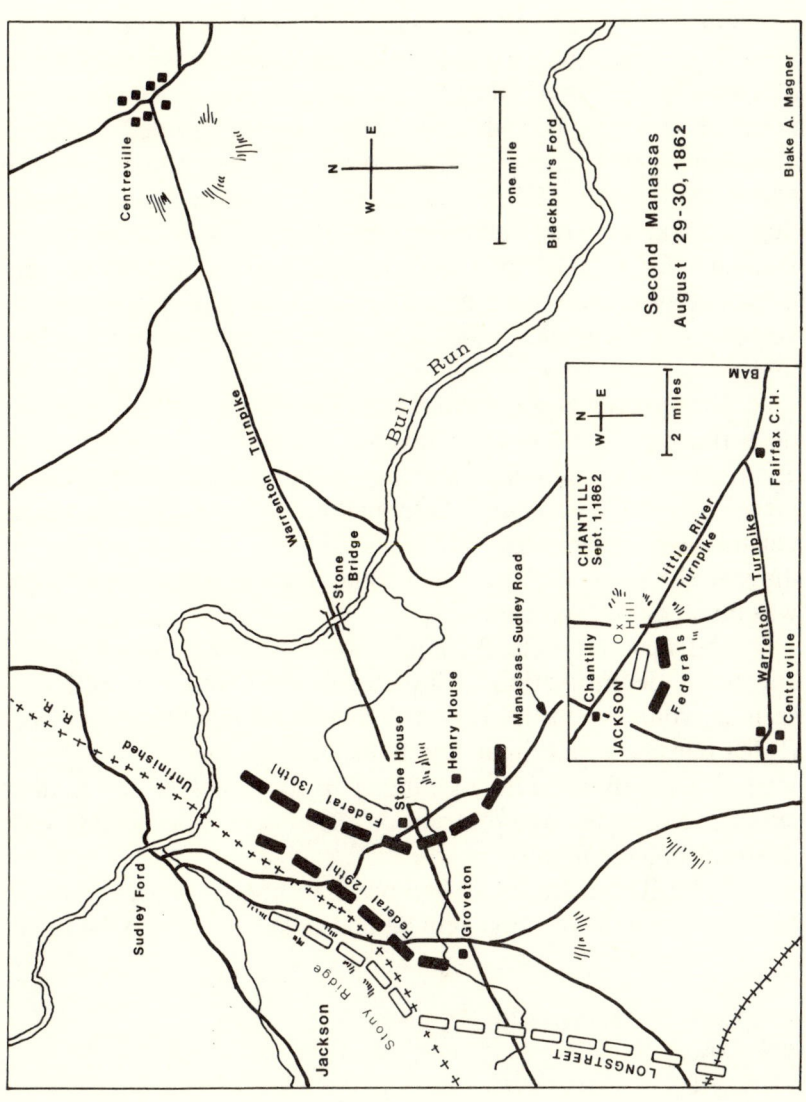

Second Manassas
August 29-30, 1862

Blake A. Magner

ments, faced parts of Ewell's and Taliaferro's divisions, about 4,500 strong, in what one historian described as "a long, desperate stand-up combat which exceeded in sheer unadulterated nerve any fight many of the officers ever saw."[89]

Once they received the word to advance, Jackson's men let loose "a hoarse roar like that from cages of wild beasts at the scent of blood." Capt. W.W. Blackford went on to relate that "long columns of glittering brigades, like huge serpents, glided out upon the open field....Then all advanced in as perfect order as if they had been on parade, their bayonets sparkling in the light of the setting sun and their red battle flags dancing gayly in the breeze."[90] Alabama Capt. William Oates remembered that "Within one minute all was enveloped in smoke and a sheet of fire seemed to go out from each side to the other along the whole length of the lines."[91]

The opponents in butternut and blue filed into expanding battle formation no more than seventy-five or one hundred yards apart, and "stood as immovable as the painted heroes in a battle-piece" marvelled Taliaferro. "Out in the...dying daylight, and under the stars, they stood, and although they could not advance, they would not retire. There was some discipline in this, but there was much more of true valor."[92]

The Federals held their ground with what Jackson called "obstinate determination."[93] Taliaferro and Ewell both fell with serious wounds and the Union division commander, Brig. Gen. Rufus King, lay sick in an ambulance at Gainesville, so brigade leaders alone directed the fighting. This may explain why neither side effectively utilized reserves or maneuvered appreciably with the troops on the field.[94]

At 9:00 p.m., after two and one-half hours of brutal combat, Gibbon broke off the engagement and faded south into the night.

[89] Vandiver, p. 364; Chambers, v. 2, p. 157.

[90] W.W. Blackford, p. 121.

[91] Oates, p. 138.

[92] *B&L*, v. 2, p. 510.

[93] *OR*, v. 12, part 2, p. 645.

[94] Alexander, pp. 199–200.

Each side suffered about 1,000 casualties, Jackson's two division commanders representing the most significant losses. Surgeons removed Ewell's leg the next day and A.R. Lawton replaced him at the head of his division. Of Taliaferro's three wounds, the ball in his arm caused the most concern. Jackson elevated Brig. Gen. William E. Starke to the top of the old Stonewall division.[95]

Indecisive tactically, the Battle of Groveton achieved Jackson's purpose of instigating a battle with Pope before that officer joined McClellan's legions nearer to Washington. His gamble would succeed only if Longstreet appeared in time to crush Pope. In the interim, Jackson knew he must face the Federals alone.[96]

Late on the night of the 28th, with this thought in mind Stonewall rode a mile or so toward the Bull Run Mountains, climbed wearily from the saddle, and put his ear to the ground to listen for Longstreet's approach. Dr. Hunter H. McGuire, medical director of the wing, witnessed the scene: "I shall never forget the sad look of the man that night as he gazed towards Thoroughfare Gap, wishing for Longstreet to come."[97] The anxious commander then remounted and rode to a house near Sudley Mills, where he retired for the evening, doubtlessly praying for guidance in the coming day's inevitable conflict.[98]

August 29 dawned on what one Confederate believed to be the most nauseating scene of carnage he ever witnessed, silent testimony to the grisly slaughter at Groveton. The campaign had reduced some regiments to the size of small companies, while many others boasted no field-grade officers.[99] Jackson planned to compensate for his thinned ranks by assuming a strong defensive posture nearly two miles in length behind the cuts and fills of an unfinished railroad. Hill's division deployed on the left, its left flank refused to cover Sudley Ford and the road to Aldie. Lawton, with two brigades, watched the left center, and Starke's division

---

[95] Freeman, *Lee's Lieutenants*, v. 2, pp. 108–10; Henderson, v. 2, p. 149; Foote, p. 627.

[96] Chambers, v. 2, p. 159. Many writers, particularly my friend Alan T. Nolan, prefer to call the engagement Brawner's Farm.

[97] *SHSP*, v. 19, p. 307.

[98] "Cavalry of Second Manassas," Hotchkiss Collection.

[99] Oates, p. 143; Freeman, *Lee's Lieutenants*, v. 2, p. 111.

guarded the right. Lawton's remaining two brigades, Early's and Forno's, protected the far right and held open the highway to Thoroughfare Gap. Jackson bolstered his 18,000 infantry with forty guns posted in effective firing positions on the rising wooded ground behind the railroad embankment. Stuart's cavalry patrolled both flanks.[100]

The wing commander emphasized to his subordinates the importance of buying time until Old Pete arrived and could provide the strength needed to assume the offensive. In the meantime, Jackson would face odds on the field of more than three to one.[101]

Pope inaugurated the action at 7:00 a.m. with a series of artillery bombardments and infantry demonstrations focused, as would be most of his aggression this day, against A.P. Hill. Maj. Gen. Franz Sigel's corps managed to dent the Light Division in several places, but each time Hill's reserves expelled Sigel's "Dutchmen." While the German hero thus spent himself with a lackluster performance, William Starke noticed dust clouds rising in the west. The freshly-minted division commander anxiously investigated the situation, then raced back to the Confederate line with welcome news. Longstreet's vanguard would be in place shortly. Stonewall's apprehensive troops burst forth with a resounding Rebel Yell, the significance of which escaped Pope for another twenty-eight hours. Brig. Gen. John Bell Hood led Longstreet's column and met briefly with Jackson about 10:30 a.m. as his men filed across the Turnpike perpendicular to Jackson's right.[102]

Following Sigel's repulse, a midday lull descended upon the battlefield. Jackson walked calmly along the railroad, examining Hill's dispositions and peering into the thick belt of woods that lapped against the Confederate line. An occasional shell exploded in the General's vicinity and a staff officer admonished Jackson for being so reckless with his personal safety. "I believe we have been together in hotter places before," the commander replied.[103]

---

[100] Chambers, v. 2, p. 159.

[101] Ibid.

[102] Henderson, v. 2, pp. 154–57; Freeman, *Lee*, v. 2, p. 319; Freeman, *Lee's Lieutenants*, v. 2, pp. 112–13; Alexander, pp. 203–205; Allan, pp. 244–48; *SHSP*, v. 33, pp. 85–86.

[103] *SHSP*, v. 13, p. 26; Heros Von Borcke, *Memoirs of the Confederate War for Independence* (Edinburgh: W. Blackford and Sons, 1866), v. 1, p. 148.

Shortly before 2:00 p.m., Pope renewed his offensive with the divisions of Maj. Gen. Jesse L. Reno and "Fighting Joe" Hooker. The morning assaults paled by comparison to this determined advanced by skilled veterans. The Federals reached the railroad and grappled hand-to-hand with brigades on Hill's right and center. Little Powell committed his reserves at precisely the right moment and North Carolinians under Brig. Gen. William Dorsey Pender smashed into the attackers, driving them out of the woods. One of Hooker's unbloodied brigades regained the Northern initiative at 3:00 p.m. and penetrated a gap in Jackson's defenses, carrying the embankment and pushing deep into the Confederate position. But once again, the Southerners responded with a counterattack against the unsupported Federal regiments that severely punished the Unionists for their short-lived success.[104]

A particularly bold Federal officer, finely mounted, attracted the attention and grudging admiration of the Confederates during this afternoon fighting. When an Alabama rifleman drew a bead on this conspicuous fellow and tumbled him from his saddle, a junior officer rebuked his troops for shooting such an intrepid enemy. Jackson materialized and overhead the lesson. "No, Captain," he scolded the speaker, "the men are right; kill the brave ones, they lead on the others."[105]

Another peaceful interlude now intruded on the day's bloody work, and Hill sent word to Jackson confessing that his exhausted troops might not stand up to another assault. The commander replied via courier, telling Hill, "if they attack [you] again [you] must beat them." Jackson then trotted toward the left where he encountered his worried subordinate and personally repeated his message. Immediately, the sound of battle again reverberated in the ears of the generals. "Here it comes," cried Hill as he wheeled to join his men. Stonewall shouted at the red-shirted Virginian as Hill faded from view. "I'll expect you to beat them."[106]

---

[104] Henderson, v. 2, pp. 157–60; Chambers, v. 2, p. 161. Brig. Gen. Cuvier Grover led the temporarily successful Union breakthrough.

[105] Oates, p. 144.

[106] Douglas, p. 138. Kelly, pp. 30–35, provides a good overview of the fighting on August 29 illustrated with useful maps.

The action that prompted this exchange began shortly after 5:00 p.m. Maj. Gen. Philip Kearny's division, supported by some Ninth Corps troops, launched one last supreme effort to turn Hill's left and break his front. Brig. Gen. Maxcy Gregg's South Carolinians met the oncoming Federals with clubbed muskets and bayonets, displaying "courage and determination...rarely equalled."[107] Still the Union momentum and strength threatened to overwhelm the Southern defense. One Palmetto Stater remembered, "Our feet were worn and weary and our arms were nerveless. Our ears were deadened with the continuous roar of battle, and our eyes were dimmed with the smoke."[108]

Just as the beleaguered Hill appeared about to lose control of affairs, Early and Forno pounded into Kearny's boiling masses and once again stayed disaster. Jackson had relieved these two brigades from his far right when Longstreet arrived, and now they rescued the far left of the army in the midst of crisis. As the blue wave receded, a courier reined in at Jackson's command post with a message for the commander. "General Hill presents his compliments and says the attack of the enemy was repulsed." Jackson smiled faintly, "Tell him I knew he would do it."[109]

All told, some 37,000 Federals tested Jackson's line on August 29, but their piecemeal assaults and Stonewall's judicious use of interior lines and local reserves carried the day. "When the sun went down," wrote a Richmond artillerist, "their dead were heaped in front of that incomplete Railway, and we sighed with relief for Longstreet could be seen coming into position on our right; the crisis was over, Longstreet never failed yet, but the sun went down so slowly."[110]

In point of fact, however, Longstreet had failed to make any direct impact on the tactical situation August 29. Lee's "Old War Horse" balked at the notion of an advance in the afternoon and conducted only a limited reconnaissance-in-force in the evening,

---

[107] Chambers, v. 2, pp. 164–65; Allan, p. 253.

[108] *SHSP*, v. 13, pp. 32–33.

[109] Douglas, p. 138; Freeman, *Lee's Lieutenants*, v. 2, p. 117.

[110] Chambers, v. 2, p. 166; John H. Chamberlayne, ed., *Ham Chamberlayne—Virginian; Letters and Papers of An Artillery Officer in the War for Southern Independence, 1861–1865* (Richmond: Press of the Dietz Printing Co., 1932), pp. 100–101.

The Deep Cut at Second Manassas circa 1900. [*Manassas Battlefield Park*]

from which he withdrew his men after dark. Jackson also pulled back in the night to conceal his reduced numbers in the deep woods behind the embankment. The Federals discovered these twin withdrawals, which Pope interpreted as the harbinger of a full-scale retreat. Refusing to believe that he now opposed the entire Confederate army, Pope prepared to "pursue" Jackson the following morning and seal the victory that had eluded him this day.[111]

In Jackson's camp, Dr. McGuire met with the General to review the extent of Confederate casualties. "General, this day has been won by nothing but stark and stern fighting," observed the physician. Stonewall shook his head. "No, it has been won by nothing but the blessing and protection of Providence."[112]

Kyd Douglas remembered Saturday, August 30 as a clear warm morning, but, he thought, "the stillness seemed unnatural."[113] Although no serious attacks marred the quiet forenoon, the grass between the lines caught fire, roasting the corpses from the previous day's fighting. Jackson's troops had replenished their stomachs, cartridge boxes, and spirits overnight, and waited in their hidden positions behind the railroad, a deployment, thought E.P. Alexander, indicative of Jackson's "instinctive desire to mystify his opponent."[114] Pope neglected to conduct an adequate reconnaissance so he persisted in his delusions regarding Confederate strength and intentions.[115]

Jackson arose early to inspect his combat-hardened troops. Riding to the right, he chatted with Col. William S.H. Baylor of the Stonewall Brigade and warned that officer to "keep your men in line and ready for action," though he predicted that Pope would not advance.[116] The General continued west to a little cabin north of the Turnpike behind Hood's line, where he conferred briefly

[111] Alexander, pp. 209–10.

[112] Dabney, p. 531.

[113] Douglas, p. 139.

[114] Moore, p. 117; Alexander, p. 212; Henderson, v. 2, p. 169.

[115] Stackpole, *Cedar Mountain to Antietam*, p. 216.

[116] *Confederate Veteran*, v. 22, p. 231.

with Lee, Longstreet, and Stuart. Then he retraced his route back to his own corps.[117] A Louisiana soldier spotted the mighty Stonewall and echoed more articulately the assessment made four days earlier at Bristoe:

> Jackson was then dressed in a sort of grey homespun suit, with a broken-brimmed cap, and looked like a good driving overseer or manager, with plenty of hard, horse sense, but no accomplishments or other talent....The remark was then made by one of us, after staring at him for a long time, that there must be some mistake about him—if he was an able man he showed it less than any man any of us had ever seen.[118]

His examination revealing no sign of imminent danger, Jackson repaired to the rear about noon and indulged in a quiet lunch seated on a rail fence and surrounded by his staff and couriers. When some Union guns swung into battery unacceptably close to the Confederate position, the General promptly dispatched the Rockbridge Artillery, which handsomely dispersed the Federal cannoneers about 2:00 p.m. Then, an eerie silence pervaded the field.[119]

Between 3:00 and 4:00 p.m. Jackson addressed a note to Lee expressing the opinion that Pope did not intend to renew the offensive. Then a single Union piece shattered the stillness. "That's that signal for a general attack," Jackson predicted.[120] A moment later, 12,000 Federals "burst like a thunder-bolt" toward the Southern ranks.[121] More than three dozen regiments belonging to Porter's corps and Brig. Gen. John Hatch's division advanced, recalled a Virginia trooper, "in magnificent style, lines straight as an arrow, all fringed with glittering bayonets and fluttering with flags."[122]

---

[117] Freeman, *Lee,* v. 2, p. 330.

[118] Quoted in Bartlett Napier, *Military Record of Louisiana* (New Orleans: L. Graham & Co., printers, 1875), p. 98 (last collation).

[119] James Power Smith to his sister, August 31, 1862, typescript at Fredericksburg and Spotsylvania National Military Park; *SHSP,* v. 6, p. 66; Freeman, *Lee's Lieutenants,* v. 2, pp. 122–23.

[120] Douglas, p. 139.

[121] Chambers, v. 2, pp. 168–69; *SHSP,* v. 6, p. 66.

[122] W.W. Blackford, p. 131.

Jackson's troops, in turn, emerged from their concealment in the woods and moved toward the embankment. "The effect was not unlike flushing a covey of quails," said a Federal officer, and the two lines crashed together with astonishing impact.[123] "It seemed to me that the very earth trembled," remembered a participant, "and surely one or the other of the armies would the next morning find itself…'all dead!'"[124]

On a front of one and one-quarter miles, Porter and Hatch hammered against Jackson's right and center. One Rebel testified that "The Federals came up in front of us suddenly as men rising up out of the ground, showing themselves at the old railroad line…in double battle phalanx and coming forward in slow time, pouring their shots into our ranks in unmerciful volume."[125] Jackson himself confirmed that "As one line was repulsed another took its place and pressed forward…by force of numbers and fury of assault."[126] The combatants struggled hand to hand with fixed bayonets, some Confederates, their ammunition expended, employing large rocks to fracture Yankee skulls. "One continuous roar" engulfed the railroad bed. When Union reinforcements struck Hill's sector of the line, the Federals managed to claw through the thin gray defense.[127]

For almost thirty-six hours Jackson alone had resisted the concentrated attacks of Pope's legions, but now, unlike circumstances on the 29th, Stonewall had no uncommitted reserves. He needed help. Couriers dashed to Lee and Longstreet requesting assistance in dislodging the stubborn Union attackers. Relief appeared instantly, not in the form of infantry—although Longstreet at last felt willing to participate in the battle—but from rows of Confederate artillery positioned by Col. Stephen D. Lee on a ridge overlooking Jackson's entire front. Lee focused on the waves of bluejacketed reinforcements who poised ready to exploit the lodgements effected by their comrades. "As shell after shell burst

[123] Quoted in Henderson, v. 2, p. 173.

[124] Oldaker, p. 43.

[125] *Confederate Veteran*, v. 22, p. 231.

[126] *OR*, v. 12, part 2, p. 647.

[127] *Ibid.*, p. 666; Casler, p. 112; Chambers, v. 2, p. 170.

in the wavering ranks, and round shot ploughed broad gaps among them," recalled an eyewitness, "you could distinctly see, through the rifts of smoke, the Federal soldiers falling and flying on every side. With the dispersion of the enemy's reserve, the whole mass broke and ran like a flock of wild sheep."[128]

Then occurred "one of those inspiring scenes which its actors will never forget, and [which make] a staunch soldier of a recruit!"[129] Longstreet's divisions stepped out splendidly "with the crimson of [their] colours gleaming like blood in the evening sun," and completely overwhelmed Pope's left, routing it "fully as much as any disciplined army can be routed."[130]

A portion of Jackson's exhausted command joined Longstreet in his countercharge, presenting a picture William Oates called "indescribably grand."[131] R.L. Dabney wrote breathlessly that, "Over several miles of hill and dale, of field and forest, the two lines now swept forward...closing upon the disordered masses of the enemy like the jaws of a leviathon." Pockets of Unionists stood fast until steam-rollered by the relentless Confederate machine.[132]

Darkness, confusion and a defense of the plateau around the Henry House of First Manassas distinction saved Pope's fleeing army from total destruction. Confederate pursuit ended about 10:00 p.m. Lee's line now formed a huge V with its point at Groveton and its arms stretched in either direction toward the fords along Bull Run.[133]

Jackson returned at last to the rear of his victorious command and stumbled upon a solitary Confederate sprawled near the railroad cut. Asking the man his unit and condition, the veteran replied, "the Fourth Virginia, your old brigade, General. I have been

---

[128] *SHSP*, v. 6, p. 66; Cooke, *A Military Biography*, pp. 297–98; Chambers, v. 2, p. 170. Lee had actually commenced his fire before receiving Jackson's plea.

[129] Worsham, p. 79.

[130] Henderson, v. 2, p. 178; Jedediah Hotchkiss to his wife, September 8, 1862, Hotchkiss Collection.

[131] Oates, p. 146.

[132] Dabney, p. 534; Chambers, v. 2, p. 172.

[133] Alexander, p. 215; Allan, p. 302.

wounded four times but never before as bad as this. I hope I will soon be able to follow you again."

Jackson recognized the serious nature of the private's injury and procured medical attention, causing the soldier to sob with a gratitude and respect akin to reverence. The General then placed his hand softly on the soldier's head. "You are worthy of the old brigade and I hope with God's blessing, you will soon be well enough to return to it."[134]

The scene that greeted Lee's army the following morning left no doubt that, for thousands of men, Manassas would mark their final campaign. Jed Hotchkiss wrote his wife, "I went on Sunday over the battlefield...and never have I seen such horrors."[135] A Southern artillerist, gazing at the unfinished railroad, claimed he "could have walked a quarter of a mile in almost a straight line on their dead bodies without putting a foot on the ground."[136] Zouave casualties studded the fields like "crimson flowers."[137]

Early on the 31st, Lee and Jackson forded Bull Run to reconnoiter, drawing a hostile fire upon themselves in the process. Then in the company of his two lieutenants, the army chieftain explained his notion to employ Jackson's corps in another envelopment designed to force Pope to evacuate the powerful defenses at Centreville. Stonewall liked the plan but merely mumbled "good" before riding off to execute his part of the work.[138]

Jackson had anticipated further action and in the morning provided for the distribution of rations and the exchange of inferior arms for captured Northern weapons. His troops were ready to march by noon. With Hill's division in the lead, the column followed the Sudley Road across Bull Run and gained the Little River Turnpike. There, they turned east, encamping at Pleasant Valley, ten miles from their starting point.[139]

Heavy rains and post-battle exhaustion prevented Jackson from reaching Pope's rear on the 31st. Still, the pace proved suffi-

[134] Douglas, p. 142.

[135] Hotchkiss to his wife, September 8, 1862, Hotchkiss Collection.

[136] Moore, p. 123.

[137] Oldaker, p. 44.

[138] Freeman, *Lee*, v. 2, pp. 338–39; Longstreet, p. 191.

[139] Oates, p. 149; Chambers, v. 2, p. 173.

ciently challenging for one observer, who wrote, "Truly Jackson was the most restless leader the world ever saw, and he seemed to have very little consideration for the bones and sinews of his men."[140]

On September 1, even an "inconsiderate" commander like Old Jack could squeeze but little additional efficiency from his dragging, famished troops. The soldiers marched very poorly and broke ranks frequently to forage for food and refill empty canteens. By early afternoon the caravan had progressed only three miles to the vicinity of an elegant old mansion named Chantilly. Jackson also felt the strain of the week's continuous action and stretched out at the foot of a tree. Pulling his cap over his eyes, his chin on his chest, and his hands crossed neatly on his breast, "he slept as peacefully as a child."[141]

Pope had learned of Jackson's approach from a local citizen and issued orders for most of his army to fall back from Centreville to Fairfax. Hooker, Reno, and Kearny sallied out toward Germantown to meet the Confederate threat and buy time for an orderly retreat.[142]

The Battle of Chantilly or Ox Hill began late in the afternoon amidst a violent storm. "The rain came down in torrents," remembered Dr. McGuire, "and the peals of thunder could hardly be distinguished from the roar of artillery close to us. I was sitting close to Jackson, who was doubled up on his horse, so that his rubber cape would shed the rain over the top of his boots...his cap ...drawn tightly over his eyes."[143] Kyd Douglas recalled that "the lightning interchanged continuous flashes with those of musketry in the gloomy woods." The Federal attack was, in the words of one sopping Secessionist, "sudden and almost as furious as the rainstorm!"[144]

Several of Hill's brigades repulsed the Union assault, killing Brig. Gen. Isaac I. Stevens in the process. The battle lines swayed back and forth, Lawton supporting Hill's left to meet the charg-

---

[140] Chambers, v. 2, p. 173; *Battle-fields of the South* (New York: John Bradburn, 1864), p. 453.

[141] Cooke, *A Military Biography*, p. 304; Freeman, *Lee's Lieutenants*, v. 2, p. 130.

[142] Stackpole, *Cedar Mountain to Antietam*, p. 249.

[143] Hunter, H. McGuire, Hotchkiss Collection.

[144] Douglas, p. 144; Worsham, p. 81.

ing Bluecoats of Reno's and Kearny's commands. At one point, an officer in Hill's division, perhaps Branch or Hill himself, requested permission to withdraw on account of rain-soaked cartridges. "Give my compliments to [the general]," snapped Jackson, "and tell him that the Yankee ammunition is as wet as his [and] to stay where he is." According to McGuire, "there was always danger and blood when he began his terse sentences with 'Give my compliments!'"[145]

In the murky twilight, while attempting to organize another counter-assault, Union General Phil Kearny's mount accidentally carried him beyond his men and into Confederate skirmishers. Whirling his horse back toward his own lines, as William Oates so delicately phrased it, the Rebels "fired and killed him, but his skin was not broken."[146] Kearny's death and the gathering darkness ended the fighting. Jackson lost five hundred men, fewer than half the number of Federal casualties.[147]

Chantilly is recorded as a Confederate victory, but strategically it accomplished nothing. It does, however, provide a discernible climax to the Second Manassas Campaign. As Lee reported, "it was found that the enemy had conducted his retreat so rapidly that the attempt to intercept him was abandoned. The proximity of the fortifications around Alexandria and Washington rendered further pursuit useless."[148]

The military events that occurred in northern Virginia between August 15 and September 1, 1862, compose one of the most significant chapters of Confederate military history. The high tide of Southern fortunes that crested once at Sharpsburg and again at Gettysburg traces its origins to these eighteen days. Not only did the Second Manassas Campaign ensure the relief of Richmond for almost two years, but it forged a command team that would bear responsibility for the best battlefield results the Confederates would ever achieve.

---

[145] Freeman, Lee's Lieutenants, v. 2, pp. 131–33; Allan; pp. 311–17; Kelly, p. 43; Worsham, p. 81; *SHSP*, v. 25, p. 99. McGuire says Hill made the request. Henderson, v. 2, p. 184, identifies the requestor only as "a brigade commander."

[146] Henderson, v. 2, p. 184; Oates, p. 151.

[147] Kelly, pp. 43–44.

[148] Chambers, v. 2, p. 176; Henderson, v. 2, pp. 189–97.

It reflects no discredit on the army commander to admit that at Second Manassas, the junior member of the Lee-Jackson partnership deserves the lion's share of credit for Pope's ruination. Jackson is not at fault for the failure to trap the Federals between the rivers, and had Lee accepted his advice for fast action, the Union army might never have crossed the Rappahannock intact. No officer could have accomplished more during the sparring between the 21st and 24th and, in fact, Stonewall deftly averted potential trouble at Fauquier Springs and Freeman's Ford.

For five days beginning August 25, Jackson exercised a command as independent as if he had been in Mexico. He received no instructions from Lee. He received no assistance from Longstreet. He possessed no line of supply or communications save for messages carried by lonely couriers over circuitous routes through the Bull Run Mountains. During this interval he managed to conduct a masterful flank march of more than fifty miles to the enemy's rear; destroy the Federal supply base while repulsing attacks from three directions; select and secretly occupy an outstanding defensive position; aggressively dissuade the Unionists from reuniting their forces beyond Bull Run; and single-handedly resist numerous assaults executed by vastly superior numbers. No wonder one of Jackson's biographers calls his Manassas generalship "an exhibition of military genius."[149]

Jackson's performance at Second Manassas eliminated whatever doubts Lee may have maintained about the Valley General's cooperative attitude in the wake of the Seven Days. E.P. Alexander secularly postulated that Stonewall's bold behavior was the result of "at least a sub-conscious appreciation that the Lord helps best those who do not trust in Him for even a row of pins...but who appreciate the whole responsibility & hustle for themselves accordingly."[150] But, of course, the moral courage displayed by Thomas Jackson in this campaign, as in all others, found its inspiration in an absolute reliance on God's will.

[149] Chambers, v. 2, p. 176; Henderson, v. 2, pp. 189–97.

[150] Freeman, *Lee's Lieutenants*, v. 2, p. 137; Gallagher, p. 132.

Following the battle, one observer paused to assess the General in the aftermath of the victorious campaign that belonged more to Jackson than to anyone else:

> There you see self-command, perseverance, indomitable will, that seems neither to know nor think of any earthly obstacle, and all this without the least admixture of vanity, assumption, pride, foolhardiness, or any thing of the disposition to exert its pretensions....He has energy enough to supply a whole manufacturing district, and enough genius to stock two or three military schools like West Point....It would be a profitable study for some of our military swells to devote one hour each day to the contemplation of the "magnificent plainness" of old Stonewall.[151]

---

[151] *Battle-fields of the South*, p. 459.

Opportunity to the South: Meade versus Jackson at Fredericksburg

PRIVATE Benjamin Ashenfelter of the 6th Pennsylvania Reserves described the experience as "the worst disaster to our army since the war began." Another soldier in the Army of the Potomac declared, "I do not recollect of ever feeling so discouraged over the result of anything we ever undertook to do."[1]

These observations followed the Battle of Fredericksburg in December 1862. To most students of the Civil War, such references create images of towering Marye's Heights and the terrible stone wall, both blazing with Confederate fire. Yet, Ashenfelter and his comrade never saw these landmarks. They fought their battle of Fredericksburg four and one-half miles south of the city, in a bloody engagement frequently overshadowed by the more famous futility at the Sunken Road. Nevertheless, the combat that pitted Robert E. Lee's most famous lieutenant, Stonewall Jackson,

---

[1] Benjamin F. Ashenfelter to Father Churchman, Dec. 23, 1862, Harrisburg Civil War Round Table Collection (HCWRTC), United States Army Military History Institute (USAMHI); Freeman Cleaves, *Meade of Gettysburg* (Norman: Univ. of Oklahoma Press, 1960), p. 92.

against the man who would lead the Army of the Potomac longer than any other individual—George G. Meade—represented the Federals' only opportunity to avert what became their most lopsided defeat of the war in Virginia.

The campaign for Fredericksburg began in early November when President Lincoln replaced the dilatory Maj. Gen. George B. McClellan with Rhode Island's leading military figure, Ambrose E. Burnside. Once convinced to accept command, Burnside reorganized the army into three Grand Divisions under Maj. Gens. Edwin V. Sumner, Joseph Hooker, and William B. Franklin, and moved his forces southeast from Warrenton toward Fredericksburg. By doing so, he hoped to cross the Rappahannock River quickly at the old colonial town, and move directly south toward Richmond before Lee could react.

Burnside's pontoons failed to arrive with his infantry, and the new Federal commander squandered the advantage of his swift march by procrastinating on the left bank of the river. As early as November 22, Maj. Gen. George G. Meade, a division commander in Maj. Gen. John F. Reynolds' First Corps, expressed doubt about the potential success of the campaign due to the delay in crossing the Rappahannock. Prophetically, he suggested that the way to capture Richmond would be to sever the railroads leading to it from the south and southwest, an operation over which he would preside some two years later! But for now, Meade and the rest of the Army of the Potomac would wait until Burnside made his decision to span the stream.[2]

Those orders came at last on December 11. Franklin's Grand Division, consisting of Reynolds' troops and Maj. Gen. William F. Smith's Sixth Corps, crossed on the bridges farthest downstream from the town. Unlike their comrades in Fredericksburg, the Left Grand Division encountered little resistance, and easily secured the right bank on the 11th. The bulk of Franklin's men marched across the next day, serenaded by regimental bands playing gay tunes, including "Dixie," which according to Luther Furst of the 10th Pennsylvania Reserves, "cheered up the troops."[3]

[2] George G. Meade to wife, Nov. 22, 1862, in George Gordon Meade, ed., *The Life and Letters of George Gordon Meade* (New York: Charles Scribner's Sons, 1913), v. 1, p. 330.

[3] Luther C. Furst diary, Dec. 12, 1862, HCWRTC.

Franklin watched as the last of his soldiers cleared the bridges at 1:00 p.m. He placed Smith's corps on his right and Reynolds' on his left. While most of the Federals faced generally west with their backs to the river, Meade's division formed practically a right angle to the main line, its left anchored on the Rappahannock to prevent surprise attacks from downstream. Thirty-six guns protected the bridgehead. Later, Brig. Gen. Daniel E. Sickles' and Brig. Gen. David B. Birney's divisions from Hooker's command marched into position to cross Franklin's pontoons at a moment's notice, which gave that officer significant reserve infantry. Counting these troops, a division from the Ninth Corps, and 3,500 men of Brig. Gen. George D. Bayard's cavalry brigade, Franklin controlled some 60,000 soldiers, more than half of Burnside's army.[4]

Once established on the far bank, Franklin threw skirmishers forward and, joined by Reynolds and Smith, began examining the ground. The Federals occupied a broad plain, defined on the east by the Rappahannock and on the west by a wooded ridge defended by the Confederates, and dominated by a modest eminence called Prospect Hill. One and one-half miles separated the river from the high ground, the distance bisected almost in the middle by the Old Richmond Stage Road, sometimes called the Bowling Green or Port Royal Road. An earthen bank and ditch bordered the highway on both sides, rendering it, as Franklin said, "an exceedingly strong feature in the defense of the ground." Between the road and the ridge in a slight depression several hundred yards in width ran the Richmond, Fredericksburg and Potomac Railroad. Trees covered the slope leading from the ridge crest to the railroad except the southernmost three hundred or four hundred yards, in some places extending across the tracks. The hills petered out in the swampy woods fringing Massaponax Creek on the far southern extremity of the plain, which effectively limited operations in this direction.[5]

Franklin and his lieutenants quickly realized that in order to reach their antagonists, they would be required to cross the stage

[4] Jacob L. Greene, *Gen. William B. Franklin and the Operations of the Left Wing at the Battle of Fredericksburg December 13, 1862* (Hartford: Belknap and Warfield, 1900), p. 11; *OR*, v. 21, pp. 449, 361, 377, 90; Chambers, v. 2, p. 279.

[5] Greene, p. 11; *OR*, v. 21, p. 499.

road, traverse almost a thousand yards of open fields, descend into the railroad cut, and then climb the wooded ridge, all within clear view of the Confederates, who themselves would be concealed amidst the trees. Such a mission demanded careful planning at the highest level of command.

Late on the afternoon of the 12th, Franklin, Smith, and Reynolds all repaired to Franklin's headquarters at the Bernard House, known locally as "Mansfield." The owner of the plantation had protested the use of his home by Federal troops but found himself hustled unceremoniously across the pontoon bridges under guard, leaving the generals alone to contemplate their course of action.[6]

The brain trust of the left wing agreed that the only logical option was to form its troops into assault columns and turn Lee's right flank at any price. Shortly after they reached this consensus, Burnside joined the conference and listened attentively as his subordinates explained their plans. Although the army commander departed without specifically endorsing what he had heard, Franklin and the others assumed they had persuaded Burnside and that formal orders would be forthcoming shortly. Franklin had emphasized the need to launch the attack before dawn and sought authorization early that evening in order to set the scheme in motion. The three generals worked out details for the offensive and remained at Mansfield awaiting Burnside's go-ahead so that they might issue immediate instructions to their subordinate commanders.[7]

Twilight faded to darkness, and soldiers like Luther Furst dropped off "into the hands of Morpheus hoping the infernal cannon will keep quiet and I will dream of onward to Richmond." But no one at Mansfield slept. Franklin paced the floor, beside himself with anxiety. He telegraphed army headquarters on Stafford Heights and sent couriers across the river, repeatedly inquiring as to why he had no orders for the morrow. At 3:00 a.m., Reynolds gave up and retired to his bed to steal a few hours' rest. All agreed

---

[6] *B&L* v. 3, p. 136. This article provides interesting detail about Union operations at Fredericksburg, although Smith is less than frank about his own responsibility for the Federal failure.

[7] Vorin E. Whan, Jr., *Fiasco at Fredericksburg* (State College: Pennsylvania State Univ. Press, 1961), p. 51; *B&L*, v. 3, p. 133.

Jackson's problematical subordinate, Ambrose Powell Hill. Did Hill's feud with Stonewall contribute to the failure to close the gap in his line at the Battle of Fredericksburg?
[*Valentine Museum, Richmond, Virginia*]

that Burnside's delay would prove costly if and when the attack was launched.[8]

December 13 dawned with heavy fog in the Rappahannock Valley. The bitter cold and windy night had been rough on the soldiers. At 7:30 a.m., a time when Franklin, Smith, and Reynolds had hoped that their all-out attack would be well under way, a staff officer from Burnside's headquarters clattered up the drive to Mansfield and delivered the long-awaited orders. Franklin's face fell when he read them: "Keep your command in position for a rapid movement down the Old Richmond Road and...send...a division at least...to seize, if possible, the height near Captain Hamilton's...taking care to keep it well-supported and its line of retreat open." The Right Grand Division, the order concluded, would assault Lee's left once Franklin carried out his mission.[9]

General Franklin found his instructions incomprehensible relative to the strategy proposed at the previous evening's conference. Not only would the attack begin too late to take advantage of the early morning mist, but Burnside had reduced the assault force from Franklin's whole command to just one division. His use of the term "seize" implied that "Old Burn" thought the Confederate ridge to be only lightly held. Officers used the word "carry" when instructing troops to attack a strong position, which Franklin knew to be the case with the high ground before him.[10] Moreover, the timid language which referred to lines of retreat could hardly inspire subordinates to audacious action, at least not in the case of the deflated Franklin.

Actually, Burnside's intention to capture the military road that Lee had constructed behind his lines and to use it to move laterally along the Rebel defenses had merit if properly executed. Control of the heights would also drive the Southerners away from their rail line to Richmond. However, in order for the plan to work, sufficient infantry, properly supported by artillery, was required. Burnside's orders, particularly as interpreted by Frank-

[8] Furst diary, Dec. 12, 1862; Greene, pp. 13–14; *B&L*, v. 3, pp. 133–34.

[9] Stackpole, *Fredericksburg Campaign*, pp. 178–79; *B&L*, v. 3, p. 134; *OR*, v. 21, p. 71.

[10] Greene, p. 18; Whan, pp. 55, 153 n. 11; Stackpole, *Fredericksburg Campaign*, p. 170; *B&L*, v. 3, p. 134.

lin, were to do something safe that could not hurt very much if it failed of its object. Weak generals frequently adopted just such a policy.[11]

Franklin moved to implement his ill-advised instructions. Because Burnside had not released Birney's and Sickles' divisions from the Stafford side of the river to protect the bridgehead, Franklin felt compelled to leave Smith's entire corps to do this job. This overly cautious decision and Smith's subsequent day-long inaction contributed significantly to the eventual outcome of the battle. Reynolds' corps remained to do the work, and that officer selected Meade's division of Pennsylvania Reserves supported by Brig. Gen. John Gibbon's division, to spearhead the advance. Whether Meade received his assignment because of his men's fine reputation, because he had recently been promoted to major general, or simply because he was nearest the point of attack, his Pennsylvanians accounted for fewer bayonets than any other division in the left wing—only 4,500 in all. As they would soon discover, their task was a formidable one.[12]

Burnside's unexpected move to Fredericksburg and his indecisiveness in crossing the Rappahannock had placed Robert E. Lee's Army of Northern Virginia in a reactive posture throughout the campaign. Lee initially brought Lt. Gen. James Longstreet's First Corps to the hills behind the town and then summoned Lt. Gen. Thomas J. Jackson's divisions to range downstream, almost as far as Tappahannock, on the alert for a Federal crossing of the lower Rappahannock. Burnside's action on the 11th, however, revealed the Union commander's intentions. Lee responded on the 12th by bringing up two of Jackson's divisions, Maj. Gen. Ambrose Powell Hill's and Brig. Gen. William B. Taliaferro's, to concentrate his forces better. He ordered the Second Corps' other two divisions, Brig. Gen. Jubal A. Early's and Maj. Gen. Daniel Harvey Hill's, to remain downriver, still not entirely certain that

[11] Whan, p. 55; *Report of the Joint Committee on the Conduct of the War,* Senate Reports, No. 108, v. 2, *(JCCW)* (Washington: U.S. Government Printing Office, 1863), p. 653; Richard Meade Bache, *Life of General George Gordon Meade* (Philadelphia: Henry T. Coates, 1897), p. 235.

[12] Stackpole, *Fredericksburg Campaign,* p. 179; Greene, p. 18; Cleaves, p. 88; Joseph R. Orwig, *History of the 131st Pennsylvania Volunteers* (Williamsport, Pa.: Sun Book and Job Printing House, 1902), p. 108.

his opponent would ignore the opportunity to threaten his far right.[13]

On December 12, Lee and Jackson, in the company of the giant Prussian aide on J.E.B. Stuart's staff, Maj. Heros Von Borcke, crept forward from Prospect Hill onto the plain now occupied by Franklin's grand division. They approached to within four hundred yards of the Federal position as Von Borcke fretted over the fate of the Confederacy should sharpshooters spot the little party. This personal reconnaissance convinced the Generals that Burnside was preparing to attack, not simply to feint at this point, and they rushed orders to Early and D.H. Hill to join the rest of the army. Those two officers marched their soldiers fifteen to eighteen miles through a winter night over frozen roads and reached the battlefield near dawn.[14]

Lee assigned Jackson's corps to only two of the seven miles defended by the Confederate army, owing perhaps to the lesser natural strength of the terrain at the southern end of the line. Therefore, Jackson was able to create a defense in depth. He anchored his right at Hamilton's Crossing near marshy Massaponax Creek and would use his military road, Franklin's objective, to facilitate the rapid movement of units to threatened points.[15]

Powell Hill bore responsibility for the first line of defense, 3,300 yards in length. Two regiments of Col. John M. Brockenbrough's Virginians along with Brig. Gen. James J. Archer's brigade protected the right, northward from Hamilton's Crossing. Brig. Gen. James H. Lane's North Carolinians guarded the center, their right separated from Archer's left by a considerable distance. Brig. Gen. William Dorsey Pender was posted on the left, where he linked up with Maj. Gen. John B. Hood's division of Longstreet's corps. On the wooded high ground some five hundred yards behind the front line, Hill posted Brig. Gen. Maxcy Gregg's South Carolinians and Brig. Gen. Edward L. Thomas' Georgians. All told, the Light Division numbered almost 13,000 men, 8,000 of whom composed the front ranks. Hill used the railroad em-

[13] *OR,* v. 21, p. 645; Freeman, *Lee* v. 2, pp. 448–50.

[14] Von Borcke, v. 2, pp. 109–10; *OR,* v. 21, pp. 643, 630.

[15] Stackpole, *Fredericksburg Campaign,* pp. 151–52; *OR,* v. 21, pp. 630–31.

bankment as a picket line, the main position of his troops being 250 to 450 yards to the rear. Early's division formed the reserve on the right, Taliaferro's on the left, and D.H. Hill served as general corps reserve, creating a line almost one mile deep.[16]

But Jackson did not expect his 35,000 foot soldiers to stand alone. Stuart's cavalry and eighteen pieces of artillery filled the interval between Hamilton's Crossing and the Massaponax on Stonewall's right.[17] Lt. Col. Reuben Lindsay Walker, reputed to be the most handsome man in the Confederacy, commanded a grand battery of fourteen pieces on Prospect Hill. Twenty-one guns posted between Pender and Lane secured the left, including twelve cannon advanced across the railroad so as to offer flanking fire against any force attacking Prospect Hill.[18] Strong as the artillery support might be, the wooded and broken character of the ground initially limited Jackson to deploying less than one-third of the available guns.[19]

Old Jack rode up and down his line late on December 12, and topographical engineer Jed Hotchkiss noted that his corps commander came back to headquarters whistling—a phenomenon never seen previously. Stonewall had reason for optimism, to be sure, but his position also had its weaknesses. Only two improvements upon the natural strength of the ground had been made: the military road and a short trench occupied by Archer and Brockenbrough. The frozen ground and a shortage of entrenching tools precluded more digging.[20]

[16] *OR*, v. 21, pp. 630, 645, 654, 656; Branch Spalding, "Jackson's Fredericksburg Tactics," in *Military Analysis of the Civil War* (Millwood, N.Y.: KTO Press, 1977), p. 68. Spalding argues unpersuasively that Jackson intentionally lured Meade into a trap by leaving the gap in Hill's line uncorrected. See also Whan, pp. 59–60.

[17] *OR*, v. 21, p. 553; Whan, p. 61; Allan, p. 480.

[18] *OR*, v. 21, pp. 636–37. Col. Stapleton Crutchfield, Jackson's artillery chief, states clearly that a total of 21 guns protected the left of Jackson's line. Jackson's report (*OR*, v. 21, p. 631) confuses the artillery strength on the left, an error repeated in several secondary accounts of the battle, notably Chambers, v. 2, p. 281; Henderson, v. 2, p. 309; and G.F.R. Henderson, *The Campaign of Fredericksburg* (London: Kegan Paul, Trench and Co., 1888), p. 62.

[19] Henderson, v. 2, p. 310. During Meade's attack, Jackson deployed fifteen additional guns on his right. See *OR*, v. 21, p. 638.

[20] Jedediah Hotchkiss diary, Dec. 12, 1862, Hotchkiss Collection; Alexander, p. 294; Whan, p. 61.

More importantly, neither Walker's guns on the right nor the batteries on the left could adequately cover the interval in the line between Archer and Lane. The wooded gap, characterized by boggy ground, contained a point of woods two hundred yards broad along the Confederate line and narrowing toward the apex of a rough triangle pointing straight at the Federals. Archer's left flank on the right of this gap was some 150 yards from the trees, and Lane's right flank on the left was about 250 yards from them; so the gap stretched nearly six hundred yards.[21]

Numerous officers remarked upon the open space. Von Borcke says he suggested the trees be felled. Lane warned Archer, Gregg, and division commander Hill of the danger, but no one acted. Hill considered the ground too swampy to be passable. Others assumed the artillery crossfire would be sufficiently severe to prevent penetration.[22] Some pointed to Gregg's brigade as capable of blunting any drive into the woods, although his Palmetto Staters were blinded by the thick forest to anything that occurred at the front. Even Jackson reportedly saw the gap at 9:00 a.m. on December 13 and said "The enemy will attack here," but did nothing about it.[23]

Perhaps Jackson's neglect stemmed from his desire to attack. Both he and Stuart pressed this notion upon Lee, but the army commander demurred. Lee recognized that the Confederate position at Fredericksburg was tactically strong but strategically weak. He would wait until the Federals wrecked their divisions against his impregnable position and then, when the odds were more even, he would consider a counterattack.[24]

Jackson dressed early on the morning of the 13th, selecting the new coat Stuart had given him, as well as new trousers, boots, saber, and spurs. His grayish-blue cap adorned with a half-inch gilt braid had just come from his wife. He thought the braid conspicuous, but feared to remove it in deference to Anna's feelings.

[21] Chambers, v. 2, p. 282.

[22] Von Borcke, v. 2, p. 106; *OR,* v. 21, pp. 54, 676. Von Borcke specifically cites Stuart as believing in the effectiveness of the artillery.

[23] *OR,* v. 21, pp. 656–57; Robert K. Krick, "Maxcy Gregg: Political Extremist and Confederate General," *Civil War History,* 19 (Dec. 1973), p. 20; Dabney, p. 610.

[24] Von Borcke, v. 2, p. 114; Bache, p. 231.

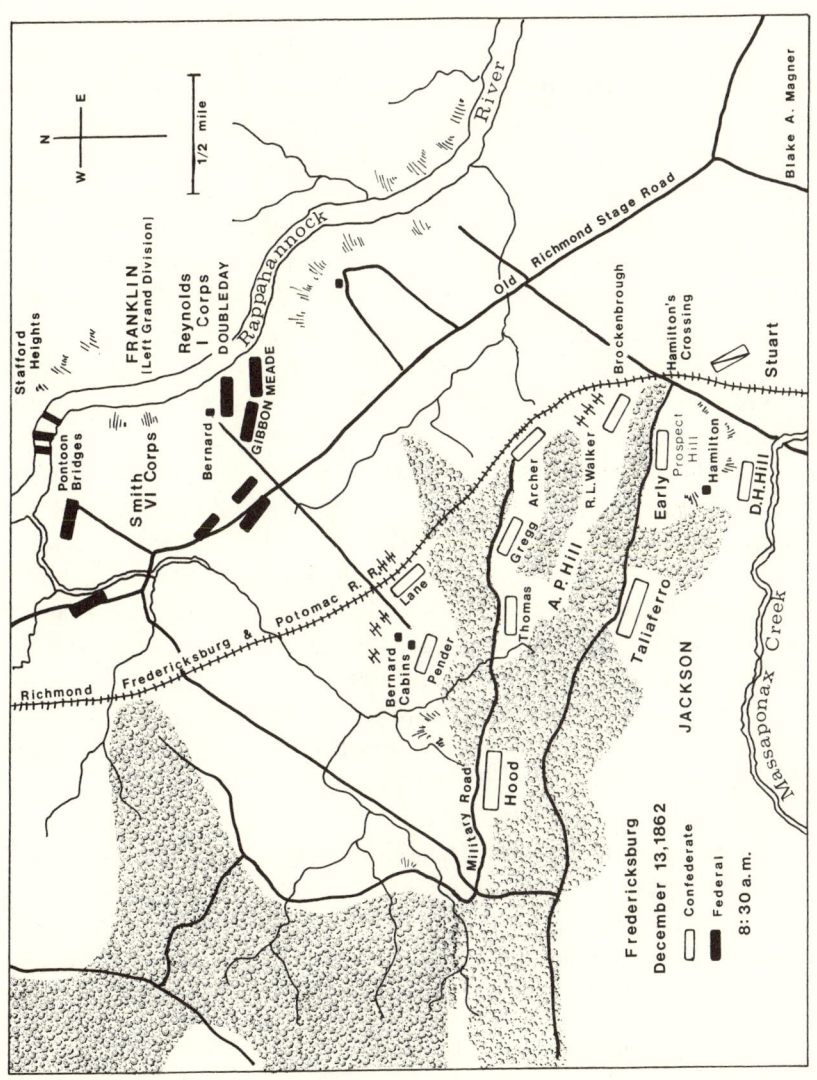

Fredericksburg
December 13, 1862

Confederate
Federal

8:30 a.m.

Stuart was beside himself with glee when Old Jack donned this finery, and the troops joked that they preferred to see Stonewall wearing his old clothes, fearing he would not get down to work attired so rakishly.[25]

Jackson and Stuart rode to Telegraph Hill, where Lee and Longstreet had their headquarters, the corps commander enduring the gibes of the soldiers and the cavalryman reveling in them. The tactless Longstreet, animated by the prospect of battle, continued to tease a somber Jackson. "General," he asked with mock concern, "do not all these multitudes of Federals frighten you?" "We shall see very soon whether I shall not frighten them," came the calm reply. The conference over, Jackson and Stuart returned to the Confederate right, and joined A.P. Hill. The officers peered into the slowly dissipating mist out on the plain, where they heard "an indistinct murmur," remembered Von Borcke, "like the distant hum of a myriad of bees" vaguely announcing the presence of a suddenly active army.[26]

Franklin's soldiers would remember the music from the regimental bands that morning, as well as the bark of commands from eager line officers. In Meade's division, those orders translated into an advance south across the fields parallel to the river at about 8:30 a.m. After covering five hundred or six hundred yards, the Pennsylvanians turned sharply right (west) and headed for the Richmond Road. The old thoroughfare was lined with thick hedgerows and was sunken in some places to a depth of six feet, presenting an obstacle to men and artillery. The soldiers unslung their knapsacks, and, still protected by the fog, tore away the bushes and bridged the ditches.[27]

Once across the road, Meade formed his attack with his first and second brigades in column, three hundred yards apart, and the third brigade deployed to the left to provide flank security. Skirmishers preceded the division in front and on the left to avoid surprise in the foggy light. Gibbon's division advanced on Meade's

[25] Dabney, p. 610; Freeman, *Lee*, v. 2, p. 454; Chambers, v. 2, p. 283; Fitzhugh Lee, *General Lee* (New York: D. Appleton and Co., 1894), p. 227.

[26] Dabney, p. 611; Freeman, *Lee*, v. 2, p. 454; Von Borcke, v. 2, p. 114.

[27] Cleaves, p. 90; Alexander, p. 296; *OR*, v. 21, pp. 453, 510; *History of the 121st Regiment Pennsylvania Volunteers by the Survivors Association* (Philadelphia: Burk and McFetridge Co., 1893), p. 26.

right, but the third of Reynolds' three divisions, Maj. Gen. Abner Doubleday's, remained east of the road, facing south.[28]

The Union officers had barely completed these arrangements when two Rebel guns suddenly opened fire on their left and rear. This artillery belonged to Maj. John Pelham, who had begged permission from Stuart to move forward a section along a hidden path to a point perpendicular to the stage road. "Here," said the 24-year-old Alabamian, "I can pour an enfilading fire on [their]... flank...and knock them down like ninepins." And knock them down he did. Each of Pelham's solid shot blasted through Meade's entire formation. Meade, fearing this cannonade would precede an infantry attack, deployed his third brigade in line of battle to the left, forming with the first brigade two sides of a square. The divisional batteries immediately returned the fire, aided by Doubleday's guns, and quickly disabled Pelham's Blakely rifle. The boy cannoneer maintained the contest with his one remaining piece, a Napoleon captured six months earlier from the Federals, and eventually drew upon himself the concentrated attention of some thirty Union guns. Stuart ordered him to disengage three times, and Lee, watching from his distant command post, remarked, "It is glorious to see such courage in one so young." At last, his ammunition exhausted, the gallant Pelham retired, enjoying the finest moment of his brief life.[29]

How long did Pelham sustain his unequal fight? Meade says twenty minutes; Jackson, an hour. In either case, Pelham disrupted the Union advance and contributed to the Federals' sensitivity about their left flank. As a result, Doubleday spent the entire day passively guarding the left, never advancing across the Richmond Road. Following Pelham's withdrawal, Franklin brought forward several batteries and bombarded the woods before him. He also called up Birney's division to augment his position, although the Sixth Corps remained virtually stationary guarding the pontoons and Sickles sat idly on the left bank.[30]

[28] *OR*, v. 21, pp. 510–11, 480; Henderson, *Fredericksburg*, p. 74; Whan, p. 63.

[29] William Woods Hassler, *Colonel John Pelham: Lee's Boy Artillerist* (Richmond: Garrett and Massie, 1960), pp. 145–47; Whan, p. 63; *OR*, v. 21, pp. 514–15; Von Borcke, v. 2, pp. 118–19; Allan, p. 482 n. 1; *SHSP*, v. 40, p. 209; Henderson, *Fredericksburg*, p. 75; John Esten Cooke, *A Life of Gen. Robert E. Lee* (New York: D. Appleton and Co., 1871), p. 183.

[30] *OR*, v. 21, pp. 511, 631, 462–63, 637, 454, 361–62, 523, 378–79; Allan, p. 483.

At about 11:00 a.m., Meade swung around his third brigade, Brig. Gen. C. Feger Jackson in command, to face the Rebel line. This extended the front presented by Col. William Sinclair's first brigade. The second brigade, under Col. Albert L. Magilton, still supported the first, three hundred yards to the rear. Reynolds had directed Meade to focus on a distinctive point of woods jutting into the plain and to use it as the object of his attack. Now, he ordered the Pennsylvanians to renew their advance.[31]

Accompanied by several batteries and the continuing covering barrage of distant Union artillery, Meade's troops stepped out unopposed. The splendid sight of the dressed lines on the open plain inspired one waiting Confederate to poetic prose:

> On they came in beautiful order as if on parade, a moving forest of steel, their bayonets glistening in the bright sunlight; on they came, waving their hundreds of regimental flags, which relieved with warm bits of coloring the dull blue of the columns and the russet tinge of the wintry landscape, while their artillery beyond the river continued the cannonade with unabated fury over their heads, and gave a background of white fleecy smoke like midsummer clouds, to the animated picture.

Von Borcke described Meade's advance as "a military panorama, the grandeur of which I had never seen equaled," and expressed concern to Jackson. "Major," Stonewall replied, "my men have sometimes failed *to take* a position, but *to defend* one, never! I am glad the Yankees are coming."[32]

Jackson may have been pleased with the course of events thus far, but the gunners of Lindsay Walker's command did not share his opinion. They, and to a lesser degree Hill's infantry, suffered from the Union bombardment but had orders not to return the fire lest their position be revealed prematurely. There is nothing quite so frustrating to a soldier as to absorb punishment and not be allowed to retaliate. Therefore, when the Yankees approached to within five hundred yards of the ridge crest and Walker gave the order to commence fire, the Southerners did so with a vengeance. All of Jackson's cannon up and down the line

---

[31] *OR*, v. 21, pp. 453–54, 511, 186, 645.

[32] Von Borcke, v. 2, pp. 116–17.

A stylized depiction of Jackson's infantry near Hamilton's Crossing. The troops belong to Brig. Gen. Harry T. Hays' First Louisiana Brigade. [*Battles and Leaders*]

opened with a metallic roar, and Meade's troops staggered. The division commander ordered his men to withdraw a short distance behind a slight crest while the Federal artillery began a counter-battery fire at the now-identified targets.[33]

Shot and shell flew continually for more than an hour, "making deep furrows in the ground and bounding like rubber balls," as one Pennsylvanian remembered. Another Unionist claimed the Confederates had driven stakes in the ground as range markers, thus making Meade's attackers easy targets. The Federal troops sustained casualties, including some wounded bounty men, new to the army. As stretcher bearers removed these greenhorns from the field, the veterans sarcastically admonished them: "Take good care of those men; they have cost the government a great deal of money!"[34]

[33] *OR*, v. 21, pp. 637–39, 645, 649, 656–57, 511, 515; Whan, p. 66; Chambers, v. 2, p. 286.

[34] Alexander, p. 297, says "over an hour"; Henderson, *Fredericksburg*, p. 77, says one and one-half hours; *121st Pennsylvania*, p. 27, claims the artillery fired for "two long hours." See also *OR*, v. 21, pp. 511, 515; "Official Record of Henry Flick," HCWRTC; *B&L*, v. 3, p. 137.

While Capt. James A. Hall of the 2nd Maine Artillery conversed with two regimental commanders, a Confederate shell suddenly destroyed a caisson parked nearby. Hall looked annoyed by this interruption. He carefully dismounted, strolled to one of his guns, sighted it and gave the signal to fire. The iron missile hurtled toward its target and, in an instant, a sudden upheaval of bursting shells, wheels, splinters, and human flesh exploded in the Rebel line. Hall's shot had struck an ammunition case, killing nearly all the men and horses around it. Confederates passing the spot later saw the men lying around the case scorched and blackened so that they looked like Negroes, the hair on their heads crisped and singed. Hall calmly returned to his horse, mounted, and continued his conversation, but the explosion emboldened the poised Federal infantry. A rousing Union cheer spontaneously swept the line, and a few minutes later Meade gave the order to fix bayonets and charge.[35]

Just as Walker's cannoneers had endured the initial Union bombardment without responding, Meade's Pennsylvanians lay in the fields for what seemed like hours waiting for the artillery duel to run its course. After hugging the ground and dreading the scream of exploding shells, the ranks welcomed Meade's directive. Up jumped the division, accompanied by the deafening boom of more than fifty Union guns. Jackson's artillery ignored its counterparts, and focused its attention strictly on the approaching infantry. This reexposed the Rebel positions, and the batteries on Prospect Hill suffered such heavy casualties among their teams that the Southern gunners called their position Dead Horse Hill. One Confederate described what he saw:

> A direct and infolding fire swept each battery upon either side, as it was unmasked; volley replied to volley, crash succeeded crash, until the eye lost all power of distinguishing the lines of combatants, and the plain seemed a lake of fire, a seething lake of molten lead covered over by incarnate fiends drunk with fury and revenge.[36]

[35] Abner R. Small, *The Road to Richmond* (Berkeley: Univ. of California Press, 1939), p. 65; *Confederate Veteran*, v. 30, p. 20; *121st Pennsylvania*, p. 28; *OR*, v. 21, pp. 511, 480.

[36] E.M. Woodward, *Our Campaigns* (Philadelphia: John E. Potter, 1865), p. 235; *OR*, v. 21, p. 186; Whan, p. 66; *SHSP*, v. 40, p. 213.

The Pennsylvania Reserves rushed across the fields, leaping obstacles and ditches, dangerously delayed by one fence near the railroad. Their objective remained the point of woods identified by Reynolds almost five hours previously. Although staggered by the devastating cannonade, Meade's intrepid men maintained their momentum and plunged into the boggy woods. To their surprise and delight, they discovered that not only did the trees protect them from the enemy's batteries, but that the woods were unoccupied by Confederate infantry! Only Meade's first two brigades, however, had penetrated the line. C.F. Jackson's third brigade on the left faced Walker's guns in front, while Gibbon's three brigades attempted to drive forward on Meade's right. It was now shortly after 1:00 p.m.[37]

The gap in the Confederate front, now occupied by Meade's brigades, was too wide and too heavily wooded for mutually supporting fire from the Confederate infantry posted around it. Of Lane's five North Carolina regiments that held the ground nearest the Confederate left of the wooded gap, the 37th stood closest to the trees, followed by the 28th, 33rd, 18th, and 7th extending to Lane's left. Upon the Federal breakthrough, the first regiments, the 37th and 28th, suddenly found themselves encircled on their right as well as assailed from the front. Their flank turned and their rear threatened, these Tarheels fired all their ammunition and that of their dead and wounded and then fell back. The other three regiments maintained their ground, some soldiers pivoting to face south toward the Union penetration.[38]

Of Archer's five units that held the ground nearest the gap on the right of A.P. Hill's line, the 19th Georgia, the 14th, 7th, and 1st Tennessee, and the 5th Alabama Battalion stood in that order extending from Confederate left to Confederate right. The first three of these regiments suffered the same surprise that shocked the North Carolinians on the other side of the trees. Before they knew it, the unseen enemy had overwhelmed them. The 5th Alabama Battalion and 1st Tennessee maintained their positions, but when

---

[37] 121st Pennsylvania, p. 28; Alexander, p. 298; Henderson, *Fredericksburg,* p. 87; *OR,* v. 21, pp. 511–12, 518–22.

[38] *OR,* v. 21, pp. 654–55.

the rest of the brigade retreated, the second of the swinging doors flew open, through which the Federal forces could stream virtually untouched.[39]

The Pennsylvanians had generated a full head of steam at this point, and what they sacrificed in tactical precision they made up in enthusiasm and bravery. Sinclair's brigade brushed by Lane and rolled forward toward the ridge crest where Maxcy Gregg's brigade awaited them. Magilton also punched ahead instead of taking Archer in flank, a maneuver that would have freed C.F. Jackson to participate in the charge to the hilltop. As it was, Meade's third brigade continued to struggle head-on with Archer's Tennesseeans and Alabamians, assisted by Brockenbrough's Virginians, and therefore did not join its comrades in the breakthrough. Nevertheless, Meade had accomplished much. More than three hundred Rebel prisoners trod sullenly to the rear, "from their dirty and ragged appearance, resembling the emptying of an almshouse," according to a member of the 2nd Pennsylvania Reserves.[40] Moreover, the Federal juggernaut had not yet run its course, as Gregg's troops soon discovered.

Incredibly, the blue wave that swept over the South Carolinians caught them almost entirely unprepared. After the battle, Archer claimed that Hill attributed Gregg's surprise to the Carolinian's deafness. Hill had ordered Gregg to advance as soon as the heavy musketry commenced, but the brigade commander probably did not hear either the guns or the orders. Busy making coffee or eating dinner with regimental colors resting atop stacked arms, Gregg's men initially mistook the attackers for a retiring Confederate force. When individual soldiers began shooting at the surging figures racing toward them through the forest, their commander endeavored to stop them. Gregg rode rapidly in front of his regiments knocking up their muskets with his hands and vainly shouting to cease fire. His erroneous identification cost him a minie ball through the spine, a painful and serious wound. Some of the South Carolinians collapsed, while others adjusted their

[39] *OR*, v. 21, p. 657.

[40] *OR*, v. 21, pp. 511–12, 518–22; Henderson, *Fredericksburg*, pp. 87–88; Woodward, p. 236.

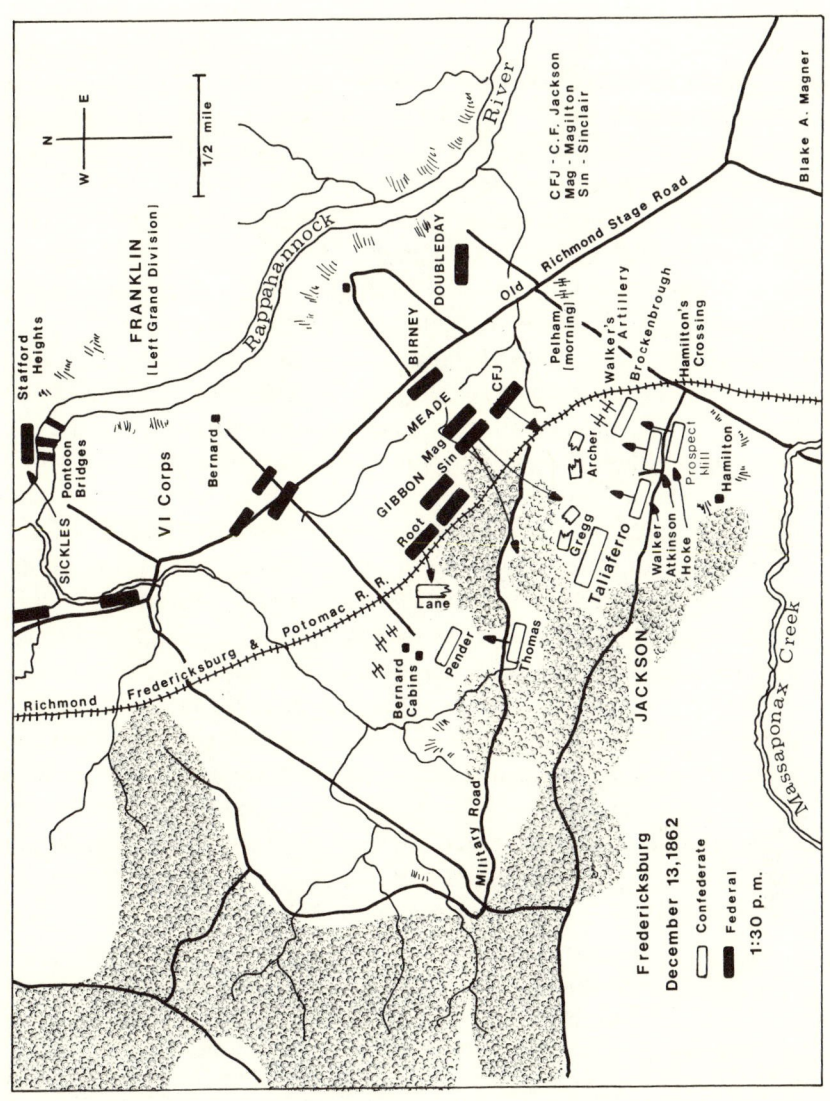

ranks to limit the damage. Meade's men pressed on in their wake, crossed the military road, and reached the crest of the heights.[41]

Meade's first and second brigades now found themselves in the midst of the Confederate position, but the charge had dissolved them into a disorganized mass. The division commander, whose hat contained a fresh bullet hole, realized that his men needed support. He could see more Confederates gathering in his front and already missiles flew about the ranks. Here was the point where a concentrated rush of Union infantry reinforcements just might have driven Jackson's reserve troops back upon themselves, but Meade stood alone. His instructions to Birney to move his division forward went unheeded, because that officer refused to obey an order not issued by a higher authority. Franklin had not advanced any other units to positions of potential support.[42]

C.F. Jackson's third brigade of Meade's division continued its futile struggle against Archer, Brockenbrough, and Walker to the left of the breakthrough. Feger Jackson fell dead while attempting to flank the Confederates at Prospect Hill, and his brigade made no further progress. Gibbon's division, which had advanced on Meade's right before the penetration, met a withering artillery and small arms fire on its front and flank. Two of Gibbon's brigades failed even to cross the railroad, but at 1:45 p.m., Col. Adrian R. Root's five regiments launched an irresistible attack. Fixing bayonets, Root's soldiers rushed across the embankment with a yell and carried the position defended by three regiments of Lane's brigade. They captured scores of prisoners from the 33rd North Carolina, but, like Meade, found themselves isolated and unsupported. Then, as Lt. Charles H. Veil of the 9th Pennsylvania Reserves remembered, "Stonewall Jackson again turned up....He always had a habit of showing up when [we] did not want him."[43]

[41] James J. Archer to his brother, Dec. 21, 1862, in *Maryland Historical Magazine,* 56 (June 1961), p. 139; "Official Record of Henry Flick," HCWRTC; Krick, "Gregg", pp. 21–22; *OR,* v. 21, pp. 646–47; Whan, p. 67.

[42] Henderson, *Fredericksburg,* pp. 88–90; Isaac R. Pennypacker, *General Meade* (New York: D. Appleton and Co., 1901), p. 103; Woodward, p. 238; Osmund R.H. Thomson and William H. Rauch, *History of the Bucktails* (Philadelphia: Electric Printing Company, 1906), pp. 235–36.

[43] *OR,* v. 21, pp. 512, 480, 486–87; Woodward, p. 237; Henderson, *Fredericksburg,* p. 89; Allan, pp. 488–89; Charles Henry Veil, "An Old Boy's Recollections," Miscellaneous Civil War Collection, USAMHI.

Jackson had first learned of the crisis in his front from an officer in Gregg's brigade who galloped wildly to corps headquarters. Upon hearing the man's report of the disaster suffered by the South Carolinians, "The General turned round as quietly as if nothing extraordinary had happened," recalled an eyewitness, "and ordered up Early's division to support the center." Early himself had received the news from a breathless artillery officer that "an awful gulf" had been left in the front line and the Federals had penetrated the position. He responded by sending three brigades to expel the invaders and restore the line.[44]

Lawton's brigade, under Col. Edmund N. Atkinson of the 26th Georgia, had been resting about three-quarters of a mile west of Hamilton's Crossing along the Mine Road when it received the word to move forward at 1:30 p.m. The Georgians advanced in fine style, joined by Early's own brigade, commanded by Col. James A. Walker, on its left. Col. Robert F. Hoke's North Carolinians, Georgians, and Alabamians fell in on Atkinson's right.[45]

Above the deep roar of the artillery there came the echo of what Early called "the cheering peculiar to the Confederate soldier...which is never mistaken for the studied hurrahs of the Yankees." Union soldiers characterized the noise as "an unearthly fiendish yell such as no other troops or civilized beings ever uttered." Atkinson and Walker slammed into Meade's two advanced brigades and engaged in vicious hand-to-hand combat. According to Private Ashenfelter, "The action was close-handed and men fell like leaves in autumn....Our boys fought bravely. It seems miraculous that any of us escaped at all." The dying Maxcy Gregg dragged himself up by grasping a small tree, and, cap in hand, waved to the troops. Meade hung on stubbornly for about twenty minutes, but by 2:15 p.m. his troops began trickling out of the Confederate position. The Pennsylvanians fell back slowly but in no semblance of order.[46]

[44] Mrs. Jackson, p. 369; *OR*, v. 21, p. 664.

[45] *OR*, v. 21, pp. 664, 669–70.

[46] *OR*, v. 21, pp. 664, 653; John C. Gregg, *Life in the Army* (Philadelphia: Perkinpine and Higgins, 1866), p. 60; Ashenfelter to Churchman, Dec. 23, 1862, HCWRTC; Krick, "Gregg", p. 22. General E.L. Thomas called Meade's resistance "stubborn." See also Freeman, *Lee*, v. 2, p. 462; *OR*, v. 21, p. 450; Cleaves, p. 91.

Root's brigade of Gibbon's division fared no better. E.L. Thomas' Georgians, who had been posted on Gregg's left, joined by some of Walker's men, pushed forward against the outnumbered Federals. Private Marion H. Fitzpatrick of the 45th Georgia relates what happened:

> Soon…our regiment fired a deafening volley which told that we were in sight of the bluecoats. In a moment more we could all see a plenty of them. I raised my rifle, took deliberate aim and fired, loaded and fired again. The Yanks retreated and we followed with a rush and a yell and poured death in their ranks at every step.

Root reported the Rebel fire to be "simply murderous," and like Meade he fell back across the railroad.[47]

On the Confederate right, Hoke reinforced Archer and drove Jackson's brigade into the open plain, capturing more than two hundred prisoners in the railroad cut. Early's men had done their job splendidly, and these veterans chided their comrades of the Light Division by boasting that "Jubal's boys are always getting Hill out o' trouble." General Lee watched this spectacle from his lofty command post, at the same time that Longstreet's corps almost casually repulsed Burnside's brigades at the Sunken Road. He turned to Old Pete and said, with a tone of wistful resignation, "It is well that war is so terrible—we should grow too fond of it."[48]

Meanwhile, Meade dashed to General Birney when the retreat began and angrily assumed the authority to order him to the relief of the Pennsylvanians. Birney released two of his brigades for the purpose, two regiments of which rushed immediately into the gap between Meade and Root. But these few troops, the only reinforcements sent by the Left Grand Division during the assault, were too little, too late. They washed away along with the initial attackers. Federal officers attempted to make a stand east of the railroad, but the units were too disorganized to reform. Moreover, Atkinson and Hoke, caught up in the emotion of the hour, raced down the hill, across the tracks and out into the open. This coun-

---

[47] *OR*, v. 21, pp. 653, 673–74, 487; Mansel Hammock, ed., *Letters to Amanda* (Culloden, Ga: privately printed, 1976), p. 30.

[48] *OR*, v. 21, pp. 672–73. Von Borcke, v. 2, p. 123, claims that an entire regiment fell captive, which is an exaggeration typical of the author; *B&L*, v. 3, p. 140; Cooke, *Lee*, p. 184.

terattack finished Meade and Gibbon for the day, and their beaten men refused to rally again until they reached the Old Richmond Road.[49]

The impetuosity of the two Confederate brigades, however, carried them too far out into the plain, where they became easy targets for Federal artillery. Union gunners employed their canister rounds with good effect, supported by the bulk of Birney's division. Atkinson fell with an arm wound and was captured. The Rebels lost heavily and received orders to retire.[50]

Not every Confederate shared the two brigades' enthusiasm. One large, fine-looking fellow, a recent conscript of the 60th Georgia, dropped out of the charge and took cover behind a tree. An officer of the regiment saw this and as he passed struck the fellow a sound whack with the flat of his sword, simultaneously saying "Up there, you coward." To his astonishment, the man dropped his musket, clasped his hands, and prayed devoutly, "Lord, receive my spirit." The officer was surprised by this display, but recovered his composure and delivered a violent kick upon the fellow's ribs, at the same time shouting, "Get up sir; the Lord would not receive the spirit of such an infernal coward." At this, the man leapt up joyfully and exclaimed, "Ain't I killed? The Lord be praised," and, grabbing his musket, sailed in like a hero.[51]

With the threat of a counterattack apparently extinguished for the moment, Birney, joined by Sickles, reestablished the integrity of the Left Grand Division by posting a line about halfway between the road and the railroad. Meade's Fredericksburg adventure had ended. The Federal attack, ironically, resembled in some ways the Pickett-Pettigrew charge against Meade's army seven months later, except the Pennsylvanians penetrated farther and received better support in their withdrawal. After his division completed its retreat, Meade encountered the First Corps commander. "My God, General Reynolds," he cried in exasperation, "did they think my division could whip Lee's whole army?" Ges-

---

[49] Thomson and Rauch, p. 236; *OR*, v. 21, pp. 368, 450; *B&L*, v. 3, p. 135 (the 38th and 40th New York made the attack); Henderson, *Fredericksburg*, p. 91.

[50] *OR*, v. 21, pp. 462, 516, 632–33, 671.

[51] Stiles, p. 135.

turing toward his thinned ranks he added, "There is all that is left of my Reserves."[52]

Meade had good reason for his distress. Of the 4,500 men who crossed the plain, more than 1,800 became casualties. The 11th Pennsylvania Reserves watched six of their color bearers fall within a few moments, and Company E of that regiment had but three men left unhurt. Company C of the 12th Reserves lost forty of forty-nine men present. Feger Jackson was killed and Sinclair wounded. Meade's division suffered such devastation, in fact, that the army completely reorganized the Reserves after the battle. The division simply ceased its affiliation with the Army of the Potomac.[53]

Meade then rode to Franklin's headquarters, calmly removing his hat and displaying two bullet holes between which and the top of his head there were but a few millimeters. Sarcastically observing that "I found it quite hot enough for me," Meade complained that his division had virtually carried the battle alone. Remarkably, Franklin claimed that until that moment he had not known that Meade had fought unsupported.[54]

Burnside then provided Franklin the opportunity to atone for his timidity by ordering him to renew the attack on his front. He wrote this order, received at Grand Division headquarters about 2:30 p.m., in an obscure fashion, and Franklin could not decide if he was supposed to attack at a single point or along his entire line. By now, however, Franklin had lost all confidence in the army commander and felt it would take too long to organize his whole force for a new advance in any case. He informed Burnside that he simply could not comply, and became content with the notion of running out the clock on this short winter day.[55]

General Jackson, however, did not share his opponent's satisfaction with the status quo. Franklin's shifting of new units to

[52] *OR,* v. 21, pp. 362–63; Francis W. Palfrey, *The Antietam and Fredericksburg* (New York: Charles Scribner's Sons, 1882), p. 158; Thomson and Rauch, p. 236.

[53] *OR,* v. 21, pp. 140, 877–79; M.D. Hardin, *History of the Twelfth Regiment Pennsylvania Reserve Volunteer Corps* (New York: published by the author, 1890), p. 137; Frederick H. Dyer, *A Compendium of the War of the Rebellion* (Des Moines: Dyer Publishing Co., 1908), v. 1, pp. 286–87.

[54] Bache, p. 240; *B&L,* v. 3, p. 136; Franklin to Meade, Mar. 25, 1863, cited in Cleaves, p. 92.

[55] Bache, pp. 244–45; *OR,* v. 21, pp. 94, 128, 118–19.

the front following Meade's repulse prompted Stonewall to expect a new Union attack. When it became apparent that the Federals planned no such advance, Old Jack's mind immediately returned to thoughts of the offensive. "Those who saw him in that hour," wrote John Esten Cooke, "will never forget the expression of intense but suppressed excitement which his face displayed. The genius of battle seemed to have gained possession and his countenance glowed as from the glare of a great conflagration." Jackson would attack! He planned, typically, to move with his entire corps. The troops would attack at sunset, artillery in the lead to measure the Union firepower. Darkness would protect his men if they were forced to retreat.[56]

Jackson's orders arrived at the various division headquarters late in the day, and subordinate commanders felt unsure of their roles. Nevertheless, just before dark, the artillery rolled out across the railroad, Stuart and Pelham on the right advancing most rapidly. The cavalry chieftain exposed himself to such fire that a minie ball tore the fur collar off his cape, and after twenty minutes, Jackson ordered him to fall back. Union artillery greeted Jackson's movement in the center so emphatically that here Stonewall aborted the attack before it fairly began. "The enemy's artillery reopened and so completely swept our front as to satisfy me that the proposed movement should be abandoned," he wrote.[57] Some evidence indicates that Jackson proposed a night assault and went so far as to distribute white bandages to the soldiers to wrap around their arms for identification, a plan supposedly vetoed by Lee.[58] In any event, Old Jack reluctantly conceded to Franklin possession of the Rappahannock's right bank. After eight hours, this Battle of Fredericksburg had concluded at last.

[56] Cooke, *Lee*, p. 232; Dabney, p. 621; *OR*, v. 21, p. 634.

[57] Von Borcke, v. 2, p. 219; *OR*, v. 21, pp. 643, 647, 652, 634.

[58] Henderson, v. 2, p. 234; W.R. Tanner, Sr., *"Reminiscences of the War between the States,"* (Chapel Hill: Univ. of North Carolina, 1931), p. 9. Tanner says, "General Jackson had the doctors of the different regiments to put a white bandage on the arm of each soldier so that we would know each other from the Federal soldiers." Tanner served in the 13th South Carolina. Freeman, *Lee*, v. 2, pp. 465–66, clearly calls this notion fictitious. He cites Walter H. Taylor, *Four Years with General Lee* (New York: D. Appleton and Co., 1877), pp. 81–82 as his authority. Taylor is a reliable source.

Casualty figures clearly demonstrate the ferocity of the fight. Franklin lost more than 2,500 men in addition to the devastation suffered by Meade. Jackson's corps lost some 3,400 troops, two-thirds of them in A.P. Hill's division.[59] Confederate brigade commanders Gregg and Atkinson joined Union division commander Gibbon and cavalryman Bayard as the highest ranking casualties of the day on this end of the battlefield.

Any rational analysis of the Battle of Fredericksburg must assign primary responsibility for the Federal debacle to army commander Burnside. That officer's confused thinking and delay severely compromised any chance for the Army of the Potomac to emerge victorious. As Meade accurately predicted in a letter home on December 16, "Burnside, I presume, is a dead cock in the pit."[60]

Early the next year, however, the Committee on the Conduct of the War determined that William Franklin bore the blame for what happened on the Union left. Clearly, what opportunity the Federals possessed at Fredericksburg lay on the ground in front of Jackson. Franklin's initial inclination to attack massively was by no means a path to certain victory, but it had the best chance of succeeding. Franklin's decision to place the most conservative and literal interpretation on the orders he received from Burnside in the morning conspired to sacrifice one of the more notable accomplishments of the war and consign it to the graveyard of forlorn hopes. Meade wrote that "the slightest straw, almost, would have kept the tide in our favor," but Franklin failed to employ Doubleday, Birney, Sickles, or any of Smith's divisions.[61]

Franklin told the Congressional Committee after the battle: "I never dreamed that this was considered as a strong attack...but supposed it was an armed observation to ascertain where the enemy was." As a member of the 2nd Pennsylvania Reserves noted, "He was subsequently suspended from his command for not being a better dreamer." If Franklin really believed what he told the

---

[59] *OR*, v. 21, pp. 133–34, 137–39, 635.

[60] Meade to wife, Dec. 16, 1862, in Meade, *Life and Letters*, v. 1, p. 338.

[61] *JCCW*, p. 57; Meade to wife, Dec. 20, 1862, in Meade, *Life and Letters*, v. 1, p. 340.

congressmen, his armed reconnaissance could have been accomplished without Meade's final attack at all. Once he committed the Pennsylvanians, though, he should have employed the remainder of his grand division, particularly because this was his initial idea, and he expressed nothing but disappointment for the orders he did receive. Private John B. Tobias of the 8th Pennsylvania Reserves summed it up well when he wrote, "All this could have been avoided had the officers done their whole duty."[62]

T.J. Jackson's conduct of the battle was not without its shortcomings as well. The Confederates blundered terribly by ignoring the point of woods and presuming it to be impassable. Even had this been the case, some units should have held it in front to deny its shelter to the attackers. Somehow, Jackson allowed his frontline division commander, A.P. Hill, to disappear all afternoon. His whereabouts are unknown at any time during the engagement.[63] Furthermore, during the counterattack, Atkinson and Hoke needlessly exposed their men by pursuing piecemeal across the plain and paid a heavy price in casualties for their poor judgment.

Nevertheless, Jackson's defense in depth and his decision to reserve his artillery fire to oppose infantry made the difference. It is difficult to agree with historians who suggest that if properly supported by Hood and Pickett, the Second Corps could have driven Franklin into the Rappahannock.[64] Reynolds' corps may have been demoralized, but too much unscathed Federal artillery and infantry remained on the right bank to expect Jackson to have accomplished more than he did.

In fact, therein lies the primary lesson of the Battle of Fredericksburg. Despite winning in the most overwhelming tactical sense, Lee accomplished nothing more than postponing the next advance against Richmond for a few months. Sagacious observers at the time recognized the ominous significance of this hollow Confederate victory. Wise men also made note of the performance

---

[62] *JCCW*, p. 56; Woodward, p. 240; "Army Life of John B. Tobias, During the Civil War, 1861–1865," p. 11, copy at Fredericksburg and Spotsylvania National Military Park.

[63] Robertson, *General A.P. Hill*, p. 168.

[64] See, for example, Henderson, *Fredericksburg*, p. 113.

of the only Federal division commander to breach Lee's line on December 13. Within days after the battle, Meade received his promotion to corps command, and a few months later, largely on the strength of his accomplishments on the plains below Fredericksburg, George Gordon Meade became the last commander of the Army of the Potomac.

The Generalship of Stonewall Jackson

He began the Civil War as a major of engineers in Virginia state service. Two years later, he died a lieutenant general and his country's most famous and revered military figure.

Thomas J. Jackson never attained promotion to full general. Five of the South's lieutenant generals outranked him, and as a major general, Jackson stood but twelfth in seniority.[1] Yet, in the estimation of the first soldier of the Confederacy, no one eclipsed him on the battlefield. "Such an executive officer the sun never shone on," wrote Robert E. Lee. "I have but to show him my design, and I know that if it can be done, it will be done."[2]

Few observers in 1861 could have predicted that this peculiar professor would rise from an uncomfortable obscurity at the Virginia Military Institute to achieve international renown. In the first months of the war, the name of Stonewall would ignite trepidation

---

[1] *SHSP*, v. 1, pp. A 10–11; 14–15. The lieutenant generals who outranked him were James Longstreet, Edmund Kirby Smith, Leonidas Polk, Theophilus Holmes, and William J. Hardee. At the major general level, David Twiggs, Polk, Braxton Bragg, Earl Van Dorn, Gustavus W. Smith, Holmes, Hardee, Benjamin Huger, Longstreet, John B. Magruder, and Mansfield Lovell were all Jackson's seniors.

[2] Quoted in Henderson, p. 699.

and awe in the North, respectful fascination abroad, and unparalleled hope and devotion in Dixie.

Forty-eight hours after Abraham Lincoln's call for volunteers to suppress an armed insurrection in Charleston, South Carolina, the Virginia secession convention voted to leave the Union. In Lexington, a few days later, Maj. Thomas J. Jackson, instructor of Natural Philosophy and Artillery Tactics at V.M.I. stood poised to lead the cadets to Richmond. Jackson's orders directed that he depart at 12:30 p.m. Although his eager young soldiers formed up early, the Major patiently waited until the exact specified minute before authorizing an advance.[3]

Jackson's brilliant record in the Mexican War and his West Point education earned him immediate attention. Governor John Letcher, a Lexingtonian, recommended his fellow townsman for a colonelcy of Virginia volunteers and command at Harpers Ferry, one of the state's most important venues. When delegates to the convention bluntly asked, "Who is this Major Jackson?", Rockbridge County delegate Samuel M. Moore replied: "I will tell you who Major Jackson is. He is a man who, if you order him to hold a post, he will never leave it alive to be occupied by the enemy."[4]

Jackson relished his assignment to the lower Shenandoah Valley, quickly mustering and organizing his men. "This place should be defended with the spirit which actuated the defenders of Thermoplyae, and, if left to myself, such is my determination," the Colonel informed Richmond.[5] He impressed wagons, supplies, and equipment and drilled his troops endlessly. When Brig. Gen. Joseph E. Johnston arrived on May 24 to assume authority in the name of the Confederacy, he inherited a surprisingly well-ordered command.[6]

Johnston assigned Jackson to command of five regiments of Virginia infantry, a unit destined to become the South's most-renowned brigade. Jackson also acquired his best-known mount at Harpers Ferry, a little sorrel selected by quartermaster John A.

[3] Vandiver, pp. 131–32.

[4] *SHSP*, v. 40, pp. 154–55.

[5] *OR*, v. 2, p. 814.

[6] Vandiver, pp. 140–43.

Harman from a carload of captured horses. The Colonel pronounced the animal's gait to be "as easy as the rocking of a cradle," and called him "Fancy," a name that stuck neither with the men nor with posterity.[7]

Three weeks after Johnston's evacuation of Harpers Ferry on June 15, Jackson learned of his elevation to brigadier general. His regiments had performed well in support of Capt. J.E.B. Stuart's cavalry during the skirmish at Falling Waters, and Johnston had recommended both officers for promotion. The commission carried the date June 17, 1861.[8]

Jackson's first test as a general came at Manassas on July 21. His Virginia brigade assumed a tactically important position on the Henry House Hill and served as a rallying point for Confederate forces. Brig. Gen. Barnard Bee, in command of a hard-pressed, then stampeded brigade, dashed up to Jackson, according to tradition, and shouted, "General, they are beating us back." The former professor replied laconically, "Sir, we will give them the bayonet."[9]

Bee saluted and rode off to rejoin his men. Exactly what he told them and how he meant it have been in dispute for generations. Lt. William M. Robbins of the 4th Alabama remembered Bee's order as "Yonder stands Jackson like a stone wall. Let us go to his assistance."[10] Maj. Gen. Dabney Maury quoted Bee as saying, "See where Jackson stands like a stone wall. Let us form behind him."[11] Dr. Hunter McGuire's rendition is the most familiar: "There stands Jackson like a stone wall—rally behind the Virginians."[12]

Most witnesses regard Bee's remark, whatever precisely it might have been, as a compliment to Jackson's tenacity. Others believe that the South Carolinian really implied a criticism. Jackson's brigade had remained concealed on the reverse crest of Henry Hill while Bee and other Confederates absorbed their beat-

---

[7] *SHSP*, v. 43, pp. 96–99 discusses the acquisition of all of Jackson's wartime mounts.

[8] Vandiver, pp. 149–51.

[9] *SHSP*, v. 35, pp. 80–81.

[10] *SHSP*, v. 19, p. 164.

[11] *SHSP*, v. 25, p. 313.

[12] *SHSP*, v. 19, p. 308.

ing. This failure to advance, an immobility reminiscent, some suggest of a stone wall, did temporarily contribute to Bee's discomfiture.[13]

Bee's mortal wounding left the matter in doubt, but the press latched on to variations of his quote, transforming it into a *nom de guerre* for the Virginians and their General. Jackson's devastating counterattack, which captured two Union batteries and turned the tide of battle, gave credence to his image as the hero of the day. Wounded in the finger, Jackson held his hand aloft to ease the pain, a gesture many interpreted as the invocation of a blessing by the pious commander. The General stood sternly near his brigade, with cap drawn close over his eyes, until the Federals began streaming from the field.[14] Then, he urgently advocated pursuit of the disorganized Union fugitives and exclaimed to President Jefferson Davis, who had arrived upon the scene, "We have whipped them! They ran like sheep! Give me 5000 fresh men, and I will be in Washington City tomorrow morning."[15]

Circumstances would not permit such an attempt, however, and the Yankees escaped safely to their capital. Still, Jackson had made an auspicious debut. "God made my brigade more instrumental than any other in repulsing the main attack," he wrote his wife. "This is for your information only—say nothing about it. Let others speak praise, not myself."[16]

Stonewall, as he now began to be known, deplored the complacency and inactivity that followed the victory at Manassas. He ceaselessly drilled and exercised his troops and they soon grew to resent the extra work. Within weeks, however, the exceptional quality of Jackson's brigade became evident, and the men derived as much pride from their reputation on the parade ground as on the battlefield.[17]

---

[13] William C. Davis, *Battle at Bull Run*, (Garden City, NY: Doubleday & Company, Inc., 1977) p. 197 examines the question of Bee's meaning. John Hennessy in *Civil War: The Magazine of the Civil War Society*, v. 8, no. 2, pp. 10–17 concludes that Bee's remark came much later in the battle than generally assumed.

[14] *SHSP*, v. 23, p. 261.

[15] Alexander, p. 42.

[16] Mrs. Jackson, p. 178.

[17] Vandiver, p. 170.

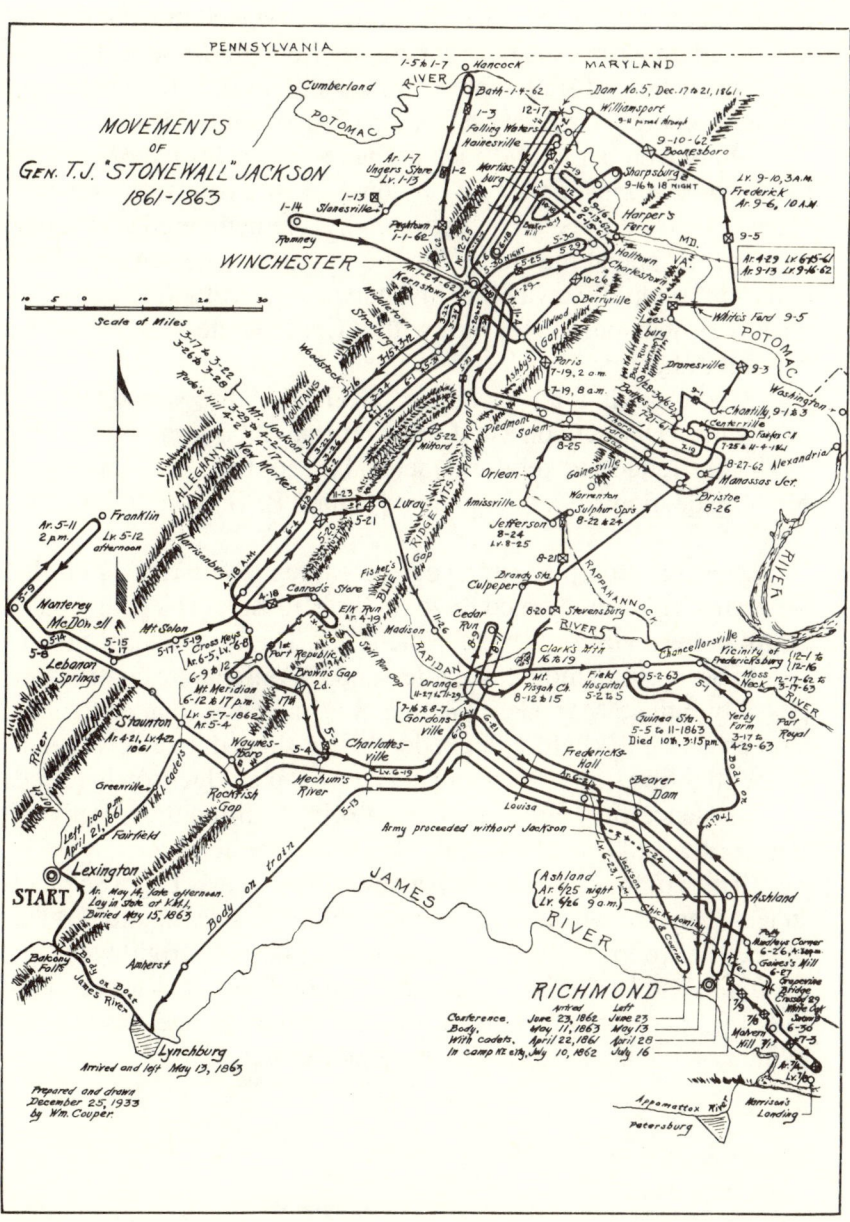

Stonewall Jackson's movements from 1861–1863.
[*Lee-Jackson Foundation*]

In October, the government rewarded Jackson with a promotion to major general. Shortly thereafter, it assigned him command of Confederate forces in the Shenandoah Valley. Although the new rank and change of station pleased Jackson, his transfer would necessitate a painful separation from the Stonewall Brigade.[18]

On November 4, Old Jack delivered a rare formal oration to his devoted troops, personally bidding them a heartfelt farewell. "He spoke from horseback, very rapidly," remembered a Virginia cannoneer, "and at the end of his short address wheeled his horse and rode so rapidly away that his men had scarcely time to choke back their tears and greet him with a Confederate yell before he was out of hearing."[19]

Upon arriving in Winchester, the General discovered that the new Valley District consisted of fewer than 2,000 troops. He immediately requested reinforcements, and joyfully welcomed his old brigade, now under Brig. Gen. Richard B. Garnett, to his little army.[20]

Jackson promptly surveyed the strategic situation in northwestern Virginia and opted to go on the offensive. His goal would be Romney, a village west of Winchester. The capture of Romney would bring a rich mountain valley under Confederate control and possibly induce Maj. Gen. George B. McClellan to attack Johnston prematurely, before the Federals had shaped themselves into proper fighting trim. In order to execute his plan, Jackson required the assistance of Brig. Gen. W.W. Loring's diminutive Army of the Northwest, located 150 miles from Winchester.[21]

The Romney expedition began on New Year's Day 1862 and in less than two weeks resulted in the bloodless occupation of the town. The troops suffered from short supplies and frigid weather, however, and Loring's men became demoralized. Jackson, consequently, cancelled plans for further campaigning and returned to Winchester, leaving Loring to garrison Romney.[22]

[18] Chambers, v. 1, pp. 400–402.

[19] *SHSP*, v. 23, p. 122.

[20] Vandiver, p. 178.

[21] Chambers, v. 1, pp. 407–408.

[22] See Vandiver pp. 188–90 for a brief review of the Romney Campaign.

On January 26, General Loring, unhappy in his isolated post, appealed directly to Richmond seeking the removal of his frozen command to a more commodious and strategically sound location.[23] Four days later, Secretary of War Judah P. Benjamin responded by ordering Jackson to withdraw the Army of the Northwest to Winchester.[24] Jackson acted instantly:

> Your order requiring me to direct General Loring to return with his command to Winchester has been received and promptly complied with. With such interference in my command I cannot expect to be of much service in the field, and accordingly respectfully request to be ordered to report for duty to the Superintendent of the Virginia Military Institute at Lexington as has been done in the case of other professors. Should this application not be granted, I respectfully request that the President will accept my resignation from the Army.[25]

Jackson sincerely resented the violation of proper military procedure and fully intended to resign. Johnston and Governor Letcher worked feverishly behind the scenes to smooth matters, and personally appealed to their indignant General's sense of duty. Their reasoning eventually prevailed. Stonewall retracted his resignation, but preferred charges against Loring. The War Department dealt with that matter by dispersing the Army of the Northwest and removing Loring from Jackson's authority.[26]

This unpleasant incident taught the Confederate War Department a valuable lesson in military protocol and usage. Moreover, for the student of Jackson's generalship, the Romney operation reveals Stonewall's willingness to divide his forces, take risks, and rely on bluff and psychological strategies to compensate for small numbers.

Those military philosophies, among others, received full application in the spring of 1862. Stonewall Jackson's Valley Campaign remains one of the most extraordinary wartime sagas in

---

[23] *OR*, v. 5, pp. 1046–48.

[24] *Ibid.*, p. 1053.

[25] *Ibid.*

[26] Vandiver, pp. 193–95.

American history. During thirty-two days in May and June, Jackson marched four hundred miles, skirmished almost daily, defeated three armies totalling twice his strength in five pitched battles, captured twenty-six guns, 4,000 prisoners, and immense quantities of supplies, and immobilized 60,000 Federals, all at a cost of fewer than 1,000 casualties.[27] Hunter McGuire considered the exploit "Jackson's greatest feat."[28]

The Valley's strategic importance resided both in its function as a Confederate breadbasket and as a natural invasion corridor aimed southwest to northeast directly toward Washington. Jackson, although too weak to contemplate a raid across the Potomac, intended to delay any Federal advance up the Valley, engaging as many Bluecoats as possible and thereby protecting Johnston's left flank at Manassas.

Ironically, Stonewall lost his first battle in the Valley—at least in a tactical sense. His grossly outgunned brigades unwisely assailed a Federal division under Brig. Gen. James Shields on March 23 at Kernstown, and received a thorough whipping. Jackson's audacity generated unreasonable consternation in Washington, however, and prompted a series of over-cautious decisions that compromised McClellan's long-anticipated Peninsula campaign against Richmond. The Lincoln administration designated armies under Maj. Gens. Irvin McDowell, John C. Frémont, and Nathaniel P. Banks to frustrate Jackson's perceived threat to the national capital, thus denying the timid McClellan reinforcements he felt he needed.[29]

Maj. Gen. Richard S. Ewell joined Jackson in the Valley on April 30. His 7,000 troops more than doubled the little Confederate force and provided Stonewall the required manpower to carry out his incredible campaign.[30]

Frémont's advance troops west of Staunton offered Jackson his first target. Sharing his plans with no one, the gray commander

---

[27] *SHSP*, v. 35, p. 82.

[28] *SHSP*, v. 19, p. 314.

[29] For a discussion of the Battle of Kernstown and its consequences, see Chambers, v. 1, pp. 463–473.

[30] Vandiver, p. 224.

crossed, then re-crossed the Blue Ridge and struck the Yankees a sharp blow at McDowell on May 8. He chased the beaten Federals across the mountains for a few days, then returned to the Valley.[31]

Massanutten Mountain bisects the Valley for fifty miles between Strasburg and Harrisonburg. Utilizing this range as a screen, on May 23 the Confederates swooped down upon the small Union garrison at Front Royal and virtually destroyed it. "Hearing loud cheering in the rear, which came nearer and nearer," reported a participant, "we soon saw that it was Stonewall himself...galloping along the column with uncovered head....The mountains echoed and re-echoed with the glad acclaim."[32]

Jackson's unexpected appearance at Front Royal alerted the Federals at Strasburg to their predicament. Banks fled northward but suffered a serious reverse at Winchester on May 25.

The Confederate reoccupation of that Valley city delighted soldiers and townsfolk alike. One unabashed Virginia maiden shouted to the liberating secessionists, "Oh! you brave, noble, ragged, dirty darlings you! I am so glad to see you!" Jackson joined the celebration, cheering and waving his cap in the air.[33] The General's efforts to interdict Banks' retreat, however, failed to prevent the Federals from crossing the Potomac on May 26. Nevertheless, Banks' losses at Front Royal and Winchester equalled one-third of his total strength.

On May 28, Jackson continued down the Valley, seizing a supply depot at Martinsburg and menacing Harpers Ferry. Meanwhile, the Federals plotted their revenge. Frémont from the west and Shields from the east would converge 37,000 strong at Strasburg, thus trapping the Rebels between themselves and the Potomac. Stonewall discovered this developing snare on May 30 and ordered his men to fall back and escape through the night. "Every man bent his energies to meet the requirement of our loved chief-

---

[31] Many sources recount details of Jackson's Valley Campaign. William Allan's *History of the Campaign of Gen. T.J. (Stonewall) Jackson in the Shenandoah Valley of Virginia* (London: H. Rees, Ltd., 1912) remains useful despite the passage of a century. Robert G. Tanner, *Stonewall in the Valley* (Garden City, N.Y.: Doubleday & Company, Inc., 1976) is the best modern treatment.

[32] *SHSP*, v. 9, p. 189.

[33] *Ibid.*, pp. 235–36.

tain," wrote one participant,[34] although some of the troops believed Jackson worried primarily about saving a large cache of lemons tucked away in the supply wagon.[35]

The Valley Army skirmished with the converging Federals and bought time for Jackson's trains, lemons and all, to roll safely south. The Yankees ultimately encountered Jackson at Cross Keys on June 8 and Port Republic on June 9, but met defeat at both places. When Shields' men began flowing northward signalling the campaign's conclusion, Stonewall turned to Ewell and said, "General, he who does not see the hand of God in this is blind, sir, blind."[36]

Indeed, Jackson's accomplishments appeared to be divinely inspired. His "foot cavalry" covered more ground in less time than seemed humanly possible, materializing where the enemy least expected them. Tactically, however, Jackson made mistakes. Banks might not have escaped at Winchester had Stonewall's mounted arm performed more efficiently. The Confederates launched their attack at Port Republic without proper reconnaissance and before all their troops arrived on the field. Nevertheless, Old Jack's remarkable achievement allowed Gen. Robert E. Lee the opportunity to rescue Richmond and perhaps destroy the Army of the Potomac.

Lee, who had replaced the wounded Joe Johnston in early June, admired Jackson's desire to resume the offensive in the Valley. The Confederate commander, however, viewed McClellan's army at the gates of Richmond as his first order of business. He planned to unite Stonewall's brigades with the divisions defending the Southern capital, then drive the "Young Napoleon" back down the Peninsula and, with luck, into oblivion.

Lee accomplished his primary objective in a series of engagements known as the Seven Days Battles. Between June 26 and July 1, McClellan retreated from the outskirts of Richmond to a fortified camp at Harrison's Landing on the James River. The Army of Northern Virginia lost some 20,000 men in the process,

---

[34] *Ibid.*, p. 276.

[35] Taylor, p. 67.

[36] Douglas, p. 91.

however, and the Unionists and their timid commander survived intact to fight another day.[37]

Blame for this failure to annihilate the Federals usually falls on Jackson's shoulders. Confederate artillerist Lt. Col. E.P. Alexander wrote, "Gen. Lee's best hopes & plans were miscarried &... he was prevented from completely destroying & capturing McClellan's whole army & all its stores & artillery by the incredible slackness & delay & hanging back which characterized Gen. Jackson's performance...."[38]

Stonewall's contemporary critics and later historians cite a variety of reasons for Jackson's alleged ineffectiveness. Unwillingness to serve as a subordinate, reluctance to fight on the Sabbath, the wish to spare his men from heavy combat, and clinical stress fatigue each enjoy their particular partisans.

Lee's plans at the Seven Days unarguably went awry. On each battlefield, except Malvern Hill, Jackson's absence or tardiness contributed to Confederate frustrations. To assume that responsibility for each tactical defeat rests with the Valley General, however, is to misread the record.

The Confederate debacle at Mechanicsville originated with ambiguous, poorly conceived orders from Lee and an impetuous, unauthorized attack by A.P. Hill. Again at Gaines' Mill, Lee misevaluated McClellan's intentions and based his strategy on erroneous assumptions. Jackson's maligned performance at Savage Station may be explained by an ill-advised directive from Lee instructing Stonewall to suspend his assault against the Union rearguard in order to resist any attempted Yankee passage of the Chickahominy River. Jackson behaved with great bravery and skill at Malvern Hill and played little part in the suicidal Confederate frontal attacks that closed the campaign.

Only at White Oak Swamp can Jackson's detractors mold a valid case. There the General's physical condition—a combination of exhaustion and an unspecified malady Jackson called

---

[37] No one has written a comprehensive study of the Peninsula Campaign and the Seven Days Battles. Clifford Dowdey's *The Seven Days: The Emergence of Lee* is quite good in treating the Confederate prespective, though in the author's opinion, too harsh on Jackson. See Essay Two.

[38] Gallagher, p. 96.

"fever and debility"—contributed to his lack of action. The comic book caricature of Stonewall blissfully dozing while the opportunity of the war slipped through his fingers, however, ignores the miscues of other Southern commanders on June 30 and oversimplifies Jackson's tactical problems at the swamp.

Any analysis of Jackson's performance at the Seven Days must consider his role at each engagement. He participated as merely one increment of a loosely-knit coalition of divisions that did not yet function as an army. Stonewall operated as a new subordinate, not as an independent commander as he had in the Valley, and he and Lee had not developed that special relationship that would later bear so much fruit. The Seven Days, therefore, qualify as a black mark on Jackson's record only when compared to his other military endeavors, not in any objective sense.[39]

No Confederate officer displayed initiative equal to Jackson's following the Seven Days. He advocated the immediate pursuit of McClellan, but Davis and Lee vetoed the idea. As the days in early July quietly elapsed, Stonewall urged the resumption of active campaigning. "We are losing valuable time here," he told a friend, "by repeating the blunder we made after the Battle of Manassas, in allowing the enemy to recover from his defeat and ourselves to suffer by inaction."[40]

The formation of a new Federal army, composed of the residue remaining from Jackson's vanquished Valley adversaries and commanded by the bombastic Maj. Gen. John Pope, presented Stonewall with the opportunity he cherished. On July 13, Lee assigned him to deal with the Yankee "miscreant," while the gray chieftain and the rest of the army kept their eyes on the nearby and potentially dangerous McClellan. "I must now leave the matter [of Pope] to your reflection and good judgment," Lee told his lieutenant, in eloquent testimony to the commander's continued confidence in Jackson, even after the disappointments around Richmond.[41]

---

[39] For a sympathetic analysis of Jackson's performance during the Seven Days, see Essay Two in this volume.

[40] *SHSP*, v. 40, pp. 180–81.

[41] *OR*, v. 12, part 3, p. 926.

Stonewall's command, consisting of his own, Ewell's, and A.P. Hill's divisions, met a portion of Pope's army at Cedar Mountain on August 9. The Confederates won the battle and drove the luckless N.P. Banks from the field. As at Kernstown and Port Republic, however, Jackson committed his forces prematurely and without adequate intelligence, and found it necessary to rally his men personally in order to save the day.[42]

Lee now determined to concentrate his entire army against Pope and defeat the distasteful Illinoisan before McClellan could arrive in northern Virginia on his transports from Harrison's Landing. The Second Manassas Campaign resulted from this calculated gamble against time, the Old Dominion's geography, and two numerically superior Federal opponents.

True to form, Marse Robert selected Jackson's wing of the army, a corps in every regard except name, to execute his plan. Jackson's task would be to march swiftly and secretly to Pope's rear, sack the Federal depots at Manassas, and somehow maneuver the Yankees so that the reunited Confederate army could bring them to battle on favorable terms.

Stonewall performed his assignment with a level of success that matched his achievements in the Valley. For five days beginning August 25, Jackson exercised a command as independent as if he had been in Europe. He received no instructions from Lee. He received no assistance from Longstreet. He possessed no line of supply or communications save for messages carried by lonely couriers over circuitous routes through the Bull Run Mountains.

During this interval, Jackson managed to conduct a masterful flanking march of more than fifty miles to the enemy's rear, destroy the Federal supply base while repulsing attacks from three directions, select and surreptitiously occupy an outstanding defensive position behind an unfinished railroad, boldly dissuade the Unionists from uniting their forces in safety beyond Bull Run, and single-handedly repulse numerous assaults from vastly superior numbers. No wonder one of Stonewall's biographers calls Jackson's Manassas generalship, "an exhibition of military genius."[43]

---

[42] The definitive work on the Battle of Cedar Mountain is Krick.

[43] Chambers, v. 2, p. 176; Essay Three in this volume.

Pope's ruination left only the dilatory George McClellan and his star-crossed Army of the Potomac to Lee, Jackson, and Longstreet. The Confederate brain trust decided to hazard a raid into Maryland, hoping to relieve Virginia from the ravages of war and recruit supposedly sympathetic Marylanders to the Bonnie Blue Flag. The ever-cautious McClellan, they guessed, would cling near his Washington defenses and permit the Rebels time to maneuver. So began the fateful Sharpsburg Campaign.

When Lee reached Frederick, Maryland in early September, he realized that the Union garrison astride his supply line at Harpers Ferry held the key to the campaign. That irritating thorn must be extracted. The gray commander first proposed the reduction of Harpers Ferry to Maj. Gen. James Longstreet, "but finding his senior lieutenant unable to appreciate the opportunity," wrote William Allan "he turned to Jackson, whose vigor and boldness better suited the enterprise."[44]

Jackson left Frederick on September 10 without seeing, much less firing upon, the bedridden, 96-year-old Barbara Fritchie, John Greenleaf Whittier notwithstanding.[45] Jackson's column splashed across the Potomac at Williamsport the next day.

In conjunction with three of Longstreet's detached divisions, Jackson encircled Harpers Ferry and induced the surrender of some 11,000 Bluecoats with seventy-three guns. Stonewall conducted this independent operation flawlessly in almost every regard. One of the Union prisoners spied the legendary Valley leader and told his comrades, "Boys, he's not much for looks, but if we'd had him we wouldn't have been caught in this trap."[46]

The strategic situation in Maryland had changed, however, when McClellan acquired a copy of Special Orders 191 detailing the dangerous division of the outnumbered Confederate army. Lee opted to concentrate his scattered forces behind Antietam Creek and make a stand near Sharpsburg. Jackson "emphatically concurred" with this controversial decision and rushed to join Lee,

---

[44] *SHSP*, v. 14, p. 105.

[45] *SHSP*, v. 7, pp. 435–38; v. 27, pp. 287–89.

[46] Douglas, p. 163.

leaving Maj. Gen. A.P. Hill in Harpers Ferry to administer the capitulation.[47]

The sanguinary combat at Antietam generated more casualties than did any other single day of the Civil War. Jackson fought on the Confederate left and calmly directed a desperate defense that teetered on the brink of disaster most of the morning. When the gunfire shifted toward the south after noon, Stonewall characteristically turned to thoughts of the offensive. "We'll drive McClellan into the Potomac," he prophesied, but this time a preliminary reconnaissance deterred him. Little Mac enjoyed a two-to-one numerical advantage and the hideous losses sustained in the morning deprived Jackson of the reserves he needed to seize the initiative.[48]

Lee chose to remain on the field the following day and even considered using Stonewall's bloodied command in a counterattack. Jackson endorsed this plan, but Southern scouts discovered the foolishness of such a notion, and Lee withdrew to Virginia.

"It was better to have fought in Maryland than to have left it without a struggle," thought Jackson.[49] In retrospect, most writers disagree. Lee took risks at Sharpsburg that promised little advantage but opened the possibility of catastrophic defeat. Jackson at Antietam, fighting tenaciously on the defensive and looking for the chance to turn the tables on McClellan, merely responded to Lee's directives.

Fortunately for the South, McClellan failed to exploit his golden opportunity to destroy the Army of Northern Virginia. Jackson easily turned back the Federals' perfunctory pursuit at Shepherdstown, then settled down to a quiet interlude of refitting his command in the lower Valley.

In October, the Richmond government authorized the creation of army corps to be commanded by lieutenant generals, and Lee naturally recommended Jackson for one of the new positions. "He is true, honest, and brave," wrote Marse Robert, "has a single

---

[47] Quoted in Vandiver, p. 392.

[48] *B&L*, v. 2, p. 679. Many excellent accounts treat the 1862 Maryland Campaign. See Allan, pp. 362–447 for a classic account of Jackson's role.

[49] Quoted in Vandiver, p. 400.

eye to the good of the service, and spares no exertion to accomplish his object."[50] Stonewall's promotion dated from October 10 and he told his staff with a smile, "Young gentlemen, this is no longer the headquarters of the Army of the Valley, but of the Second Corps of the Army of Northern Virginia."[51]

Old Jack also upgraded his wardrobe, thanks to Jeb Stuart. The cavalry officer presented his friend with a new coat to replace the garment savaged in September by adoring souvenir hunters en route to Harpers Ferry. Stonewall thought the coat to be "much too handsome for me," but promised to preserve it as a memento.[52] The daily mails buried Jackson with food, handkerchiefs, scarves, and even furniture from a nation of admirers. He implored his wife: "Don't send me any more socks, as the kind ladies have given me more than I could probably wear out in two years.[53]

Maj. Gen. Ambrose E. Burnside's accession to Union command presaged the beginning of a new campaign. The ruff-whiskered Rhode Islander abandoned McClellan's course and marched southeast toward Fredericksburg. Burnside's inability to negotiate the Rappahannock River allowed Longstreet to assume a defensive position west and south of the city. Lee then summoned Jackson to Fredericksburg but permitted his subordinate discretion as to how, where, and when to arrive. On November 29, Stonewall rode forty miles ahead of his men to meet with Lee, and two days later the Second Corps filed onto the scene.[54]

Jackson did not like what he saw. Although Longstreet occupied an impressive seven-mile line, the Yankee high ground on the opposite shore dominated the valley. "We will whip the enemy, but gain no fruits of victory," he predicted.[55] Lee shared this opinion and preferred to defend the North Anna River, twenty-five miles to the south. But President Davis objected to the voluntary

---

[50] *OR,* v. 19, part 2, p. 643.

[51] *SHSP,* v. 40, p. 206.

[52] Von Borcke, v. 1, pp. 295–97.

[53] Mrs. Jackson, p. 349.

[54] The Fredericksburg Campaign, like the Seven Days, still needs a comprehensive study. Jackson's role is treated with characteristic grace and thoroughness in Freeman, *Lee's Lieutenants,* v. 2, pp. 317–58; 369–76.

[55] Quoted in Vandiver, p. 420.

surrender of the rich Rappahannock basin and Lee decided to draw his line at Fredericksburg.[56]

Initially, the Second Corps extended Longstreet's front some fifteen miles downriver to the vicinity of Port Royal, reflecting Lee's uncertainty as to where Burnside might attempt a crossing. On December 11, the Federals revealed their plans by spanning the Rappahannock at three places near Fredericksburg. Jackson's four divisions rushed north and relieved the First Corps of the lower two miles of its responsibility.

Just as at Sharpsburg, Jackson would fight on the defensive during the Battle of Fredericksburg. He carefully created a line almost one mile deep to compensate for the modest natural strength of his assigned terrain. He concealed his artillery in the woods and ordered it to reserve its fire until Federal infantry reached canister range. Old Jack personally investigated the Federals' deployment and ordered deserters to be shot to stimulate discipline in the looming struggle. Stonewall's preparations left him anxious for the contest. "My men have sometimes failed *to take* a position, but *to defend* one, never!" he told an officer on Stuart's staff. "I am glad the Yankees are coming."[57]

Jackson's only gaffe at Fredericksburg might have cost him the battle. A.P. Hill bore responsibility for the front-line defense, but Little Powell permitted a six-hundred yard gap to exist midway in his division. Jackson noticed the gap on the morning of December 13 and remarked "the enemy will attack here," but did nothing to correct it.[58] Maj. Gen. George G. Meade's division did exploit this breach and penetrated deep within the Confederate position. Unfortunately for Meade, few Union troops supported him. Stonewall's splendid counterattack repulsed the Pennsylvanians with frightful losses.[59]

True to form, Jackson organized a counter-offensive in the early evening but cancelled the assault when he realized that Fed-

---

[56] Stackpole, *Fredericksburg Campaign,* p. 71; Freeman, *Lee,* v. 2, pp. 430–31.

[57] Von Borcke, v. 2, p. 117.

[58] Dabney, p. 610.

[59] For a detailed examination of the Confederate right at Fredericksburg, see Essay Four in this volume.

eral artillery still controlled the field. Both he and Lee deeply regretted Burnside's eventual escape across the river, but in reality, the Confederates possessed no means to prevent it.

Stonewall spent a pleasant winter season attending to army business at the hospitable Moss Neck estate in Caroline County. His hard work and attention to detail contributed to soaring morale in the Second Corps, despite shortages of food and supplies that necessitated Longstreet's detachment to Southside Virginia in February.

The winter also produced yet another Union commander. "Fighting Joe" Hooker, the personal and moral antithesis of Jackson, shared Stonewall's preference for the offensive. Maj. Gen. Hooker designed a brilliant plan that he thought would force the Confederates to retreat toward Richmond. Lee divined the Union strategy, however, and opted to challenge the Federals west of Fredericksburg in the green hell of the Wilderness.[60]

During the predawn hours of May 1, a grayclad column wound its way west from the Fredericksburg defenses toward a roadside tavern called Chancellorsville. Col. Risden T. Bennett of the 14th North Carolina remembered:

> Suddenly the sound of a great multitude who had raised their voices in accord came over tips of the bayonets. The very air of heaven seemed agitated....The horse and rider cross our vision. The simple Presbyterian Elder, anointed of God, with clenched teeth, a very statue, passes....No artist could express on canvas the face of that man in moments of excitement....I have been transported to the summit of action...by his presence. He was God's hermit.[61]

Lee had merely ordered Jackson to "make arrangements to repulse the enemy."[62] Earlier, the gray commander directed one Confederate division to fortify a strong ridge running between two churches three-and-one-half miles east of Chancellorsville.

---

[60] Of the many fine accounts of Chancellorsville, Jed Hotchkiss and William Allan, *Chancellorsville*, (New York: D. Van Nostrand, 1867) remains a most useful study of the Confederate perspective.

[61] *SHSP*, v. 34, p. 55.

[62] *OR*, v. 25, part 2, p. 762.

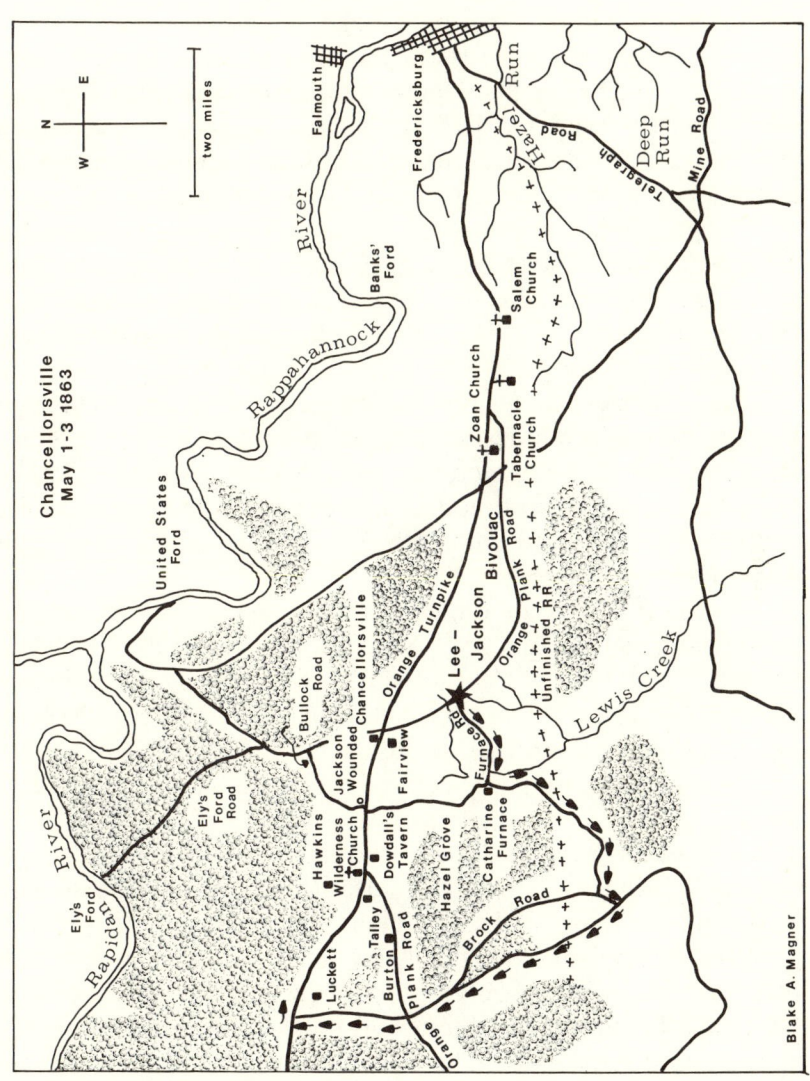

Jackson might reasonably have assumed that Lee wished him only to reinforce these defenses. Instead, when Stonewall arrived at the high ground, he told the Confederates there to drop their shovels, pick up their rifles, and prepare to attack.

The Rebels moved forward and encountered Hooker's advancing columns on the Orange Turnpike and Orange Plank Road. This bold and unexpected display of aggression persuaded the Union commander to surrender the initiative and withdraw his army to a defensive perimeter around Chancellorsville.

Jackson's daring course of action on May 1 set the stage for the most dramatic battle of the Civil War. In a campaign dictated by critical command decisions, this one rates among the most pivotal, although it is frequently overshadowed by the events of the following day.

Lee and Jackson met on the night of May 1–2 and conducted perhaps the most famous strategy session in American military history. Stonewall predicted that Hooker would retire across the river, but Lee disagreed and Confederate scouts confirmed the continued presence of Union troops. The question now became what to do.

Both officers favored the offensive, despite their staggering numerical disadvantage. Any debate as to who devised the flank attack is moot. Lee and Jackson jointly endorsed a stratagem that each had independently conceived. Stuart, Brig. Gen. Fitzhugh Lee, Capt. Jedediah Hotchkiss, Reverend Beverly T. Lacy, and local guides all contributed pieces of the puzzle needed to execute the plan.

The events of May 2 that led to the defeat of Hooker's right wing and ultimately Jackson's mortal wounding may be divided into two endeavors. Jackson's flank march across the front of a powerful enemy, on roads barely sufficient to accommodate four men abreast, covered twelve to fourteen miles, depending upon the unit. The notion that Stonewall conducted an unnecessarily slow operation patently ignores the physical and logistical requirements of the enterprise.

The Valley General administered the march as efficiently as possible. He prevented deliberate straggling by posting colonels at the rear of their regiments. He regularly rested his men to preserve their strength for the afternoon attack. He displayed flexibility and ingenuity in choosing his route, altering his plans where necessary and intentionally deceiving the enemy as to his destination.

The success of the flank attack itself knows few parallels. Maj. Gen. Oliver O. Howard's Eleventh Corps, despite displaying more courage than that with which they are usually credited, abandoned the field to Stonewall's onrushing warriors. Due to the length of his marching column, an attack against his rear guard at Catharine Furnace, and the miscalculation of a Georgia brigadier, only eight of Jackson's fifteen brigades actually participated in the attack. Nevertheless, nothing but darkness and the inevitable intermingling of Jackson's triumphant units arrested the progress of his assault. "The intense energy of General Jackson's nature was never more in evidence," thought a participant, and it is difficult to quarrel with the results which that energy achieved.[63]

Stonewall's tragic wounding occurred in the midst of typical Jacksonian circumstances. Not satisfied with the destruction of the Federal right, the General wished to eliminate the entire Army of the Potomac. He ordered A.P. Hill's relatively fresh division to prepare a night attack aimed at blocking Hooker's escape routes across the rivers. Then, in cooperation with Lee, he would assail the Yankees from three directions and crush them.

Was such an operation feasible? Probably not. Hooker had been reinforced, and the likelihood of 40,000 Confederates annihilating 80,000 Federals at night in a tangled Wilderness simply does not ring true. Still, Jackson sought a decisive victory, and he rode forward of his lines, without informing all local commanders, to ascertain the dispositions of the enemy.[64]

The volley that struck Jackson has been described as one of the great ironies of the war. There, at the apex of his finest hour, Stonewall fell mortally wounded at the unknowing hands of his own men. In a sense, however, what transpired in that impenetrable Virginia thicket was inevitable. Risk-takers realize that they

---

[63] *SHSP*, v. 40, p. 72.

[64] The circumstances surrounding Jackson's wounding on May 2, 1863, have been the subject of countless contemporary accounts, no two of which agree in their entirety. The best synthesis of these conflicting sources appears in Chambers, v. 2, pp. 409–19.

place their destiny in others' hands—fate's, lady luck's or God's. In Jackson's mind, his Heavenly Father had called him home.

The accomplished historian Allan Nevins lists Thomas Jackson as one of the six great combat commanders of the Civil War.[65] He, along with Lee, were the "two men whom the South could not spare."[66] Federal Col. Theodore Dodge called Jackson the war's "most able lieutenant,"[67] and Stonewall's Chancellorsville opponent, O.O. Howard, wrote, "In bold planning, in energy of execution, in indefatigable activity and moral ascendancy, Jackson stood head and shoulders above his confreres, and after his death General Lee could not replace him."[68]

Any number of writers have commented upon what combination of qualities explains Jackson's success on the battlefield. The General's aide, James Power Smith, identifies no fewer than fourteen such characteristics.[69] Other contemporaries such as Fitzhugh Lee, J. William Jones, Moses D. Hoge, and Hunter H. McGuire all contributed essays on the subject in the *Southern Historical Society Papers*.[70] Each of Stonewall's many biographers crafted his own particular interpretation of what made Jackson one of the Great Captains.

It seems possible, however, to distill these various analyses into half-a-dozen constituent parts: deception and secrecy; celerity on the march; strong discipline; decisiveness in combat; belief in total victory; and personal bravery and modesty.

Jackson's ability to mask his strategic intentions lay at the heart of his most impressive victories. In the Valley at McDowell and Front Royal, during the movement from the Shenandoah to the Chickahominy, all through the Second Manassas Campaign, and on the flank march at Chancellorsville, Stonewall deceived his opponents and mystified his friends.

---

[65] Allan Nevins, *The War for the Union,* (New York: Charles Scribner's Sons, 1960), v. 2, p. 94. The others are Lee, Grant, Sherman, Thomas, and Farragut.

[66] *Ibid.,* p. 452.

[67] *SHSP,* v. 14, p. 292.

[68] *SHSP,* v. 43, p. 103.

[69] *Ibid.*

[70] *SHSP,* v. 7, p. 583; v. 19, pp. 147–56; v. 13, pp. 321–25; v. 25, pp. 94–96.

Jackson frequently arranged for the capture of Confederate volunteers whom he had coached to repeat misleading information for the benefit of eager Federal interrogators. He conducted staged conversations within earshot of Yankee prisoners whom he promptly released to spread the tall tales they had overheard. He habitually concealed his troops behind hills or in the woods. When Jackson knew his men would be in sight of the enemy, he would march them in a direction opposite from their true destination to create the desired effect, then double back on some hidden byway.[71]

Stonewall guarded his thinking from his friends almost as assiduously as he did from his foes. "If my coat knew my plans, I would burn it at once," he proclaimed. "If I can keep my movements secret from our own people, I will have little difficulty in concealing them from the enemy."[72]

The General instilled this thinking throughout his entire command, as an episode in June 1862 illustrated. Jackson and two aides, whom he instructed to call him "Colonel," were en route from Fredericks Hall to Richmond to meet secretly with Lee. They encountered a straggling soldier on the road and Jackson asked the boy his unit.

"I do not know," answered the private.

"What state are you from?"

"I do not know, sir."

"What *do* you know, then, sir?"

"Nothing at all, sir, at this time. Old Stonewall says that we must be know-nothing until the next battle, and I am not going to violate orders."[73]

Of course, Jackson's reticence frustrated his immediate subordinates, who took umbrage at their superior's apparent lack of trust. Loring bitterly complained during the Romney Campaign that he would inherit control of an army about which he knew practically nothing if Jackson fell in battle.[74] Ewell considered

---

[71] *SHSP*, v. 35, p. 87.

[72] *SHSP*, v. 35, pp. 83–84.

[73] *SHSP*, v. 35, p. 87.

[74] *SHSP*, v. 16, p. 90.

Stonewall to be "as mad as a March hare" because Old Baldhead could not decipher Jackson's plans in the Valley.[75] Jed Hotchkiss, the General's topographical engineer, reported that Old Jack would often study a map in one direction for hours, then nimbly march the opposite way.[76]

When Lee dispatched A.P. Hill's division to Jackson prior to Cedar Mountain, he counseled his lieutenant, "Hill you will...find a good officer, with whom you can consult, and by advising with your division commanders as to your movements much trouble will be saved you in arranging details, as they can act more intelligently.[77] This suggestion made little apparent impact. Even in Jackson's final battle, none of Stonewall's subordinates knew enough about his plans to execute them following the fateful volley.

The foot cavalry rarely may have known their objective, but they learned to expect hard marching along the way. "Old Jack always starts at early dawn," observed one veteran, "except when he starts the night before."[78] Fitz Lee wrote that like Napoleon's, Jackson's success "must be attributed to the rapid audacity of his movements."[79] Stonewall himself harbored no illusions about the demands he made upon his troops. "Colonel, I yield to no man in sympathy for the gallant men under my command," he once told an officer in the Stonewall Brigade," but I am obliged to sweat them tonight, that I may save their blood tomorrow."[80]

The General issued strict instructions regarding his marching regimen. Canteens were to be filled before departure or during designated halts only. He allowed nothing but entrenching tools and cooking utensils in baggage wagons, and no one could leave the ranks except in cases of illness or necessity. Jackson carefully

---

[75] *SHSP*, v. 9, pp. 364–65.

[76] *SHSP*, v. 43, p. 61.

[77] *OR*, v. 12, part 3, p. 918.

[78] *SHSP*, v. 19. p. 149.

[79] *SHSP*, v. 7, p. 583.

[80] J.B. Avirett, *The Memoirs of General Turner Ashby and his Compeers*, (Baltimore: Selby & Dulany, 1867), pp. 196–97.

enforced a ten-minute rest period each hour and usually broke formation between noon and 1:00 p.m. for dinner.[81]

As a result of these practices, Stonewall's most renowned campaigns invariably included the element of rapid, lengthy marching. The Valley, Second Manassas, Harpers Ferry, and Chancellorsville all meet this criterion.

James Power Smith, with perhaps one of the greater understatements ever uttered, noted that his General "expected fidelity and efficiency from all his officers and men."[82] Another staff member, Henry Kyd Douglas, phrased it differently. "Jackson was as hard as nails in the performance of a duty....I never knew him... to temper justice with mercy; his very words were merciless."[83]

In February 1862 during a meeting with a frustrated colonel, Stonewall revealed *his* perspective on the importance of strict discipline:

> I regret to hear from an officer that it is *impossible* to execute an order. If your cavalry will not obey your orders you must *make them* do it, and, if necessary, go out with them yourself. I desire you to...arrest any man who leaves his post, and prefer charges and specifications against him, that he may be court-martialed. It will not do to say that your men cannot be induced to do their duty. *They must be made to do it.*[84]

On another occasion, Jackson encountered a brigade commander whose regiments were not in their specified marching position. The officer explained, in a rather rollicking tone, that because the army would not be in combat that day, he felt it made no difference where his unit appeared in the column. "How do you know that we are not going to fight today?" Jackson growled, "Besides, colonel, I want you to distinctly understand that you must obey my orders first, and reason about then afterwards. Con-

[81] Vandiver, pp. 232–33.

[82] *SHSP*, v. 43, p. 78.

[83] Douglas, p. 214.

[84] *SHSP*, v. 43, pp. 140–41.

sider yourself under arrest, sir, and march in the rear of your brigade."[85]

During one sharp engagement, a brigadier reined up to Stonewall and inquired, "General, did you order me to move my brigade across that plane [sic] and charge that battery?"

"Yes, sir, I sent you that order," Jackson replied.

"Have you obeyed it?"

"Why, no! General, the enemy's artillery will sweep that field, and my brigade will be literally annihilated if I move across it."

Jackson responded in a clear, deliberate voice. "General, I always try to take care of my wounded and bury my dead. Obey that order, sir, and do it at once."[86]

"Jackson probably put more officers under arrest than all others of our generals combined," theorized J. William Jones.[87] On August 22, 1862, for instance, Stonewall confined all five colonels of Brig. Gen. Maxcy Gregg's South Carolina brigade for nothing more than allowing the demolition of a neighboring civilian's picket fence.[88] Jackson relentlessly pursued and incarcerated deserters, for whom he frequently prescribed the death penalty.[89] He took precautions against the debilitating presence of alcohol in his corps and told a colleague at Manassas Junction that he feared the stockpiled Yankee liquor more than Pope's army.[90]

Jackson believed in stern but pragmatic discipline. For example he ordered Brig. Gen. Charles Winder to suspend the institution of brutal corporal punishment when other officers argued that bucking, gagging, and flogging would likely result in a breakdown of morale.[91] Soldiers with clean records experienced relatively light penalties for first offenses. By establishing his expectations and authority from the outset, however, Stonewall forged an efficient military machine that responded to his every command.

---

[85] *SHSP*, v. 35, pp. 88–89.

[86] *Ibid.*

[87] *SHSP*, v. 19, p. 155.

[88] *SHSP*, v. 14, pp. 209–10.

[89] Vandiver, p. 404.

[90] *SHSP*, v. 43, p. 145; v. 23, pp. 333–34.

[91] Freeman, *Lee's Lieutenants*, v. 2, p. 3.

The manner in which Jackson determined those commands also revealed his remarkable military capacity. "His mind, under the stimulus of the excitement and peril of the conflict," wrote a member of the Stonewall Brigade, "apparently acted with calmness and coolness, and yet with the celerity of lightning and the certainty and precision of a rifle ball driven straight to its mark."[92]

Jackson's chief of staff, Maj. Robert L. Dabney, remembered that Stonewall "asked questions of all; sought counsel of none; gave no account to any man of his matters."[93] When in March 1862 a conference of his officers elected to retreat from Winchester, against Jackson's better judgment, the General slammed his fist into his palm and declared, "that is the last council of war I will ever hold.[94]

Jackson knew how to distinguish the decisive points of a military problem from the unessential ones, and once committed to a course of action he followed through with an iron will. That is not to suggest that changes in the strategic picture paralyzed him. "Urgent and critical peril," wrote Dabney, "did not agitate or confuse his reason, nor make him hang vacillating, uneasy and impotent to decide between the alternatives, but only nerved and steadied his faculties....He ever thought best where other men could think least."[95] Jackson's decisions to attack at Gaines' Mill, engage Pope at Groveton, and lengthen his march at Chancellorsville all bear witness to this claim.

Numerous vignettes capture Stonewall under complete control during moments of crisis: plucking peaches at Sharpsburg; recommending the bayonet to Bee at Manassas; escaping from near capture at Port Republic. His crisp, concise orders on every battlefield often spelled the difference between triumph and tragedy.[96]

Moreover, there could be no mistaking the nature of the victory Jackson always coveted. "War means fighting," he told Dr. McGuire. "March swiftly, strike the foe with all your strength, and

[92] *SHSP,* v. 40, p. 159.

[93] *SHSP,* v. 11, p. 130.

[94] *SHSP,* v. 25, p. 97.

[95] *SHSP,* v. 11, p. 146.

[96] *SHSP,* v. 25, pp. 99–102.

take away from him everything you can. Injure him in every possible way, and do it quickly."[97]

Stonewall's legions understood his philosophy. In June 1862, two Irish volunteers paused at Rockfish Gap during their march to join Lee at Richmond.

"I wish all the Yankees was in hell," said one.

"And faith, and I don't wish anything of the sort," replied his companion.

"The divvil you don't, and why don't you?"

"Because Old Jack would have us standing picket at the gate before night and in there before morning—and it's too hot where we is to suit me."[98]

Jackson once justified his periodic dozing at strategy sessions by explaining, "I always have one single, simple opinion ...and that is to attack the enemy wherever we find him. God has not endowed me with the power of impressing my views upon other people, and when I have stated them, I have done all I can for the conference."[99]

Of course, Stonewall did impress his views on subordinates. For example, he once arrested a Georgia colonel who had abandoned a position without suffering any casualties. "Do you call that much of a fight?" Jackson asked scornfully, before lowering the boom.[100] During the Valley Campaign, another Confederate officer expressed regret at the slaughter of so many intrepid Federal soldiers. "No, shoot them all," advised Jackson. I do not wish them to be brave."[101]

The General's record clearly demonstrates his preference for the offensive. Even when circumstances dictated that he parry the enemy's blows, as at Sharpsburg and Fredericksburg, he ceaselessly searched for the chance to counterattack.

---

[97] *Ibid.*, p. 104.

[98] Blackford, pp. 84–85.

[99] *SHSP,* v. 21, pp. 26–27.

[100] Freeman, *Lee's Lieutenants,* v. 1, p. 417. The unfortunate officer was Col. Z.T. Conner of the 12th Ga.

[101] Dabney, p. 397.

Dr. Hunter Holmes McGuire, medical director of Jackson's corps, wrote extensively about his general after the war. He was only 27 years old when Stonewall died.
[*The Confederate Cause and Conduct in the War Between the States*]

Some historians, with the benefit of hindsight, believe that this aggressive philosophy, which Jackson shared with Lee, led to the Rebels' demise. Only by adopting the strategic defensive could the South have hoped to outlast the Unionists' will to win. Recent scholarship like James M. McPherson's widely acclaimed *Battle Cry of Freedom* argues that the Confederacy *could* have won its independence on the battlefield.[102] But in order to do so, it had to maintain the initiative—Jackson's credo.

The final weapon in Jackson's arsenal had more to do with personal than martial philosophy. Stonewall possessed a single-minded commitment to duty that superseded all matters of self-consideration. He had little tolerance for individual indulgence, private ambition, or disregard for the safety and welfare of others in the army. He wasted no energy on ego gratification. Moreover, as Reverend Hoge observed, Jackson maintained "a sublime indifference to personal danger, to personal comfort, and personal aggrandizement.[103] By doing so, he set an example for his officers and men that greatly enhanced morale, and partially explains the sacrifices and exertions they willingly made for the cause.

Although Stonewall demanded almost as much from others as he did from himself, he always evinced a concern for the health and well-being of his men. He replenished tents, supplies, and clothing whenever possible. More importantly, his administrative style maximized the efficiency of his command. Jackson advocated the promotion of officers by merit rather than election, only sparingly approved furloughs, and replaced spit and polish with an emphasis on training and readiness.[104]

Furthermore, Jackson admired his men and revered the goals for which they struggled. He told McGuire that "the patriotic volunteer, fighting for country and his rights, makes the most reliable soldier on earth."[105] The order Stonewall published following the Battle of Winchester typified the esteem he felt for his troops:

---

[102] James M. McPherson, *Battle Cry of Freedom,* (New York: Oxford Univ. Press, 1988), pp. 857–58.

[103] *SHSP*, v. 13, p. 325.

[104] Vandiver, pp. 167–69, 201–202, 217.

[105] *SHSP*, v. 25, p. 103.

> The General commanding...warmly express[es] to...his command his joy in their achievements and his thanks for their brilliant gallantry in action and their patient obedience under the hardship of forced marches, often more painful to brave soldiers than the dangers of battle.[106]

Jefferson Davis wrote after the war, "Jackson gave his whole heart to his country and his country gave its whole heart to Jackson."[107] On the one hand, Stonewall revealed his patriotism by instructing his wife to invest their money in Confederate bonds, but not to cash the coupons so as to spare the treasury.[108] He honored Virginia women, whether they were the ladies of Winchester, whom he pronounced "the truest people in the South,"[109] or simple country matrons searching for their soldier sons.[110] In return, the citizens of the Confederacy poured out a stream of affection that continually fueled Jackson and his corps and sustained the hopes of the noncombatants.

Jackson's stature and popularity, particularly within the army, evolved over time. Brig. Gen. William B. Taliaferro noted that not until the Valley Campaign did the troops learn to trust Stonewall with absolute confidence.[111] Through the spring of 1862, Jackson's officers variously labeled him "that enthusiastic fanatic,"[112] "a crazy lemon-squeezer,"[113] and "our crack-brained general."[114] Ewell called Stonewall "an idiot," but by June 1862 Old Baldhead had changed his tune. "Jackson is no fool; he knows how to keep his own counsel, and does curious things, but he has method in his madness."[115] Maj. Gen. George E. Pickett, who

---

[106] Mrs. Jackson, p. 263.

[107] *SHSP,* v. 9, p. 218.

[108] Mrs. Jackson, pp. 206–207.

[109] Douglas, p. 55.

[110] *SHSP,* v. 19, p. 308.

[111] Mrs. Jackson, pp. 511–12.

[112] Percy G. Hamlin, ed., *The Making of a Soldier: Letters of General R.S. Ewell* (Richmond: Whittet & Shepperson, 1935), p. 108.

[113] Thomas T. Munford quoting Richard Taylor in *SHSP,* v. 7, p. 523.

[114] John A. Harman, quoted in Vandiver, p. 216.

[115] *SHSP,* v. 7, pp. 527, 530.

never even belonged to Stonewall's command, spoke for most of the Army of Northern Virginia when he said, "I only pray that God may spare him to see us through."[116]

Similarly, Jackson reserved his praise and respect for only those officers who achieved success. William Allan remembered that:

> To his mind, nothing ever fully excused failure, and it was but rarely that he gave an officer the opportunity of failing twice. Jackson used to say "The Service cannot afford to keep...a man who does not succeed. Get rid of the inefficient man at once, and trust Providence for finding a better."[117]

The commanders who did win Jackson's approbation often did so posthumously. Brig. Gens. Turner Ashby and Charles S. Winder, for instance, received glowing Jacksonian tributes that they never lived to read.[118]

More than any other figures, Robert E. Lee and Jeb Stuart earned Jackson's esteem. Stonewall openly admired them both. "So great is my confidence in General Lee that I am willing to follow him blindfolded," Jackson averred. "His perception is as quick and unerring as his judgment is infallible."[119]

Stonewall's feelings toward Stuart transcended respect. Old Jack truly exulted in the company of the bold dragoon. According to James Power Smith, "No guest [to headquarters] received so cordial a welcome as General Stuart, whose gaiety and exuberance of spirit gave [General Jackson] the greatest delight."[120] The cavalryman could tease the usually dour Jackson into fits of laughter and propagate more levity in his presence than any other man. Stuart and Jackson performed well together on battlefields like Manassas, Sharpsburg, Fredericksburg, and Chancellorsville which helps explain their congeniality around the campfire.[121]

---

[116] Arthur C. Inman, ed., *Soldier of the South; Gen. Pickett's War Letters to his Wife* (Boston and New York: Houghton Mifflin Company, 1928) pp. 27–28.

[117] *SHSP,* v. 9, pp. 470–71.

[118] *OR,* v. 12, part 1, p. 712; part 2, p. 183.

[119] *SHSP,* v. 40, pp. 180–81.

[120] *SHSP,* v. 43, p. 80.

[121] Vandiver, p. 140.

Of course, not every officer in Confederate service maintained such a healthy working relationship with the Valley General. Many continued to resent Stonewall's taciturnity and authoritative, unforgiving command style.[122] Two men in particular, Generals Richard B. Garnett and A.P. Hill, suffered from General Jackson's unbending judgment.

Garnett replaced Jackson at the head of the Stonewall Brigade in the autumn of 1861. At the tactically disastrous Battle of Kernstown the following March, Garnett ordered his men to fall back under overwhelming pressure from superior numbers. Jackson had not sanctioned the retreat, and when he arrived upon the scene it appeared for all the world that Garnett's withdrawal had lost the battle. Stonewall arrested his brigadier and removed him from his post.

The men of the Stonewall Brigade expressed outrage at his injustice, and every one of Garnett's colonels defended their general's decision to disengage. None of this impressed Jackson one iota. He prepared a list of charges that festered until August.

A formal court-martial was assembled at that time and Garnett eloquently defended himself, raising questions concerning Jackson's motives in the proceedings. Although Stonewall did not shrink from prosecuting his case, the opportunity to strike Banks at Cedar Mountain relieved him from a potentially embarrassing outcome. Garnett returned to duty in Pickett's division of Longstreet's corps, and the affair never again officially surfaced.[123]

Jackson's feud with A.P. Hill caused even greater problems for the army. Lee assigned the proud, easily offended Little Powell to Jackson's wing in July 1862 because of Hill's dispute with Longstreet following the Seven Days. The red-bearded Virginian soon embroiled himself in a controversy with his new superior— an acrimonious association that endured until Stonewall's death.

Hill quickly earned Jackson's disapproval by botching the approach to Cedar Mountain, although Stonewall's failure to clar-

---

[122] *SHSP*, v. 38, p. 282.

[123] A brief summary of Garnett's arrest and court-martial may be found in Chambers, v. 1, pp. 473–75; v. 2, pp. 103–104. The best analysis of this controversy is by Robert K. Krick, "Jackson vs. Garnett," in *Blue and Gray Magazine*, 1985, v. 3, no. 6, pp. 27–32.

ify a change in his orders contributed to Hill's confusion.[124] When
Little Powell marched poorly at the outset of the Maryland Campaign, Jackson replaced him with one of his brigadiers. Old Jack
restored Hill in time for the fiery Virginian to play a hero's role at
Sharpsburg, but the division commander refused to let the matter
drop. He demanded that either he be censured or that Jackson be
punished for "making loose charges against an officer who has
done and is doing his utmost to make his troops efficient."[125]

Jackson drew up conventional specifications but forwarded
them with an unusually restrained qualification: "As the object in
arresting Gen. Hill, which was to secure his stricter compliance
with orders, has been effected, I do not consider further action on
my part necessary."[126] Lee breathed a sigh of relief, and declined
to call a court-martial.

Hill resented Stonewall's implication that the corps commander's discipline had born fruit:

> I beg leave to disclaim any credit which General Jackson
> may have given me for the good results of his punishment, as to
> my better behavior thereafter, and that its only effect has been to
> cause me to preserve every scrap of paper received from corps
> headquarters to guard myself against any new eruptions from this
> slumbering volcano.[127]

Jackson and Hill maintained only the most stilted relations
throughout the autumn and winter, and one wonders what influence this may have wrought upon the flawed defense at Fredericksburg. Their animosity flared up anew over Jackson's right to
issue direct orders to Hill's staff without first clearing them with
division headquarters. When Little Powell continued to press the
matter, Jackson at last recommended that his subordinate be removed. Lee agonized over this debilitating distraction. Only
Stonewall's mortal wounding relieved Marse Robert of the need

---

[124] Freeman tells the story of Hill's problems in Orange in *Lee's Lieutenants,* v. 2, pp. 12–15.

[125] *OR,* v. 19, part 2, p. 730.

[126] *Ibid.,* p. 731.

[127] *Ibid.,* p. 733.

to resolve the hostilities by depriving his army of one of its two best generals.[128]

Neither Hill nor Jackson emerges from this melodrama untainted. Little Powell reacted over-sensitively to his superior's disciplinary decisions. Stonewall judged Hill's actions too harshly. More importantly, both officers allowed essentially irrelevant matters to imperil the army's smooth operation.

Jackson's dealings with Hill betray the Achilles heel of Stonewall's generalship. Old Jack possessed a literal mind that demanded literal obedience. At times, this orientation prevented him from grasping the bigger picture—understanding the ends beyond the means.

For example, the General withheld his praise from the 33rd Virginia after First Manassas because that regiment had executed its highly successful charge before Jackson had authorized it.[129] Similarly, one winter day at Moss Neck Lee sent Jackson a note requesting a meeting at his lieutenant's convenience. Stonewall mounted immediately and reached Lee's tent after plowing twelve miles through a violent snowstorm. Lee reproached his visitor for unnecessarily exposing himself to the elements: "You know I did not wish you to come in such a storm; it was a matter of little importance; I am so sorry that you have had this ride." Jackson saluted and replied, "I received your note, General Lee."[130]

Capt. Randolph Barton, Assistant Adjutant-General of the Stonewall Brigade, explained Jackson's behavior thusly:

> His intense accuracy in obeying orders had somewhat narrowed his capacity to make allowance for changing circumstances. His intense self-reliance made him feel that in battle, as far as he governed its movements, his plans, and *his alone* must be followed.[131]

This inflexible confidence found its inspiration in large part in Jackson's religious philosophy. He viewed his military responsibilities as a duty from the Lord, to be discharged according to

---

[128] Vandiver summarizes the Hill-Jackson controversy nicely on pp. 407–409.

[129] *SHSP,* v. 38, p. 276.

[130] *SHSP,* v. 43, pp. 41–42.

[131] *SHSP,* v. 38, pp. 276–77.

the Creator's grand design. "General Jackson was the incarnation of a Christian soldier," wrote I.C. Haas. "His sublime faith in God dominated all else."[132]

Battlefield glories always belonged to the Heavenly Father. In fact, Stonewall's fundamental goal in the war was to make holy the people of the South and implore God's forgiveness of their sins. This accomplished, the Lord would watch over the fortunes of the Confederacy.[133] Although Jackson never permitted his religion to interfere with tactical decisions (he fought many of his most famous battles on Sundays),[134] in matters such as the selection of his staff, secular considerations did not always prevail.

Where, then, does Stonewall Jackson belong in the Confederate pantheon? Might his continued presence have altered the outcome of the war? Would he have succeeded independent of Lee's control?

Douglas Southall Freeman believed that "the death of Jackson was the turning point in the history of the Army of Northern Virginia.[135] General Lee confessed that he did not know how to replace his fallen lieutenant[136] and later speculated that had Jackson been at Gettysburg, "we would have won a great victory."[137]

"If Lee was the jove of the war," wrote Charles E. Fenner, "Stonewall Jackson was his thunderbolt."[138] No subordinate general shares Jackson's battlefield record. Lee's aide, Col. Charles Marshall, pointed out that Marse Robert usually relied upon Jackson to execute the army's critical movements.[139] Sgt. John F. Sale of the 12th Virginia wrote in December 1862, "Genl. Longstreet to whose corps we belong is a real bulldog man. They always send

---

[132] *SHSP*, v. 32, p. 97.

[133] Various wartime letters express this sentiment. See, for example, Mrs. Jackson, pp. 258, 390; also Rev. James R. Graham in Mrs. Jackson, pp. 505–506.

[134] Kernstown, Cross Keys, First Manassas, for example.

[135] Freeman, *Lee,* v. 3, p. 153.

[136] *SHSP*, v. 35, pp. 96–97.

[137] *SHSP*, v. 20, p. 31.

[138] *SHSP*, v. 14, p. 87.

[139] *SHSP*, v. 37, p. 106.

The last photograph taken of Jackson, made in April 1863. Mrs. Jackson complained that "a strong wind blew in his face, causing him to frown, and giving a sterness to his countenance that was not natural."
[*Leib Image Archive*]

him to give them open fight, but if there is any near business to be done, in goes old Stonewall and out goes the Yankees."[140]

James Power Smith believed that Jackson would have sparkled on his own, an opinion shared by Stonewall's biographers. "He was...most successful when in independent command," wrote Smith. "He had the will of a vast energy, and he imparted this energy to those under [him]."[141]

There can be no doubt that whenever Lee dispatched Jackson to operate alone, Old Jack performed brilliantly. Every campaign from the Valley through Chancellorsville confirms this opinion. Only at the Seven Days, where Jackson received a type of unmalleable orders that Lee never issued him again, did Stonewall stumble.

Still, apart from battlefield behavior, a commanding general must act as final authority on all matters of army business. Jackson's rigid relationship with some junior officers raises questions about his capacity to cope creatively with personality problems. In this regard, might department commander Jackson have more resembled Braxton Bragg than Lee?

In the final analysis, however, Thomas Jackson deserves the boundless acclaim rendered him during the century-and-a-quarter since his death.

> No general made fewer mistakes. No general so persistently outwitted his opponents. No general better understood the use of ground or the value of time. No general was more highly endowed with courage, both physical and moral, and none ever secured to a greater degree the trust and affection of his troops.[142]

We might add only one thought to G.F.R. Henderson's assessment. No revisionist appraisal will succeed in reducing either the breadth of Stonewall Jackson's military achievements or the perception of those achievements by his venerative contemporaries.

---

[140] Photocopy of manuscript letter, Dec. 12, 1862, in Bound Volume 3 in the collection of Fredericksburg and Spotsylvania National Military Park.

[141] *SHSP*, v. 43, p. 66.

[142] *SHSP*, v. 40, p. 155.

He's in the saddle now. Fall in!
Steady, the whole brigade!
Hill's at the ford, cut off. We'll win
His way out ball and blade.
What matter if our shoes are worn?
What matter if our feet are torn?
Quick step!
We're with him before dawn
That's Stonewall Jackson's way.[143]

---

[143] "Stonewall Jackson's Way," a song by Dr. John Willamson Palmer in *SHSP*, v. 2, pp. 136–37.

INDEX